ESPECIALLY FOR

....

FROM

....

DATE

....

DAILY WISDOM FOR MEN

2025
DEVOTIONAL COLLECTION

BARBOUR
PUBLISHING

INTRODUCTION

Happy New Year! Welcome to the 2025 edition of *Daily Wisdom for Men*!

The theme for this year's *Daily Wisdom for Men* is *Strong Faith*. The word *faith* appears hundreds of times in the Bible, and words such as *believe* and *trust* appear many other times.

Faith very important to God. Our relationship with the Lord is based on faith, which the Bible defines as "confidence in what we hope for and assurance about what we do not see" (Hebrews 11:1 NIV). The Bible also says, "Without faith it is impossible to please God, because anyone who comes to him must believe that he exists and that he rewards those who earnestly seek him" (Hebrews 11:6 NIV).

The inspiration for this year's daily devotionals is taken from scripture readings in our popular Read Thru the Bible in a Year Plan. Each day's readings are listed at the top of the page. That will help you to read the daily Bible passages and then spend a few minutes reading that day's devotional writing.

God wants to grow you into a man of strong faith, a man who fully believes God and each and every one of His promises recorded in scripture. It is the hope of the men who played a part in writing this year's *Daily Wisdom for Men* devotionals, as well as the people at Barbour Publishing, that God will use your daily Bible reading, as well as the writings in this book, to help make you a man who believes God with all his heart.

The Editors

Genesis 1–2 / Matthew 1 / Psalm 1

BE THE TREE

And he shall be like a tree planted by the rivers of water
that brings forth its fruit in its season. His leaf also shall
not wither, and whatever he does shall prosper.

PSALM 1:3 SKJV

Human as we are, guys need new beginnings, fresh starts, opportunities to shake off mistakes and look to the future with hope.

For many, the turn of a new year is a good reminder that "things can be different this time." Birthdays may serve the same purpose, or even our weekly attendance at church. And God provides sunrises as proof that His mercies "are new every morning" (Lamentations 3:23 SKJV).

Hopefully, as we mature in faith, our mistakes become less frequent and severe. Ideally, we grow to be like the "blessed" (or happy) man of Psalm 1, who has chosen not to walk, stand, or sit with the ungodly (verse 1). Instead, we make time for scripture—"the law of the LORD"—mulling it "day and night" (verse 2).

By consciously doing these things—avoiding evil, pursuing God's Word—we become like a tree on the riverside. We'll grow deep roots that strengthen us in our faith and healthy branches that protect and nourish others.

If you've already experienced salvation, the greatest of new beginnings, commit this year to growing like that tree. If you have yet to truly follow God, what better time than today?

Lord, You want me to be forgiven, healthy, and
growing. Make me like a tree by the riverside.

Genesis 3–4 / Matthew 2 / Psalm 2

SECOND-GUESSING GOD

*Now the serpent was the most cunning of all the wild animals
that the LORD God had made. He said to the woman,
"Did God really say, 'You can't eat from any tree in the garden'?"*

GENESIS 3:1 HCSB

Our culture second-guesses God constantly. Whether on the matter
of origins, or morality, or the afterlife, or any of a million other topics,
the plain teaching of God's Word is bent, twisted, upended, or tossed
aside entirely.

But that's nothing new. Satan himself second-guessed the Lord,
thinking a created angel could make a better ruler of the universe than
the perfect, infinite God. And then Satan took his insinuations to the
very first woman, getting her and her husband to second-guess God
as well. We have all suffered for their error.

Though we can't escape our sinful environment, we don't have to
make it worse either. As Christian men, temples of God's Holy Spirit,
we have every opportunity to reject the voice of doubt and rebellion
that nags at our minds and hearts. We can choose to immerse ourselves
in God's Word, in prayer, in the denial of our natural impulses. As we
do, we'll find ourselves better able to resist the next time temptation
comes.

Our enemy is cunning. But we are not "ignorant of his schemes"
(2 Corinthians 2:11 HCSB). Be ready and be firm. Don't ever allow
yourself to second-guess God.

Lord, You are the standard for everything. May I always defer to You.

Genesis 5–7 / Matthew 3 / Psalm 3

KEEP YOURSELF IN PERSPECTIVE

*"Someone is coming soon who is greater than I am—so much greater
that I'm not worthy even to be his slave and carry his sandals."*

MATTHEW 3:11 NLT

"Don't think you are better than you really are."

Maybe a parent taught that as you were growing up. Maybe your
girlfriend or wife has said something similar. If so, take heed. . .it's
a message God Himself spoke through the apostle Paul (Romans
12:3 NLT).

Perhaps Paul was thinking of John the Baptist when he wrote
those words. It was John—miracle baby, prophesied forerunner of the
Messiah, the greatest of all time in the estimation of Jesus (Matthew
11:11)—who spoke today's scripture. Whatever John's goodness (and it
was impressive) he recognized he was nothing in comparison to Jesus.

And whatever our intelligence, ability, looks, wealth—anything
we take pride in—*we* are nothing in comparison to Jesus. The most
impressive men of history have been (or will be) felled by death.
That is everyone's destiny. But if we keep ourselves in perspective, if
we acknowledge Jesus as "the way, the truth, and the life" (John 14:6
NLT), we gain all of His perfections and can look forward to eternal
life in His presence.

Don't think you are better than you really are. In fact, be very
skeptical of yourself. Intentionally and regularly direct all the glory
to Jesus.

*Lord, forgive me for my pride. Help me humble
myself before You, today and every day.*

Genesis 8–10 / Matthew 4 / Psalm 4

SPARE NO EXPENSE?

You have put more joy and rejoicing in my heart than [they know]
when their wheat and new wine have yielded abundantly.

PSALM 4:7 AMPC

The Vanderbilt family epitomized the Gilded Age of the late nineteenth century. Descendants of "The Commodore," Cornelius Vanderbilt plowed the vast wealth he'd gained from shipping and railroads into immense homes and lavish social gatherings designed to outdo all others. Fellow Americans were stunned by their prodigality.

A century later, Arthur Vanderbilt II wrote *Fortune's Children,* an account of the wild spending that erased the family wealth. In one intriguing account, the author quoted a newspaper reporter's conversation with another Gilded Age figure. When the former said that the Vanderbilts "spared no expense in the pursuit of pleasure," the latter disagreed. "No, they spare no pleasure in the pursuit of expense."

Wealth is a double-edged sword. Certainly, it's nice not to worry about groceries or the electric bill. But money can subtly become a hard taskmaster, driving us to compete with others. When that happens, pleasure gives way to pain. . .stresses like envy and one-upmanship.

The solution is to find our wholeness in God, who can "put more joy and rejoicing" in our hearts than anyone or anything else. And why not? Having created all the other things, God is far beyond any amount of wealth, any person or home or experience we could ever imagine.

I have vast wealth in simply knowing You,
Lord. Please help me to be content.

Genesis 11–13 / Matthew 5:1–20 / Psalm 5

LET THE OTHER GUY WIN

*Abram said to Lot, "Let's not have any quarreling between you
and me, or between your herders and mine, for we are close relatives.
Is not the whole land before you? Let's part company. If you go to
the left, I'll go to the right; if you go to the right, I'll go to the left."*

Genesis 13:8–9 NIV

Between sinful people in a cursed world, conflict is inevitable. But
as Christian men, we can diminish tensions by relinquishing our
supposed rights in unimportant matters.

Of course we can't compromise the clear teachings of scripture.
But when we disagree, let's always aspire to be as gracious as Abram
was with his nephew Lot.

Chosen by God to lead a specially blessed people, Abram fled a
famine in his promised land by sojourning in Egypt. Returning home,
the two relatives, owners of much livestock, realized they couldn't live
near each other without conflict between their herdsmen. As the elder
and "God's friend" (James 2:23 NIV), Abram could have thrown his
weight around, demanding whatever land he preferred. Instead, he
spoke the gracious words of today's scripture.

By giving up his rights, Abram allowed God to work out His
perfect plan. Abram got Canaan as he should have. Lot chose Sodom,
which would ultimately be destroyed for its sin.

Hold your "rights" loosely. Trust that God will work things out
for you.

*Your plan is always better than mine, Lord.
May I defer to You every time.*

Genesis 14–16 / Matthew 5:21–48 / Psalm 6

MAKE THE FIRST MOVE

"Say you're out on the street and an old enemy accosts you.
Don't lose a minute. Make the first move; make things right with
him. After all, if you leave the first move to him, knowing his
track record, you're likely to end up in court, maybe even jail."

MATTHEW 5:25–26 MSG

Jesus' Sermon on the Mount can be daunting. Commands like "love your enemies" are impossible in our own strength. Only in God's power can we live up to Jesus' principles in Matthew 5–7.

But we still have responsibility, and today's scripture highlights one key: *make the first move.* Those four words are a paraphrase but an apt summary of various translations: "Agree with thine adversary quickly" (King James Version); "Settle matters quickly with your adversary" (New International Version); "Come to terms quickly with your accuser" (Amplified Bible, Classic Edition). Each of those verbs is directed toward us and implies making the first move.

Our sinful nature often resists that. *The other guy wronged me,* we may think. *Why do I have to make things right?*

Well, we make the first move because it reflects what God does in our lives: He "demonstrates his own love for us in this: While we were still sinners, Christ died for us" (Romans 5:8 NIV). The deeper our roots grow into Him, the further our grace spreads to others.

Lord, empower me to make the first move.
I want to reflect You in all I do.

Genesis 17–18 / Matthew 6:1–18 / Psalm 7

WHAT GOD CALLS YOU

*"I am changing your name. It will no longer
be Abram. Instead, you will be called Abraham,
for you will be the father of many nations."*

GENESIS 17:5 NLT

A childless man when he stepped onto the biblical stage, Abram bore an ironic name: it means "exalted father." But after God promised to give Abram a child and make his descendants into a great nation, he was renamed Abraham, "father of a multitude."

He'd grown up pagan in Ur of the Chaldeans, among people who "worshiped other gods" (Joshua 24:2 NLT). But the real God had big plans for Abram, as indicated by that new name.

In a way, God renames each of us when He calls us to faith. The apostle Paul identified sexual sinners, the greedy, drunks, abusers, and idolaters as the kind of people naturally separated from God (1 Corinthians 6:9–10). But when, in His love, the Lord reaches out and we respond to Him, He has much better names for us: "cleansed. . . made holy. . .made right with God by calling on the name of the Lord Jesus Christ" (verse 11 NLT).

Now, like Abram, we please God by simply believing what He says (Genesis 15:6). If God calls you a clean, holy, righteous man through faith in Christ, accept that truth and live in it.

*Lord, thank You for calling me worthy through my faith in
Jesus. Help me to live up to the honor that You've shown me.*

Genesis 19–20 / Matthew 6:19–34 / Psalm 8

INSPIRED BY SCRIPTURE

. . .and the fish in the sea, all that swim the paths of the seas.
PSALM 8:8 NIV

Inspired by today's scripture, Matthew Fontaine Maury revolutionized sea travel. The pioneer oceanographer, born in Virginia in 1806, oversaw the charting of winds and currents in oceans worldwide. His work was said to cut nearly seven weeks off the New York to San Francisco passage. Maury comes down through history as the "Pathfinder of the Seas."

When read and studied consistently, scripture will inspire all of us in some way—conceivably to some new scientific discovery, certainly to revelations about ourselves and God, sin and salvation. But we must launch into this ocean, choosing to explore its depths.

A devotional book like this is helpful, but it's only a starting point. When you're finished with this entry, why not go deeper into some passages highlighting the Bible's view of itself: 2 Timothy 3:14–17 (concerning God's role in transmitting scripture to humanity); 2 Peter 1:16–21 (describing the human element of the Bible's creation); Hebrews 4:12 (regarding the power of God's Word); Matthew 5:17–19 (concerning the enduring nature of God's Word).

God inspired (literally, "breathed out") His Word so that we could be inspired (to holy living) by its truth. If the Bible also leads you to some useful practical knowledge like it did Matthew Maury, well, that's just a nice bonus.

Your Word is always true and helpful, Lord.
Open my heart to what it says.

Genesis 21–23 / Matthew 7:1–11 / Psalm 9:1–8

"DO NOT JUDGE"

*Do not judge and criticize and condemn others, so that you may
not be judged and criticized and condemned yourselves.*

MATTHEW 7:1 AMPC

Here is one of the world's most popular Bible verses. For many
people—including professed Christians—it means any questioning
of others' beliefs or behaviors is off-limits.

But as is usually the case, a single verse needs context to be
properly understood. In this case, the next four verses elaborate Jesus'
true meaning. It's not that we as Christians can never challenge other
people—but we must never attack others for things that we ourselves
are doing. Jesus described this kind of hypocrisy as a "beam of timber"
in our eyes while we're seeking to remove the "very small particle"
from another's eye (Matthew 7:3 AMPC).

Elsewhere, Jesus taught, "Be honest in your judgment and do
not decide at a glance (superficially and by appearances); but judge
fairly and righteously" (John 7:24 AMPC). As Christian men, we have
a biblical responsibility to challenge those on a bad path, believers
and unbelievers alike (see 1 Thessalonians 5:14; Jude 1:22–23). But
we must only judge according to biblical standards, and always with
mercy and grace.

Finally, let's admit that the only person any man can judge with
total accuracy is himself. We should expend our greatest energy in
dealing with our own faults and failures before we ever attempt to
judge anyone else.

Lord, help me to judge fairly and righteously, starting with myself.

Genesis 24 / Matthew 7:12–29 / Psalm 9:9–20

DO NOT DELAY

Her brother and mother said, "Let the girl stay with us for about 10 days. Then she can go." But he responded to them, "Do not delay me, since the LORD has made my journey a success."

GENESIS 24:55–56 HCSB

In scripture, waiting is good. Delay, not so much.

The difference? Waiting is our response to God, a conscious choice to calm ourselves and allow Him to work, however long that takes (see Psalm 27:14, 37:7; Proverbs 20:22; Zephaniah 3:8). Delay is a hesitation to do what God clearly expects.

In Genesis 24, Abraham's servant saw delay as an affront to God, who had answered his prayer for success in finding a wife for Isaac. Given the deciding vote, Rebekah herself chose to leave immediately.

Sadly, the nation that descended from this couple, through their son Jacob, delayed when given the chance to enter their promised land. A report of giants caused them to hesitate and rebel—and, as punishment, only two men from that entire generation would live to see Canaan (see Numbers 13–14). Decades later, when Israel was finally in the land, Joshua still had to prompt the people to do what God had said: "How long will you delay going out to take possession of the land that the LORD, the God of your fathers, gave you?" (Joshua 18:3 HCSB).

When you know what God wants, just do it. Delay only brings trouble.

Help me, Lord, to obey You, confidently and quickly.

Genesis 25–26 / Matthew 8:1–17 / Psalm 10:1–11

HOW TO SURPRISE JESUS

The centurion answered and said, "Lord, I am not worthy that You should come under my roof. But only speak the word, and my servant shall be healed. For I am a man under authority, having soldiers under me. And I say to this man, 'Go,' and he goes; and to another, 'Come,' and he comes; and to my servant, 'Do this,' and he does it."

MATTHEW 8:8–9 ɛKJV

Have you ever been pleasantly surprised? We can assume that most people enjoy it when things go better than expected. Even Jesus experienced that in dealing with a Roman centurion who had requested healing for his paralyzed servant. In response to the soldier's words above, Jesus "marveled" (verse 10 sKjv), or "was amazed" (NIV). Then He made the man's faith a teaching opportunity for others and spoke the healing word.

Exactly how the infinite, all-knowing God could be amazed by anything is a debate for scholars, though certainly, as a man, Jesus temporarily put aside many of His divine powers. Whatever the case may be, wouldn't you like to amaze Jesus with your faith? Simply believing that He has the power and the passion to help is a great place to begin. This faith grows as we study God's Word, spend time with Him in prayer, and commit ourselves to living our lives on His terms.

Even if I can't surprise You, Jesus, I'd like my faith to please You. Live Your life through me today.

Genesis 27:1–28:9 / Matthew 8:18–34 / Psalm 10:12–18

DON'T "HELP" GOD

Jacob said to his father, "I am Esau your firstborn. . . .
Please sit up and eat some of my game, so that you may give me
your blessing." Isaac asked his son, "How did you find it so quickly,
my son?" "The LORD your God gave me success," he replied.

GENESIS 27:19–20 NIV

Have you noticed how many Bible heroes were flawed? Consider the patriarchs of Israel.

Jacob was the son of Isaac and grandson of Abraham. God had promised that their offspring would become a great nation. It would be called Israel, a new name God gave to Jacob (Genesis 32).

Though Jacob was a younger son, God had promised him leadership over his older twin, Esau. But rather than trust God's Word, Jacob obeyed his mother's urging to help the Lord's plan along. They schemed to steal the blessing that Isaac planned for Esau in spite of God's prophecy when the boys were still in Rebekah's womb (Genesis 25:23). Jacob even dragged God's name into this dishonesty! Their conniving isn't surprising, perhaps, considering that Abraham had once tried to help God by having a baby by his wife's servant girl (Genesis 16).

God's good plan ultimately transpired, no thanks to the selfish, sneaky behavior of His people. Let's not be like that—when God makes a promise, let Him fulfill it no matter how long it takes.

Lord God, Titus wrote that You never lie.
May I never dishonestly "help" Your plans.

Genesis 28:10–29:35 / Matthew 9 / Psalm 11

WHAT CAN I DO?

"When the foundations are being destroyed, what can the righteous do?"
PSALM 11:3 NIV

In recent years, many—possibly most—committed Christians have asked questions like the one above. When the foundations of civil government crumble, what can the righteous do? When the foundations of churches and denominations dissolve into mush, what can the righteous do? When the foundations of basic reality are jackhammered by obvious falsehoods, what can the righteous do?

On their own, very little. But the righteous are never really "on their own." They have God on their side, and that changes everything.

Notice the quotation marks around today's scripture. They indicate that these words were spoken by someone other than the psalmist. The question was posed by fearful people who couldn't accept the writer's declaration: "In the LORD I take refuge" (verse 1). The writer, possibly David, believed strongly in God's protection, so he asked, "How then can you say to me. . . 'When the foundations are being destroyed, what can the righteous do?'" (verses 1, 3).

Sure, bad things were happening then; they still do today. But "the LORD is in his holy temple; the LORD is on his heavenly throne" (Psalm 11:4). And "on the wicked he will rain fiery coals and burning sulfur" (verse 6; all quotations NIV).

What can the righteous do? Trust God for protection and ultimate justice. He'll come through.

You are my refuge, Lord. Thank You for standing
strong in this crumbling world.

Genesis 30:1–31:21 / Matthew 10:1–15 / Psalm 12

STOP COMPARING

Now these are the names of the twelve apostles (special messengers): first, Simon, who is called Peter, and Andrew his brother; James son of Zebedee, and John his brother; Philip and Bartholomew [Nathaniel]; Thomas and Matthew the tax collector; James son of Alphaeus, and Thaddaeus [Judas, not Iscariot]; Simon the Cananaean, and Judas Iscariot, who also betrayed Him.

MATTHEW 10:2–4 AMPC

Ever heard of Alexander Pope? Even if not, you probably recognize a line from his 1711 work "An Essay on Criticism": "To err is human." For this devotional, let's revise that and say, "To *compare* is human." It happens all the time. Often—when comparison leads to envy or other ill feelings—to compare is to err.

Even Jesus' disciples succumbed to this sin: "a controversy arose among them as to which of them might be the greatest" (Luke 9:46 AMPC). That's when Jesus called a small child as a visual aid in His teaching, "he who is least and lowliest among you all—he is [the one who is truly] great" (verse 48 AMPC).

After three years of learning from Jesus, and after receiving His Holy Spirit at Pentecost, the Eleven (all but Judas Iscariot) ultimately "got it." Though Peter was clearly the leader and John was Jesus' closest friend, everyone on today's list accepted his role and did his job—very effectively, as it turns out. May we humbly do the same.

Lord Jesus, in You I have everything I need. Please make me content.

HOW GOD SPEAKS

*The previous night God had appeared to Laban the Aramean in
a dream and told him, "I'm warning you—leave Jacob alone!"*

GENESIS 31:24 NLT

For most of us, nighttime dreams are a strange concoction of our accumulated pleasures, hopes, and fears. We might dream of a girl we used to know, of finding a stash of money, or of inexplicably being naked in public. A former radio announcer often dreamed of being unable to reach the studio in time to prevent the dreaded "dead air," years after his last stint behind the microphone.

In scripture, though, dreams were important messages from God. That's interesting enough, but especially so when you see how often He spoke to pagan people through dreams. Sneaky, selfish Laban is joined by Abimelech, king of Gerar (Genesis 20), the pharaoh of Egypt (Genesis 41), and a Midianite soldier (Judges 7) in receiving nighttime revelation. And though scripture doesn't specifically say it was from God, Pilate's wife likely heard from the Lord in her troubling dream about Jesus (Matthew 27:19).

The point for us, as Christian men today: while God has sometimes chosen to get unbelievers' attention through dreams, He's given us both His Word and His Spirit to guide our thoughts and actions. We don't have to wait and wonder about His will—God has provided everything we need, right now. Are you taking full advantage of it?

*Lead me deep into Your Word, Lord,
and speak to me by Your Spirit.*

Genesis 32:22–34:31 / Matthew 10:37–11:6 / Psalm 14

IMPORTUNATE PRAYER

The man said, "Let me go, for it is daybreak." But Jacob replied, "I will not let you go unless you bless me."

GENESIS 32:26 NIV

Importunate isn't a terribly common word, but it's sometimes used in connection with prayer. The noun form appears in the King James Version, where Jesus compares prayer to a man doggedly begging a neighbor for late-night loaves of bread: "I say unto you, Though he will not rise and give him, because he is his friend, yet because of his importunity he will rise and give him as many as he needeth" (Luke 11:8 KJV).

Defined as "troublesomely urgent" or "overly persistent in making a request," *importunate* is an attitude God likes in His people. When Jacob clung to and demanded a blessing from the mysterious "man" at Peniel (identified as God Himself in Genesis 32:30), he got what he wanted. Jesus elaborated on Luke 11:8 by approving of an importunate widow (Luke 18:1–8) and a foreign mother who persisted until He agreed to heal her daughter (Matthew 15:21–28). He taught, "Ask and it will be given to you; seek and you will find; knock and the door will be opened to you" (Luke 11:9 NIV).

"Some people think God does not like to be troubled with our constant coming and asking," the nineteenth-century evangelist D. L. Moody said. "The only way to trouble God is not to come at all."

Lord, I come to You, asking earnestly for. . .

Genesis 35–36 / Matthew 11:7–24 / Psalm 15

A POWERFUL PROMISE

LORD, who shall abide in Your tabernacle?
Who shall dwell on Your holy hill?

PSALM 15:1 SKJV

The "Christian era" answer to the questions above is simple: those who put their faith in Jesus. Living as we do after the life, death, and resurrection of Christ, we can understand God's plan more clearly than the Old Testament heroes did.

Even before Jesus arrived as a baby in Bethlehem, faith was the key to pleasing God (Genesis 15:6). But once we're saved—by God's grace, through our faith in Christ (Ephesians 2:8)—there are things we must do to honor the Lord. Jesus taught, "If you love Me, keep My commandments" (John 14:15 SKJV).

Psalm 15 lays out several commands to be kept—ways to honor our Lord and demonstrate membership in His congregation. We will abide in His tabernacle (the Old Testament worship tent, perhaps an allusion to the church today) and dwell on His holy hill (a reference to the eternal New Jerusalem) by obeying the balance of Psalm 15: doing right, speaking truth, avoiding slander and other harm to our fellow man, not being greedy, and so on.

When we do these things, we have a promise from God: "He who does these things shall never be moved" (Psalm 15:5 SKJV). In a world of constant upheaval, that is a powerful promise indeed.

Lord God, I want to abide in Your tabernacle and dwell on Your
holy hill. Strengthen me today to obey Your commandments.

Genesis 37–38 / Matthew 11:25–30 / Psalm 16

ROAD TO SUCCESS

*The Midianite traders arrived in Egypt, where they sold Joseph
to Potiphar, an officer of Pharaoh, the king of Egypt.*

GENESIS 37:36 NLT

So begins Joseph's rise to prominence and power. It was a long and winding road.

A quick recap of the story: Joseph was a son of Jacob, born in the patriarch's old age to his favored wife, Rachel. This eleventh of twelve boys was daddy's favorite, and his older brothers hated him—so much that they wanted to kill him. In the end, they traded Joseph for money, selling him to traveling merchants. Resold to an Egyptian official, he spent years in prison after the man's wife—furious that Joseph had spurned her advances—accused him of sexual misconduct. In prison he interpreted dreams of fellow detainees and ultimately explained Pharaoh's strange dreams. Impressed by Joseph's God-given wisdom, the king named the Israelite second-in-command of all Egypt.

The mistreatment Joseph suffered is almost unimaginable. But throughout his story, scripture says the Lord was with him (Genesis 39:2, 3, 21, 23). God's presence and guidance helped him survive every reverse—and not only survive, but thrive. From hated kid brother to second most powerful man on earth is a story only God could write.

Our road probably won't be as dramatic. But the same God who helped Joseph also helps us. Stick with Him, work with Him, and see what He'll do in your life.

Lord, be with me—and accomplish great things through me.

Genesis 39–40 / Matthew 12:1–29 / Psalm 17

DON'T BE A PHARISEE

"Is there a person here who, finding one of your lambs fallen into
a ravine, wouldn't, even though it was a Sabbath, pull it out?"
MATTHEW 12:11 MSG

Why is it so easy to be critical? Even in the Christian life—maybe
especially in the Christian life—we fall prey to judgmental attitudes.

It's one thing to stand firm on the clear teachings of scripture.
We must do that, though as graciously as possible. It's something else
entirely to impose our preferences on others in the name of scripture.
Or to give ourselves a pass on biblical rules while expecting everyone
else to observe them. The Pharisees of Jesus' day were famous for
such hypocrisy.

In Matthew 12, Pharisees accused Jesus' disciples of breaking God's
rule against working on the Sabbath. Walking through a field of ripe
grain, the disciples had grabbed some kernels as a snack. Apparently,
they were harvesting on the day of rest!

Jesus defended His disciples with two Old Testament cases of
"rule breaking" (verses 3–5), then infuriated the Pharisees by healing a
man's crippled hand (verses 11–14). The Lord noted that any Pharisee
would help his animal on the Sabbath—so why not help people?
Then, quoting God's pronouncement through the prophet Hosea,
Jesus told the Pharisees, "I desire mercy, not sacrifice" (verse 7 NIV;
see Hosea 6:6).

Let's keep that truth in mind ourselves. Let's not be Pharisees.

Lord, grant me Your perfect balance of grace and truth.

Genesis 41 / Matthew 12:30–50 / Psalm 18:1–15

ANGRY GOD

*Then the earth quaked and rocked, the foundations
also of the mountains trembled; they moved and were
shaken because He was indignant and angry.*

PSALM 18:7 AMPC

Read the first six verses of Psalm 18 to understand what made God so angry: the mistreatment of David.

This psalm is repeated in 2 Samuel 22, which begins, "David spoke to the Lord the words of this song on the day when the Lord delivered him from the hands of all his enemies and from the hand of Saul" (verse 1 AMPC). Those are essentially the words of the title ("superscription") of Psalm 18.

If God chose to record this song twice, what should we learn from it? For one thing, that God loved and protected David, the "man after His own heart" (1 Samuel 13:14 AMPC). David was simply a shepherd boy when God set him on the path that would truly change the world. When anyone tried to stand in David's way, God became angry—enough to shake the world.

Though David was unique in many ways, he was chosen by God just as each of us are. Every follower of Jesus was chosen "before the foundation of the world" (Ephesians 1:4 AMPC) and promised eternal glory with God. He loves and protects us as He did David, and will one day shake the earth to punish those who trouble His own.

Lord, I thank You for protecting me—on this earth or in heaven to come.

Genesis 42–43 / Matthew 13:1–9 / Psalm 18:16–29

REFLECTIONS

*With the faithful You prove Yourself faithful; with the blameless
man You prove Yourself blameless; with the pure You prove
Yourself pure, but with the crooked You prove Yourself shrewd.*

PSALM 18:25–26 HCSB

A real estate agent was showing a house. The potential buyer asked,
"What are the people around here like?" The agent responded with his
own question: "What are your current neighbors like?" "Oh, they're
awful," the customer replied. "They're cold and selfish and unhelpful."
"I'm sorry," the real estate man said. "You'll find the same thing here."

Days later, the same agent was showing the same house to another
person, who posed a similar question. After asking about the man's
current neighbors, the agent was told, "They're great—we get along
beautifully." "Wonderful!" the real estate man responded. "You'll find
the same thing here."

That agent knew something about human nature: our relationships
often reflect our own personalities. Not in every case, but the way we
view and treat others inevitably affects our human interactions.

Our relationship with God definitely reflects the way we view
and treat Him. When we choose to pursue Him, through His Word
and prayer and humble obedience, God shows His faithfulness,
blamelessness, and purity to us. But if we're "crooked"—if we're
skeptical, selfish, or sensual—we'll find that He is shrewd. God
immediately recognizes our deceit and deals with us accordingly.

Isn't the right choice obvious?

I want You to honor me, Lord—so I commit to honoring You.

Genesis 44–45 / Matthew 13:10–23 / Psalm 18:30–50

A HARVEST STORY

"The seed cast on good earth is the person who hears and takes in the News, and then produces a harvest beyond his wildest dreams."

MATTHEW 13:23 MSG

Today's scripture is from a passage many Bible versions call "The Parable of the Sower." But *The Message* takes a different tack with its headline: "A Harvest Story."

We can focus on the different types of "soil" the parable's sower encountered. His "seeds"—the gospel message (verse 19)—landed on different kinds of ground, including the hard pathway, the rocky, and the weedy. These all represent people who, for various reasons, can't or won't accept the good news and be saved.

But Jesus also described a good soil—hopefully, everyone reading this devotional—who welcomes His message, lets it sink deep inside, and sees it ultimately produce fruit. That's the spiritual fruit of a changed life, and according to today's scripture quote, it's "beyond [your] wildest dreams." More traditional translations say the good soil yields thirty, sixty, or a hundred times what was sown.

When we're truly saved from our sins, we'll want to grow and produce for the God whose grace makes new life possible. Growth can be slow, and the full harvest takes time. Just be sure you're staying close to Jesus (John 15:5) so that nothing interrupts your development.

Lord God, I thank You for making me receptive to the seed of Your gospel. Now keep me close and produce much fruit in my life.

Genesis 46:1–47:26 / Matthew 13:24–43 / Psalm 19

RELATIONSHIP TO LEADERSHIP

Pharaoh said to Joseph, "Your father and your brothers have come to you, and the land of Egypt is before you; settle your father and your brothers in the best part of the land. Let them live in Goshen. And if you know of any among them with special ability, put them in charge of my own livestock."

GENESIS 47:5–6 NIV

For the past few centuries, Christians in Western nations have enjoyed an unusual position of public acceptance and leadership. That's changing quickly—we as believers are finding ourselves in much more common circumstances, ruled by those with little understanding of or commitment to our God.

That was often the case for God's people in Bible times—sadly, even during Israel's history, when many kings who knew better rejected the Lord.

But notice how often believers, by their faithful goodness, won the trust and friendship of pagan leaders: Joseph with Pharaoh, in today's scripture; Nehemiah with Artaxerxes, Esther with Ahasuerus, Daniel with Nebuchadnezzar and Darius.

Now, in New Testament times, we are called to serve all leaders well. The apostle Paul urged "that petitions, prayers, intercession and thanksgiving be made for all people—for kings and all those in authority, that we may live peaceful and quiet lives in all godliness and holiness" (1 Timothy 2:1–2 NIV).

Maybe, just maybe, our good behavior will point our own leaders to the God we serve.

Lord, please draw our leaders, at all levels of government, to Yourself.

Genesis 47:27–49:28 / Matthew 13:44–58 / Psalm 20

NEVER TAKE JESUS FOR GRANTED

Jesus said, "A prophet is taken for granted in his hometown and his family." He didn't do many miracles there because of their hostile indifference.

MATTHEW 13:58 MSG

What would it have been like to live in Jesus' day and actually see and hear Him in person?

Well, consider how many people had that privilege and hated Him. Or, like those in today's scripture, saw and heard Jesus so often that they just took Him for granted.

Though none of us have experienced the physical presence of Jesus, we Christians today have a huge advantage over the people who surrounded Him two thousand years ago: His Holy Spirit lives within us to teach and to guide.

Still, even now, it's possible to take Jesus for granted. Sometimes we are so blessed—with health and family and resources and pleasures—that our Lord can fade into the background of our lives. Hopefully, we never exhibit a "hostile indifference" to Jesus, but any indifference is problematic. He deserves every bit of attention and affection we can give Him, and our lives are fullest when we make Him the priority.

A devotional book is a nice start. Thoughtful reading and study of scripture is much better. And focused, quiet time in the Lord's presence is absolutely essential.

Jesus gave His all for you. Never take Him for granted.

Thank You, Lord Jesus, for everything. Please remind me, every day, of the incredible privilege I have in knowing You.

Genesis 49:29–Exodus 1:22 / Matthew 14 / Psalm 21

JESUS' EXAMPLE

When Jesus landed and saw a large crowd,
he had compassion on them and healed their sick.

MATTHEW 14:14 NIV

At its simplest level, spiritual growth is our increasing resemblance to Jesus. To achieve that, we have to know what Jesus is like, knowledge gained through Bible study. We must talk to Him in prayer and quietly listen for His response through the Spirit. Then we need to practice what we learn.

Of His life on earth, Jesus said He "did not come to be served, but to serve" (Matthew 20:28; Mark 10:45 NIV). That is obvious in today's scripture passage. After learning of the beheading of His relative John the Baptist, Jesus "withdrew by boat privately to a solitary place" (Matthew 14:13 NIV). But the crowds, tipped off to His movement, rushed to His presumed landing spot. Jesus, in His humanity undoubtedly distressed by the death of John, immediately began serving the people.

What about us? When needs arise, will we leave our comforts to serve others? Yes, "self-care" is important—we want to maintain the well-being of our bodies, "temples of the Holy Spirit," in the apostle Paul's words (1 Corinthians 6:19 NIV). But if Jesus could rouse Himself from a quiet time of rest to serve people in need, shouldn't we do the same?

It won't be easy. But never forget that every good thing we accomplish is done in God's strength anyway.

Make me more like You, Jesus, ready to serve whenever needed.

Exodus 2–3 / Matthew 15:1–28 / Psalm 22:1–21

STAND UP FOR YOUR PEOPLE

And it came to pass in those days, when Moses was grown,
that he went out to his brothers and saw their burdens.

EXODUS 2:11 SKJV

Salvation isn't just about you.

Conversion is personal, in the sense that we have to humble ourselves before Jesus and repent of our own sins. But once we've done that, we become part of God's family, with responsibilities to our spiritual siblings.

Moses felt that obligation as an Israelite raised in the palace of Egypt. You may recall that he was born to parents from the tribe of Levi at a time when Pharaoh's attitude had turned against God's people. They'd been welcomed in Joseph's time; now, many years later, Pharaoh ordered newborn Hebrew boys thrown into the Nile. Moses' mother placed her baby in the river, but in a floating basket. Miraculously, Pharaoh's daughter found him and decided to keep Moses as her own—after paying his birth mom to nurse him.

As a man, Moses took up the cause of God's people. Though at times reluctantly, Moses did what God told him to do, and he changed the world. Today, we are to "bear one another's burdens, and so fulfill the law of Christ" (Galatians 6:2 SKJV). You may not change the world—but you'll certainly change the world of that person you stand up for.

Give me eyes to see needs and the will to meet them,
Lord. May I always stand up for my people.

Exodus 4:1–5:21 / Matthew 15:29–16:12 / Psalm 22:22–31

MARVELOUS AND MYSTERIOUS

*Disciples: We'll never find enough food for all these
people, out here in the middle of nowhere!*

MATTHEW 15:33 VOICE

Imagine yourself as one of Jesus' disciples. You follow Him, as thousands of other people tag along. The Lord is always imparting wisdom, sometimes specifically to your group of twelve, sometimes to you and the accompanying multitude.

Jesus takes in the scene: you're all in a remote place, and none of the eager listeners have eaten for a long while. He wants to feed this crowd; you respond in the words of the scripture above. You've never seen anything like what Jesus suggests.

Except you *have* seen this movie before. This is "the feeding of the four thousand"; not so long ago, you actually helped to feed a thousand people more, handing out a young boy's loaves and fishes that Jesus multiplied by His marvelous, mysterious power (Matthew 14:13–21).

How could the Twelve so quickly overlook or forget Jesus' previous miracle? There's no good answer—but neither is there a good answer when *we* doubt His power and goodness. All of us have seen God, through Jesus, doing marvelous, mysterious things in our lives. All of us should hold on to those memories in faith, believing that God will do similar or even greater things in our next time of need.

*I know You are good and kind, Lord. Forgive my doubt and strengthen
my faith. I thank You in advance for providing for my needs.*

Exodus 5:22–7:24 / Matthew 16:13–28 / Psalm 23

DO THINGS RIGHT

Moses and Aaron did just as the LORD had commanded.
EXODUS 7:20 HCSB

Tell an eight-year-old to clean his room, and you may be disappointed. There's a good chance he'll argue, probably for longer than it takes to actually do the job. There's an equally good chance that the finished work won't rise to your adult standards. "Pick everything up and put it away" ultimately looks like a few things shoved under the bed, with toys, clothes, and candy wrappers still dotting the landscape.

But give that boy a few years, and he'll do better. Someday, hopefully, he'll do everything exactly as he should. That's a growth process all of us should pursue, in every aspect of life—especially the spiritual.

In Exodus 7, Moses and Aaron followed God's instructions perfectly as they initiated the plagues that would free Israel from slavery to Pharaoh. Soon, as they left Egypt, the people "did just as the LORD had commanded" regarding the Passover (Exodus 12:50 HCSB). Centuries later, their king, David, "did exactly as the LORD commanded him, and he struck down the Philistines all the way from Geba to Gezer" (2 Samuel 5:25 HCSB).

Exacting obedience to God's commands brings blessing. Carelessness and rebellion bring trouble. The New Testament puts it succinctly: "It is a sin for the person who knows to do what is good and doesn't do it" (James 4:17 HCSB).

Father, I want to do things right. Help me to know and obey Your will.

Exodus 7:25–9:35 / Matthew 17:1–9 / Psalm 24

FEAR, BUT DON'T BE AFRAID

When the disciples heard it, they fell facedown and were terrified.
Then Jesus came up, touched them, and said, "Get up; don't be afraid."

MATTHEW 17:6–7 HCSB

The phrases "fear God," "fear of God," and "fear of the Lord" appear fifty-five times in the Holman Christian Standard Bible, from which today's scripture is drawn. While it's true that *fear* implies an element of strong respect for God, in many cases in scripture, it's an actual terror of the Lord's holiness and power.

Matthew 17 describes Jesus' transfiguration, when He granted Peter, James, and John a preview of His coming glory. That must have inspired awe: Jesus, accompanied by the long-ago prophets Moses and Elijah, "was transformed in front of them, and His face shone like the sun. Even His clothes became as white as the light" (verse 2 HCSB). But when God's voice from heaven silenced Peter's babbling about erecting tents for Jesus and the prophets, the disciples fell on their faces in abject fear.

Jesus' response to them is the same He has for us: "Don't be afraid." The fearsome God of the universe proved His love by sending Jesus to die for our sins (Romans 5:8). And when we follow Jesus by faith, however imperfectly, we are blessed with "every spiritual blessing in the heavens" (Ephesians 1:3 HCSB). So fear, but don't be afraid.

Jesus, thank You for making Your Father my
Father as well. I don't to have to be afraid!

Exodus 10–11 / Matthew 17:10–27 / Psalm 25

A PRAYER FOR EVERY OCCASION

*Show me the right path, O LORD; point out the road for me to follow.
Lead me by your truth and teach me, for you are the God who saves me.*

PSALM 25:4–5 NLT

The Book of Common Prayer, used by the world's Anglican churches, dates back nearly five centuries. Its current edition includes written prayers covering a wide variety of topics, such as "For Peace," "For the Mission of the Church," "For the Good Use of Leisure," "For Agriculture," and "For a Birthday."

A far older book of prayer, the Psalms, includes one that applies to every imaginable situation: "Show me the right path, O LORD; point out the road for me to follow. Lead me by your truth and teach me, for you are the God who saves me."

While prayers for specific circumstances have a place in our Christian walk, Psalm 25:4–5 is an "umbrella prayer" that covers everything. Asking God to point out His right way, to teach us His truth, will serve every need—whether for peace, the mission of the church, the good use of leisure. . .even for our birthdays and agricultural pursuits.

Whether you're confused or sad or enjoying victory or angrier and more frustrated than you've ever been, this is the prayer to pray:

> *Show me the right path, O LORD; point out the road
> for me to follow. Lead me by Your truth and teach
> me, for You are the God who saves me.*

INTEGRITY

I do not sit with the deceitful, nor do I associate with hypocrites.
PSALM 26:4 NIV

Generations of Americans laughed (and often cringed) with Charlie Brown, creation of cartoonist Charles Schulz. Over fifty years and nearly eighteen thousand strips, the Peanuts gang entertained readers, occasionally making them consider deeper things. For example, the June 9, 1952, comic.

The neighborhood kids are wearing western hats and carrying toy pistols. Patty declares, "I'll be the good guy." Shermy responds, "I'll be the bad guy." When Patty asks what Charlie Brown will be, he replies, "I'll be sort of in-between. . . . I'll be a hypocrite!"

With all due respect to "good ol' Charlie Brown," hypocrites *are* bad guys. Actually worse, since they know what's good but still do the wrong thing. May we as Christians make every effort to remove hypocrisy from our own lives.

Jesus hammered the hypocrisy of religious leaders who claimed to love and serve God while keeping others from Him (Matthew 23:13–33). King David, in today's scripture, refused even to associate with hypocrites.

As with any kind of deceit, hypocrisy dishonors our truthful God. . .and creates needless stress in our lives. Things are hard enough without trying to remember who to be from interaction to interaction.

Learn what God wants through His Word. Then commit to doing it. He'll be happy to help, and you can leave those unnecessary burdens behind.

Lord, I want to be a man of integrity. Empower my complete obedience.

WAITING TO SEE GOD'S GOODNESS

*I remain confident of this: I will see the goodness of the
LORD in the land of the living. Wait for the LORD;
be strong and take heart and wait for the LORD.*

PSALM 27:13–14 NIV

When we need or want God to do something for us—especially
something we see as important—the last thing most of us want to do
is *wait*. But David, the writer of today's scripture passage, understood
that he—and other believers—would see God's goodness on full
display. . .as long as he was willing to confidently wait for the Lord.

Sometimes God answers our prayers quickly with a big "yes" or
a big "no." But He sometimes answers by instructing us to simply
wait. Those times of waiting can be very trying indeed, but we can
see them as times God uses to help us mature and to strengthen and
grow our faith.

Times of waiting can be difficult, but they are tools in God's
hand to put us in a place where He can bless us beyond anything
we asked for.

*Lord, thank You for never abandoning me or leaving me on my
own as I wait on You to act on my behalf. You are 100 percent
dependable 100 percent of the time and in 100 percent of my
tests in life. I believe You and trust in You in all things.*

Exodus 15–16 / Matthew 19:1–15 / Psalm 28

A SONG OF PRAISE AND THANKSGIVING

"The LORD is my strength and my defense; he has become my salvation. He is my God, and I will praise him, my father's God, and I will exalt him. The LORD is a warrior; the LORD is his name."

EXODUS 15:2–3 NIV

Exodus 15 is mostly a song of praise Moses and the people of Israel sang to the Lord after He had so miraculously delivered them from slavery and oppression in Egypt and given them the freedom to travel to their rightful homeland, where they could live for Him and worship Him in peace.

In leading the people in this song, Moses set a tremendous example of how we should respond when God miraculously acts on our behalf and does something we could never have done for ourselves. Instead of just moving on to the next thing, Moses stopped to open his mouth and honor the Lord as his *strength*, his *defense*, his *salvation*. . .his *God*.

God loves to bless and deliver His people, and He loves sharing Himself with us further as we praise Him for His strength and goodness.

All-powerful God, You truly are a warrior who fights my battles for me. You are worthy of my trust and of my praise and adoration. Even when You seem silent, even when I can't understand what You're doing, I choose to trust You and believe in my heart that You will faithfully act on my behalf.

Exodus 17–19 / Matthew 19:16–30 / Psalm 29

DELAYED GRATIFICATION

*"And everyone who has given up houses or brothers or sisters or
father or mother or children or property, for my sake, will receive a
hundred times as much in return and will inherit eternal life."*

MATTHEW 19:29 NLT

Many men, maybe *most* men, don't fully buy into the idea of delayed gratification—meaning reaping rewards in the future for the work we do and the sacrifices we make today. We tend to want those rewards *now*, without having to wait.

In today's scripture verse, Jesus addresses the very human desire for immediate reward for our service when He, in effect, told His followers that they would receive an enormous return on their investment of time and sacrifices for Him.

A life of faith is a life of sacrificial service. . .to Jesus and to the people He brings into our lives. We are to be motivated by pure, selfless love. When that kind of love defines our lives and guides us in our actions, the rewards—in this life and in the life to come—will take care of themselves.

Generous, loving God, I will trust You and follow You with my whole heart as I work to complete those tasks You have assigned me. I firmly believe that You will empower me to do Your work here on earth. . .and that You will richly reward me in the eternal life to come. Thank You!

Exodus 20–21 / Matthew 20:1–19 / Psalm 30

FILLED WITH JOY

You have turned my mourning into joyful dancing.
You have taken away my clothes of mourning and clothed
me with joy, that I might sing praises to you and not be
silent. O LORD my God, I will give you thanks forever!
PSALM 30:11–12 NLT

It is believed that King David wrote Psalm 30 during a special time during his reign: the dedication of his royal palace. He wrote of enduring some terrible time in both his private and public life, but he contrasted these difficult memories with words of thanks and praise for the God who was with him the whole time—and who in the end filled his heart with joy.

David's story is one filled with many struggles and difficulties—some brought on through his enemies and some the results of his own sinful actions. But the Lord never completely abandoned or disowned His servant. As a man of unfailing faith, David never stopped praising God or begging Him for help. God responded to that faith in a wonderful way.

The joy David felt can be yours today—if you choose to walk closely with God in faith during even the most difficult of times.

Thank You, Father, that You can take my mourning
and pain and fill my heart instead with inner joy and
songs of praise for You. I trust You in all things.

Exodus 22–23 / Matthew 20:20–34 / Psalm 31:1–8

PERSISTENT PLEADING

Two blind men were sitting beside the road. When they heard that Jesus was coming that way, they began shouting, "Lord, Son of David, have mercy on us!" "Be quiet!" the crowd yelled at them. But they only shouted louder, "Lord, Son of David, have mercy on us!" When Jesus heard them, he stopped and called, "What do you want me to do for you?"

MATTHEW 20:30–32 NLT

Sometimes we might feel as though we need to audibly hear Jesus asking us the same question He asked two blind men who had the courage and the faith to call out to Him even louder as a crowd of people tried to make them quiet down.

What do you want me to do for you?

Life in this world can be noisy, and if we're not careful, it can be easy to let the noise distract us from calling out to Jesus when we need Him to do something for us. So keep shouting out to Jesus, even when the world seems to saying, "Be quiet!"

What do you want Jesus to do for you today?

Lord Jesus, I know You desire to do for me what I can't do for myself when I simply ask in faith. Help me to block out all the noise around me and simply focus on You when I need Your help. Thank You for always being there for me.

Exodus 24–25 / Matthew 21:1–27 / Psalm 31:9–18

HE'S ALWAYS IN CONTROL

But I am trusting you, O LORD, saying, "You are my God!" My future is in your hands. Rescue me from those who hunt me down relentlessly. Let your favor shine on your servant. In your unfailing love, rescue me.

PSALM 31:14–16 NLT

Throughout Psalm 31, David celebrates the goodness, might, and dependability of the God in whom he had placed his faith. This psalm is a prayer of thanks and confidence in the God who has full control over his future.

As a child of the living, loving God, your life is not under the control of other people. The course of your future isn't a matter of happenstance or of certain events being "in the cards." No, your life and times are under the control of the one who is called your rock, your shelter, your refuge.

A heart and mind controlled by faith in such a good, loving, powerful God as this will find peace and comfort. A man who embraces these truths can pray with David, "How abundant are the good things that you have stored up for those who fear you, that you bestow in the sight of all, on those who take refuge in you" (Psalm 31:19 NIV).

Thank You, Lord, that everything about my life—the big things and the small things alike—is in Your hands and under Your control. I believe this, and I take great comfort and confidence in knowing that nothing will happen to me without Your say-so.

Exodus 26–27 / Matthew 21:28–46 / Psalm 31:19–24

LOVING THE LORD

Love the LORD, all his faithful people! The LORD preserves
those who are true to him, but the proud he pays back in full.
Be strong and take heart, all you who hope in the LORD.

PSALM 31:23–24 NIV

In today's scripture verses, David clearly states what may be the most important themes in scripture when he writes, "Love the LORD, all his faithful people!"

Loving God is the most important thing a Christian man can do, for out of that love will spring our faith in the Lord, our genuine love for other people, and a heart of obedience to God's commands.

That's a pretty good summary of what the Christian life should look like, isn't it?

Strong faith in God will always lead to a deep love for Him, and that love will lead to a life marked by obedience. And you can be assured that God will always bless those who love Him and His Word so much that they can't help but live a life that pleases Him.

My Lord and God, thank You for loving me more deeply than I
can understand. Help me to grow in my love for You as I grow
in my faith in You. I want to love You in a manner fitting who
You are, not just what You do for me. Help me to express that
love through the words I speak and in my acts of obedience.

THE GREATEST COMMANDMENTS

"'Love the Lord your God with all your heart and with all your soul and with all your mind.' This is the first and greatest commandment. And the second is like it: 'Love your neighbor as yourself.' All the Law and the Prophets hang on these two commandments."

MATTHEW 22:37–40 NIV

The Bible teaches that true faith and love are inseparable. In other words, if we have an authentic, growing faith in Jesus, it must demonstrate itself in our love for both God and for other people. Furthermore, our love for God demonstrates itself in obedience (John 14:15) while our love for people shows itself in devoted service (1 John 3:18).

Loving God as He is worthy can sometimes be challenging, but consistently loving imperfect, fallen humans can seem impossible. You probably know that already, don't you?

The simple truth is that we can do neither in our own strength or good will, no matter how hard we try. But when we've placed our faith in Jesus, the Holy Spirit empowers and motivates us to live a life marked by radical faith—and radical love.

Loving God, thank You for the words of Jesus in today's scripture passage. My heart's desire is to love You with everything I am and to love others as I love myself. I can't do either through my own efforts, but I have faith that You can empower me to love like that. Help me to make love the defining feature of my life.

Exodus 29 / Matthew 23:1–36 / Psalm 33:1–12

JOYFUL PRAISE

Sing joyfully to the LORD, you righteous; it is fitting
for the upright to praise him. Praise the LORD with the
harp; make music to him on the ten-stringed lyre. Sing to
him a new song; play skillfully, and shout for joy.

PSALM 33:1–3 NIV

Psalm 33 begins with the wonderful encouragement for God's people to lift their voices and joyfully praise their God, for it is only fitting for us to do so because of who He is and what He does for them.

God's Word gives us many reasons and reminders to be joyful in Christ, starting with bringing us into His forever kingdom of heaven. This is one reason why the apostle Paul enjoins us to, "rejoice always" (1 Thessalonians 5:16 NIV).

A life of faith should be marked by a joyful attitude, not one of negativity, pessimism, or anger. When we focus on the benefits of faith in Jesus—especially the eternal ones—we can't help but joyfully speak (or sing) words of praise to the God who loves us with His whole heart and who daily gives us His very best.

You, Lord, are infinitely more than worthy of my praise. I praise You
for saving me and reserving for me a place in Your eternal kingdom.
I praise You for Your goodness and for caring for me in more ways
than I can count. And, most of all, I praise You for who You are.

WELL-PLACED TRUST

We put our hope in the LORD. He is our help and our shield.
In him our hearts rejoice, for we trust in his holy name. Let your
unfailing love surround us, LORD, for our hope is in you alone.

PSALM 33:20–22 NLT

As a man making his way through life in this fallen world—a fallen world filled with fallen people—you have no doubt learned that we Christians are not immune to many of the same challenges and difficulties nonbelievers face every day.

The difference in how we as followers of Christ handle our crises, however, is that we have placed our hope in a mighty God who has promised to either get us *out* of our problems or *through* them.

This is a kind of hope the world does not know or understand. It is a hope strongly rooted in a strong faith in a supremely loving God who never takes His eyes off us.

The word *hope* in today's scripture verses expresses absolute confidence. It doesn't convey an attitude of "I *hope* God will come through for me" but "I *know* God can and will keep every one of His promises."

That's a great word picture of a living, active faith!

Lord, You never promised that I would never face opposition
or crises in this life—in fact, You promised exactly the
opposite. But I have real hope in You, simply because You
have promised in Your Word to be my help and my shield.

Exodus 32–33 / Matthew 24:29–51 / Psalm 34:1–7

PATIENT FAITH

When the people saw that Moses was so long in coming down from the mountain, they gathered around Aaron and said, "Come, make us gods who will go before us. As for this fellow Moses who brought us up out of Egypt, we don't know what has happened to him."

EXODUS 32:1 NIV

Do you consider yourself a man who is patient with God? That might seem like an odd question, but a life of faith sometimes requires that we patiently wait for God to do what He has said He would do.

Moses had ascended Mount Sinai to meet with God. But when he didn't return as soon as the Israelites wanted him to, they demanded that Aaron make a "god"—a calf made of gold—which they made offerings to and worshipped. Only Moses' fervent intercession persuaded God to spare the people from terrible judgment.

When you're waiting for God to move on your behalf or give you direction, don't give in to impatience and run out ahead of God. Instead, be patient and cling tightly to your faith and know that God hasn't forgotten you.

Heavenly Father, I confess that I can become impatient as I wait for You to act on my behalf. I know that impatience can lead to even greater sin, so I ask that You give me the faith I need to patiently wait for You, even when I don't know when You will come through for me.

Exodus 34:1–35:29 / Matthew 25:1–13 / Psalm 34:8–22

THE CRIES OF THE RIGHTEOUS

*The righteous cry, and the LORD hears and delivers them out
of all their troubles. The LORD is near to those who are of a
broken heart and saves those who have a contrite spirit.*

PSALM 34:17–18 SKJV

There are few things in this life worse than feeling alone in times of
grieving, stress, sickness, or heartbreak. Loneliness is never easy, but
it's magnified in our hearts when we believe we have no one to share
in our pain.

David understood this probably better than anyone. He endured
all kinds of life storms—threats on his life and the rebellion against
him by his own son, just to name a few. But he understood that even
in the worst of times, his God was faithful to hear the cries of the
righteous and deliver them.

As men God has declared righteous in Christ, we have the same
access to God today. Paul wrote: "Because of our faith, Christ has
brought us into this place of undeserved privilege where we now
stand, and we confidently and joyfully look forward to sharing God's
glory" (Romans 5:2 NLT).

Even in times of crisis and overwhelming loneliness, we are never
truly alone.

*Loving God, thank You for hearing me when I cry out to You.
I know there is nothing in me that makes me worthy of deserving
Your hearing ear. But I believe You when You say You delight in
drawing near and listening to the broken and contrite in spirit.*

Exodus 35:30–37:29 / Matthew 25:14–30 / Psalm 35:1–8

A GOD WHO FIGHTS FOR YOU

Contend, LORD, with those who contend with me;
fight against those who fight against me. Take up
shield and armor; arise and come to my aid.

PSALM 35:1–2 NIV

David was in a tough place in life when he wrote Psalm 35. He had many enemies—vicious, cruel enemies who tried to kill him (verse 4), set traps for him (verse 7), and slandered him. Worse yet, these were men David had believed were his friends.

David knew he had nowhere else to turn, so he asked God to fight on his behalf, to "contend. . .with those who contend with me" and "fight against those who fight against me." He begged God to be a warrior who brandished his weapons and battled his enemies for him (Psalm 35:2–3).

Perhaps you can relate to what David was going through when he wrote this psalm. Maybe you've felt betrayed or even persecuted for your faith. When that happens, resist the temptation to handle things yourself. Instead, ask the Lord to set things right—and even change some hearts.

Dear Lord, thank You that You are a God who fights on my behalf,
who defeats even my worst enemies for me. May I always trust
in You during difficult times, times when I am opposed, accused,
persecuted, and slandered. May my enemies all be put to shame.

Exodus 38–39 / Matthew 25:31–46 / Psalm 35:9–17

FOLLOWING GOD'S DIRECTIONS

*The Israelites had done all the work just as the L*ORD *had commanded
Moses. Moses inspected the work and saw that they had done it
just as the L*ORD *had commanded. So Moses blessed them.*

EXODUS 39:42–43 NIV

Some men pay close attention to detail, and it shows in the quality
of their work. Others, however, have a difficult time closely following
instructions. Care to guess which of these two groups are more richly
rewarded at their year-end reviews?

Today's scripture verses tell us of a group of men who had followed
God's directions for the construction of the tabernacle, including its
interior, to the last detail. Their efforts didn't go unnoticed. When
Moses inspected their work and saw that they had done it exactly as
God commanded, he blessed them for their work.

God has given the Christian man all the directions he needs
to build a life pleasing to Him—a blessed life—and they are found
in the pages of scripture. It is an act of faith when we carefully and
consistently obey what He says to do in those pages.

*Lord God, may I have the strength of faith it takes to follow Your
clear directions for my life as You have provided in Your written Word.
May I always defeat the ever-present temptation to do things my own
way. May I always seek Your will and Your ways above everything else.*

Exodus 40 / Matthew 26:1–35 / Psalm 35:18–28

WHEN TO STAY PUT

*Now whenever the cloud lifted from the Tabernacle, the people of
Israel would set out on their journey, following it. But if the cloud
did not rise, they remained where they were until it lifted.*

Exodus 40:36–37 NLT

The Lord had given the Israelites a visible guide to let them know
when to move forward in their wilderness journey and when to stay
put. God led the people using a cloud during the day and a pillar
of fire at nighttime. They were commanded to move only when the
cloud had lifted from the campsite. If it did not move, they were to
stay where they were and wait.

We men tend to want to always be on the move. We feel that
if we are not doing something, not moving forward, then we're not
doing what God has given us to do.

But there will be times in our walks with Jesus when the Lord
gives us a stand-in-place command. When we know that the Lord
has given us a task to complete, we do well to have a strong enough
faith to be willing to wait for His perfect timing to move forward.

*Lord, there are times in my life when You guide me into
something You want me to do. May I always listen for
what You want me to do. But also increase my faith as
I patiently wait for You to give me the go-ahead.*

Leviticus 1–3 / Matthew 26:36–68 / Psalm 36:1–6

KEEP WATCH AND PRAY

*Then he returned to the disciples and found them asleep.
He said to Peter, "Couldn't you watch with me even one
hour? Keep watch and pray, so that you will not give in to
temptation. For the spirit is willing, but the body is weak!"*

MATTHEW 26:40–41 NLT

Jesus never promised a life free of temptation and testing. Even men of unshakably strong faith will find themselves tempted to sin against the Lord. Even Jesus Himself—God in the flesh and the Son of the living God—faced severe temptation at the beginning of His earthly ministry (Matthew 4:1–11).

Now, as Jesus faced His final hours on earth, He spoke words that apply to any man of God when He told His sleepy, emotionally exhausted disciples, "Keep watch and pray, so that you will not give in to temptation."

Jesus' words speak this important wisdom into our lives: if we're going to fight a winning battle against sin and temptation, we're going to have to remain spiritually alert for temptation. . .and we're going to pray for strength and wisdom.

*Lord Jesus, like Your disciples who stayed behind, I find that
my spirit is willing, but my flesh is weak when it comes to
remaining in You and living in a way that glorifies You.
May I always remain alert, pray continually, and rely on You
in all ways so that I may be strengthened in my faith.*

Leviticus 4:1–5:13 / Matthew 26:69–27:26 / Psalm 36:7–12

LOVE PERSONIFIED

How priceless is your unfailing love, O God! People take refuge
in the shadow of your wings. They feast on the abundance of
your house; you give them drink from your river of delights.
For with you is the fountain of life; in your light we see light.

PSALM 36:7–9 NIV

We humans often tend to think in terms of "deserving." If something good happens to us, we believe we deserve it because of some good we've done. But one thing we can never do enough to deserve is God's love.

The Lord loves us simply because it's His nature to do so, not because there's anything inherently lovable about us. None of us deserves God's love, mercy, and favor. We've all gone astray from Him and rebelled against Him, and if God dealt with us as we deserve, we'd all receive eternal condemnation.

But God, because He is love personified, gave us His own Son as a sacrifice so that we could "drink from [His] river of delights."

In today's scripture verses, David marveled at God's unfailing love and unmerited favor. You can do the same today and every day.

Heavenly Father, I thank You and praise You for Your amazing love,
grace, and mercy. I don't deserve any of it. In fact, I deserve Your
eternal judgment for my sin. But because my faith is in Your Son, Jesus
Christ, I will dwell with You forever in an eternal home called heaven.

Leviticus 5:14–7:21 / Matthew 27:27–50 / Psalm 37:1–6

TRUST AND CONTENTMENT

Trust in the LORD, and do good, so you shall dwell in the land and truly you shall be fed. Delight yourself also in the LORD, and He shall give you the desires of your heart.
PSALM 37:3–4 SKJV

Psalm 37 is a great read any day, but especially in those times when you sense worry or envy over the prosperity of the ungodly rising up in your heart. In this psalm, David instructs the man of God to put aside those negative thoughts and instead focus on trusting Him in all things and glorifying Him with every word and action.

God wants us to delight in Him every day, in every way, and above anything else. That is a true exercise of faith in today's world, where most men are inwardly focused and constantly chasing contentment and satisfaction through anything and everything but God.

Nothing can satisfy our souls like fully trusting in the Lord and taking delight in Him every day.

Lord, today I choose to trust You in all things and to take delight in You and in everything You do for me every day. I want to be content in You and in where You've placed me and in what You've given me to do in this world. Please guide me closer every day toward true joy and contentment in You and Your will for me.

Leviticus 7:22–8:36 / Matthew 27:51–66 / Psalm 37:7–26

CONSECRATED

*Then Moses took some of the anointing oil and some of the
blood from the altar and sprinkled them on Aaron and his
garments and on his sons and their garments. So he consecrated
Aaron and his garments and his sons and their garments.*

LEVITICUS 8:30 NIV

After the tabernacle was completed, it was time for Moses to consecrate Aaron and his sons to serve as God's tabernacle priests. In those days, that meant sprinkling anointing oil and blood on the men and their garments. This meant they were dedicated for service to God and the people.

Today, God sets each Christian aside for His use. But instead of oil and the blood of an animal, He purifies us and consecrates us through the blood of Jesus.

Paul wrote of the idea that God has set aside every Christian man for a special purpose: "For we are God's handiwork, created in Christ Jesus to do good works, which God prepared in advance for us to do" (Ephesians 2:10 NIV).

You are set aside, called, and prepared to do good things for the Lord. He has good works for you to do. The best way to find out what He has for you to do is to ask Him!

*Lord Jesus, by Your shed blood You have cleansed me from my
sin and set me apart for Your own purposes. Strengthen my faith
and guide me so that Your will be done in me and through me.*

OUR RESCUER AND FORTRESS

The LORD rescues the godly; he is their fortress in times of trouble. The LORD helps them, rescuing them from the wicked. He saves them, and they find shelter in him.

PSALM 37:39–40 NLT

No one enjoys going through difficulties. Financial difficulties, work difficulties, health difficulties, relationship difficulties, or any number of other difficulties can send even the strongest man of faith into crippling bouts of anxiety and even depression.

But there's a better way—a *much* better way.

Rather than dwelling on your problems, run to God and place them at His feet—and leave them there. Then just step back and see how He works the outcome that is best for you. . .and that glorifies Him.

Psalm 37 encourages "the righteous" to place their faith and trust in the God who promises to be their rescuer and deliverer. While all men will have trouble in this world (John 16:33), those whose faith in the living God (the "godly") have the privilege of turning to Him for rescue and protection.

God loves you, and He desires that you seek security in Him alone.

Lord God, Your written Word shows me that even the most faithful of Your people suffered in this world. But You called them to trust You fully and in all situations. I know You've called me to do the very same thing in every situation. Father, I trust You as the stronghold of my life and my place of refuge.

Leviticus 11–12 / Mark 1:1–28 / Psalm 38

FOLLOWING JESUS

*As Jesus walked beside the Sea of Galilee, he saw Simon and his
brother Andrew casting a net into the lake, for they were fishermen.
"Come, follow me," Jesus said, "and I will send you out to fish
for people." At once they left their nets and followed him.*

MARK 1:16–18 NIV

Simon (Peter) and his brother Andrew were simple fishermen who
would do great things for God's kingdom simply because they said
"yes" when Jesus called them to "Come, follow me."

They didn't yet know Jesus well, and they had no idea where He
would take them, yet they started their lives as His disciples when
they responded to His invitation to *follow.*

"At once they left their nets and followed him." No questions, no
taking time to give their father notice that they were leaving the family
business, and no announcements to their families. They just dropped
everything and followed the man who would completely change the
course of their lives.

What an act of faith! And what an example Simon and Andrew
set for us Christian men today!

*Jesus, today I commit myself to following You with my whole
heart and body. I don't know what this day will hold for me,
but You do—and I will act in faith as I go where You lead me and
do what You want me to do. Lead me today, and I will follow.*

QUIET TIME

*And in the morning, rising up a great while before day, He went
out and departed to a solitary place and prayed there. And Simon
and those who were with Him followed after Him. And when they
had found Him, they said to Him, "All men are seeking for You."*

MARK 1:35–37 SKJV

In order to be revitalized and strengthened in our faith, we need to
spend "quiet time" with God—just like Jesus did during His ministry
here on earth.

Jesus spent much of His time ministering to hurting, needy people.
There was always another person to heal or people who desperately
needed to hear what He had to say. And while Jesus was indeed God
in the flesh, He was still a man who needed the encouragement and
strength that spending time alone with His Father provided.

When you spend "quiet time" with the Lord—reading your Bible
and communicating with Him in prayer—you're drawing close to your
source of strength and encouragement to live the way God wants you
to live and do the things He wants you to do. Not only that, you'll
find your faith deepened and strengthened.

*Lord Jesus, You set the perfect example for what every man
desperately needs when he is feeling the pressure of dealing
with needy, hurting people. When I feel the pressure, may I do
as You did: spend time in the Father's presence. That is where
my faith and my resolve are renewed and strengthened.*

Leviticus 14 / Mark 1:40–2:12 / Psalm 40:1–8

CONFIDENCE IN AN ANSWER

I waited patiently for the LORD; he turned to me and heard my
cry. He lifted me out of the slimy pit, out of the mud and mire;
he set my feet on a rock and gave me a firm place to stand.
He put a new song in my mouth, a hymn of praise to our God.

PSALM 40:1–3 NIV

How do you respond when you've been fervently and persistently praying about something but it seems like you receive nothing in return but silence? Answers to prayer don't always come quickly; in fact, praying in faith usually requires an investment of time and effort.

David, the writer of Psalm 40, understood the value of waiting patiently for his God to respond to his cries for help—and he set an example any praying Christian man should follow.

We can't always know why God waits to respond to our cries for help. But one thing we can know for sure: the waiting can help strengthen our faith and help us to learn patience.

Lord God, thank You for Your love, and thank You for hearing my prayers when I cry out to You in patience and faith. I don't always understand why You sometimes wait before You respond to my cries for help, but I remain confident in an answer. In the meantime, help my faith in You to grow stronger and deeper each day.

Leviticus 15 / Mark 2:13–3:35 / Psalm 40:9–17

INNER CLEANLINESS

"You must keep the Israelites separate from things that make them unclean, so they will not die in their uncleanness for defiling my dwelling place, which is among them."

LEVITICUS 15:31 NIV

The Bible consistently tells us that it's important for us believers to keep ourselves from taking part in behaviors and thinking that will make us "unclean." For example, James 1:27 (NIV) says, "Religion that God our Father accepts as pure and faultless is this: to look after orphans and widows in their distress and to keep oneself from being polluted by the world."

Sadly, too many professing believers engage in "unclean" activities such as lying and gossip, pornography, sexual immorality, drunkenness, foul language, and others. Many tell others they are Christians but don't seem any different from nonbelievers.

God calls us to something much different. We grow in our faith and in our witness for Jesus when we guard our bodies, our minds, and our speech from the things that displease our heavenly Father.

Holy God, living in such a sinful world, it's too easy for me to become desensitized to sin. Please restore my sensitivity to sin and help me to remember the damage it does to my relationship with You. Give me the faith I need to believe that You are faithful and just to forgive me when I turn to You in repentance, and also empower me to turn from sin.

Leviticus 16–17 / Mark 4:1–20 / Psalm 41:1–4

GOD'S MERCY

"O LORD," I prayed, "have mercy on me.
Heal me, for I have sinned against you."

PSALM 41:4 NLT

Many centuries ago, the apostle John wrote, "If we confess our sins, he is faithful and just and will forgive us our sins and purify us from all unrighteousness" (1 John 1:9 NIV).

Faithful and just. That means that God will keep His promise to forgive us when we come to Him and confess our wrongdoing. In today's scripture verse, David gave further voice to this truth when he cried out to the Lord to have mercy on him and to heal his heart, for he had sinned against Him.

Sin carries with it very severe consequences, namely eternal punishment and separation from God. But God mercifully forgives and cleanses the believer who recognizes and confesses his sin. God truly desires to forgive and restore the penitent believer.

Are you aware of some sin in your life that has created separation between you and God? Then run to Him now and confess—then believe in your heart that He has forgiven and cleansed you.

Lord God, I thank You for Your mercy upon a miserable sinner
like me. When I sin against You, may I run to Your throne
and seek mercy, forgiveness, cleansing, and restoration—
not away from You in shame and discouragement. You truly
are a God who delights in showing Your people mercy.

Leviticus 18–19 / Mark 4:21–41 / Psalm 41:5–13

QUIETING STORMS

*When Jesus woke up, he rebuked the wind and said to
the waves, "Silence! Be still!" Suddenly the wind stopped,
and there was a great calm. Then he asked them,
"Why are you afraid? Do you still have no faith?"*
MARK 4:39–40 NLT

Jesus' disciples once found themselves stuck in the middle of the Sea of Galilee as a violent storm brought them to panic. The disciples believed they would die that night. . .until Jesus rescued them by simply speaking to the storm: "Silence! Be still!"

Speaking confidently and quietly, Jesus quieted a raging storm— and His disciples' fearful hearts and minds—with three simple words, showing His disciples that He had absolute power over all things, even the weather.

You may never have to face a literal life-threatening weather event, but your life on this earth will most certainly include different types of storms—some relatively mild and some terrifyingly severe. But the account of Jesus calming a violent storm can comfort you as it shows you that He has authority over all things—even your worst life storms.

*Lord Jesus, life can sometimes be chaotic and frightening.
When the storms of life overtake me, help me to rely on You to
get either out of them or through them. No matter how bad the
storms, I will choose to rely on You to get me through them.*

Leviticus 20 / Mark 5 / Psalm 42–43

JUST BELIEVE

While Jesus was still speaking, some people came from the house of Jairus, the synagogue leader. "Your daughter is dead," they said. "Why bother the teacher anymore?" Overhearing what they said, Jesus told him, "Don't be afraid; just believe."

MARK 5:35–36 NIV

In good times, in times when nothing tests our faith, it's easy to say we trust God in all things. But what about when we're going through the dark valley of severe testing—when we've lost the job that provided for ourselves and our family, when we or a loved one is going through a serious health crisis, or when an important relation is in peril?

Life here on earth can test the faith of even the most grounded Christian in countless ways. When you are in the midst of a time of stress, sorrow, or sickness, Jesus speaks into your situation these comforting, encouraging words: *Don't be afraid; just believe.*

The choice is yours. Will you dwell in your fear, or will you just believe?

My precious Jesus, life in this fallen world is sure to take me through times of loss and heartache—serious illnesses, the death of a loved one, and others. When those times come, comfort me with Your words to Jairus the synagogue leader: "Don't be afraid; just believe." When I'm hurting, draw me nearer to You than ever.

Leviticus 21–22 / Mark 6:1–13 / Psalm 44

THE GOD WHO RESCUES

*With your hand you drove out the nations and planted our
ancestors; you crushed the peoples and made our ancestors
flourish. It was not by their sword that they won the land,
nor did their arm bring them victory; it was your right hand,
your arm, and the light of your face, for you loved them.*

PSALM 44:2 3 NIV

In Psalm 44, the sons of Korah recall how God had performed many
amazing deeds on Israel's behalf, driving out nations and settling the
Israelites in the promised land and winning many battles they could
never have won in their own strength.

God defeated Israel's enemies for one reason: "you loved them."
God had chosen Israel to be His own special people and had promised
the people that He would always be their God and they would be His
people. And God would remain faithful to them forever.

As a man who has come to the Lord through faith in Jesus Christ,
you too are the object of His love and faithfulness, and He will keep
His promise to be with you and care for you every day of your life.

*Lord God, You show Your love and faithfulness to Your people
in so many wonderful ways—including in how You've used my
own past—the good and the bad—to shape me and teach me.
May I use what I've learned to glorify You and teach others about
Your goodness and faithfulness to those You call Your own.*

Leviticus 23–24 / Mark 6:14–29 / Psalm 45:1–5

TOUGH TRUTH

John had been telling Herod, "It is not lawful for
you to have your brother's wife!" So Herodias held a
grudge against him and wanted to kill him.
MARK 6:18–19 HCSB

The world loves the idea of knowing the truth. Scientists dedicate their lives to the quest for knowledge. Celebrities are idolized for being honest about their personal lives. And countless books, movies, and songs repeatedly quote Jesus' famous line: "The Truth will set you free" (John 8:32 AMPC).

But what happens when the truth is something that people don't want to hear? What happens when a world that's in love with its sin hears that Jesus died to rescue them from sin? Do they stick to their guns and accept it like they do everything else? For some people, yes. Otherwise, the Church would be long gone. But usually people react much in the same way Herodias acted when John told Herod the truth: anger. Even we Christians can become upset when brothers and sisters in Christ point out flaws in our lives that need to change.

But it's our responsibility to uphold the truth, whether they (or we) like it or not. When confronted with hostility, strong faith doesn't back down—it doubles down. By planting your roots in the truth, your faith will stand when the world's lies turn to ashes.

Jesus, You are the Truth upon which I want to build my life.
May I never succumb to the easy lies around me.

Leviticus 25 / Mark 6:30–56 / Psalm 45:6–12

MISSION: SURVIVE

They laid the sick in the marketplaces and begged
Him that they might touch just the tassel of His robe.
And everyone who touched it was made well.

MARK 6:56 HCSB

"If I can only hold out God permitting I will eventually be seen."

These are the frantic words pilot Bob Gauchie scrawled in his personal journal, nearly seven weeks after making an emergency landing on a remote, frozen lake in Canada. The conditions were atrocious—high winds, circling wolves, and temperatures that hovered in the seventies (on the *wrong* side of zero) were all conspiring to make sure this poor man didn't make it through the night. But he did make it. And when he was finally found, the pilot who picked him up remarked that he looked like "he was waiting on a bus."

How did Gauchie preserve his sanity? Simple: by holding on each day to the one thread of hope he could see—he was still alive.

That's the kind of hope today's verse describes. A crowd of desperate, hurting people with no earthly hope were now in sight of the very embodiment of hope: Jesus. So what did they do? They hung on, knowing that if they could touch just the fringe of His clothing, then their long-awaited healing would finally arrive.

Are you clinging to Jesus with that kind of desperation?

Savior, help me value You more than life itself.
You're my only hope in this cold, barren world.

Leviticus 26 / Mark 7 / Psalm 45:13–17

FERTILE GROUND

"If you follow my decrees and are careful to obey my commands,
I will send you the seasonal rains. The land will then yield its
crops, and the trees of the field will produce their fruit."

LEVITICUS 26:3–4 NLT

Today's verse was meant to be taken literally. It was written to a budding nation whose primary concern didn't lie in health care programs or government stability but in basic, day-to-day survival. And for that survival to happen, naturally, they would need food. It was a simple system: good crops, good life; no crops, no life. As a result, God's literal promise to always keep them fed if they followed His commands held infinitely more weight than it does for us today.

But this verse still hasn't lost its impact, even for those of us living in first world countries with instant access to groceries and imported exotic foods. Why? Because God's promise is also true spiritually. If you want your walk with God to thrive, you have to nourish it by following His will. Just as you can't grow a healthy garden without watering it, you can't grow your spiritual walk without prayer and Bible reading.

And as satisfying and delicious as fruit from a healthy tree can be, the fruits for keeping God's commandments are much, much better.

Father God, may I never treat Your commands like
optional assignments. Teach me to follow Your will so
that Your blessings may overflow in my life.

Leviticus 27 / Mark 8 / Psalm 46

A CROSS TO BEAR

*"Whoever wants to be my disciple must deny themselves
and take up their cross and follow me."*

MARK 8:34 NIV

When asked if we'd be willing to die for Christ, many of us are eager to raise our hands. Hearing stories of missionaries who are killed by natives, we feel inspired and ready to face death for a cause we believe in. But why does it seem we're often more willing to die for Christ than to *live* for Him?

At worst, it might be because deep down we all know how improbable such scenarios are, so we feel safe in plugging ourselves into the stories. But maybe the answer is something less cynical. Maybe it's because the act of making a sudden, dramatic decision is easier than living a quiet, consistent life. When it comes to the daily grind—the consistent refusal of temptation in a world that mocks us, the willpower to show kindness toward those who annoy us, and the quiet dedication that drives daily devotions—noble sentiments tend to fade fairly fast.

But this is exactly the kind of life to which Christ calls us—a life born not of emotion or a sense of self-importance but of dedication to the one who dedicated His life to saving us. Are you willing to make that sacrifice?

*Lord, fill my heart not with shallow notions of grandeur
but with a deep longing for Your righteousness.*

Numbers 1–2 / Mark 9:1–13 / Psalm 47

ASHES TO ASHES

For God is the King of all the earth; sing praises in
a skillful psalm and with understanding.

PSALM 47:7 AMPC

Today, millions of Christians around the world will "celebrate" Ash Wednesday. In reality, this day is less of a celebration than it is a memorial—a time to reflect deeply on our own mortality. "You were made from dust, and to dust you will return" (Genesis 3:19 NLT) is the mantra that gets repeated as ash is ceremonially placed on the foreheads of those who observe this day.

But today's verse shows that even on Ash Wednesday, Christians can rejoice. Why? Because despite the fallen nature of this world and the death that awaits us all, we can take solace in the fact that *God is still King.* Even better, we know something that the psalmist did not: Jesus, the perfect Son of God, has conquered death once and for all. The moment a child of God closes his eyes in death is the moment he awakens in the fresh light of eternal life. And when Jesus comes again, our rent bodies and the torn earth beneath our feet will be gloriously transformed. All ash will vanish forever, replaced by the life-bringing glow of God's love.

Today, dwell on this final victory, letting it guide your journey with Christ and strengthen your faith in His power.

Almighty God, thank You for offering a hope
that's stronger than even death itself.

Numbers 3 / Mark 9:14–50 / Psalm 48:1–8

FAKE OR FAITHFUL?

Immediately the boy's father exclaimed,
"I do believe; help me overcome my unbelief!"

MARK 9:24 NIV

How often does the world look to the church for answers, only to see a crowd of people just as clueless as they are. . .but never willing to admit it? Perplexed by personal issues and hounded by doubts, we often shove these thoughts deep within our subconscious, choosing to repeat lifeless platitudes rather than grapple honestly with the God who invites us to ask Him anything.

No wonder the world sees us as fakers!

Today's verse shows that it's okay to be honest with God, admitting your failures and your lapses of faith. After all, no tree begins as a mighty oak—its roots begin from a place of weakness. Apostle Pauls and Billy Grahams aren't born overnight—each mighty man of God started out like the man in today's verse, crying out for God to strengthen his frail spiritual bones.

And even if you've been walking with God for quite some time, you'll still find that the only way to grow stronger is to admit when you feel weak. Growth isn't defined by your ability to hold a smile on your face—it's defined by where your sincerity leads you.

So come to God with the things you're ashamed to admit. . .and He will take it from there.

Heavenly Father, give me the humility to admit my helplessness
and the strength to press through the weakness.

Numbers 4 / Mark 10:1–34 / Psalm 48:9–14

FINISHING LAST

"But many who are first will be last, and the last first."
MARK 10:31 NIV

The Iraqi dictator Saddam Hussein had everything he needed to make him happy. Wealth, power, control, and unfathomable levels of protection should've given him the peace that so many men spend their lives trying to obtain. . .right?

Wrong.

Hussein was one of the most miserable men alive. His entire life was now a house of cards. Nothing and nowhere was safe. Everybody either envied him, hated him, or both. Most wanted him dead. In fact, his paranoia was so great that he even ordered certain men to be surgically altered and sent out as body doubles of himself. Not only that, he'd become so completely separated from the general population (which he oppressed relentlessly) that his loneliness must've been suffocating.

Others who craved the kind of power he had probably saw him as the luckiest man alive—when in reality, no curse is greater than the one that rested upon his head. By reaching toward the sky, he'd lost his roots—spiritually, emotionally, and mentally. He'd placed first in the race of worldly recognition. . .but failed to even cross the starting line in the only race that matters.

God, whenever I'm tempted to value money or popularity ahead of loyalty to You, remind me of the great rewards that come to those who "finish last" in this world's meaningless competitions.

Numbers 5:1–6:21 / Mark 10:35–52 / Psalm 49:1–9

SUPERFICIAL

Why should I fear when evil days come, when wicked deceivers surround me—those who trust in their wealth and boast of their great riches?

PSALM 49:5–6 NIV

In the world's eyes, the parable of Lazarus and the rich man might be one of Jesus' most depressing stories. Lazarus never gets the money he needs to get by. In fact, he dies alone—perhaps of starvation. And the rich man, despite his temporary success, has his life cut short by fate.

But it's what happens next that forms the crux of the parable's point. The rich man's odds are suddenly reversed, and he finds himself in a world of suffering, the likes of which he'd only caught glimpses of when he'd looked into the eyes of poor Lazarus. Lazarus, on the other hand, finds himself in a place where joy never ends—an eternal reward for his quiet, faithful suffering.

In short, what the world sees as success, God sees as abject failure—a fundamental misunderstanding of the purpose of life and a tragic waste of all the years He's given us. So how do we gain the spiritual understanding to look past our superficial misfortunes? By being attuned to God's will, learning about His nature each day through prayer and study of His Word.

Knowledge of God brings understanding, understanding brings purpose, and purpose brings peace.

God, grant me the strength to endure whatever suffering may come. Through it all, I want to remain faithful to You.

Numbers 6:22–7:47 / Mark 11 / Psalm 49:10–20

TICKING CLOCKS

We aren't immortal. We don't last long.
Like our dogs, we age and weaken. And die.
PSALM 49:12 MSG

It's not hard to find examples of God's ultimate power. . .and our weakness. And today, as Daylight Saving Time begins, we see an especially stunning illustration of this truth. When we tamper with the constant forward march of the clock's hands, we show just how dependent we are on the natural cycles which God has ordained.

God created days and seasons and even time itself, and all mankind can do is measure it in creative and useful ways. We can't stop time, bend it, turn it backward, or even slow it down for a single nanosecond. What's more, we're not even capable of altering the natural ways in which time is measured. Man can turn the clock—only God can turn the sun.

So. . .what does that mean for us? What can we do with the free but fleeting gift of time? Simple: "Fear God and keep His commandments, for this is the whole duty of man" (Ecclesiastes 12:13 SKJV). Time is a resource that's as precious as it is limited. You can choose to waste it on sinful pursuits or spend it learning about God and preparing for the eternity that awaits. The clock is ticking—make your choice.

Teach me to number my days, Father, and give me
the wisdom to know what to do with them.

Numbers 7:48–8:4 / Mark 12:1–27 / Psalm 50:1–15

THE POWERS THAT BE

"Give back to Caesar what is Caesar's and to God what is God's."
MARK 12:17 NIV

It can be easy for Christians to adopt an attitude of spiteful rebellion against the government, especially when the people in charge are pushing policies with which they disagree. "I serve God, not man," they may say, "so why should I pay taxes or obey their foolish laws?" But this is just a willful twisting of God's Word, perhaps to justify their attitude of rugged individualism or their tendencies toward sinful rebellion.

Today's verse says we should never use our service to God as an excuse for disobeying our earthly leaders. In fact, Romans 13:1 (NIV) says, "Let everyone be subject to the governing authorities, for there is no authority except that which God has established."

God has set our government up for a reason, and our willingness to comply with the laws of the land (so long as they don't conflict with God's laws) will better enable us to comply with God's commands. Earthly obedience is another way to foster spiritual discipline. Besides, what will nonbelievers think of us when they see our belligerence and angry rebellion? Certainly not the faith or love we're supposed to display!

So today, spend some time thanking God for the men and women who work to make this country a better and safer place.

Jesus, give me the wisdom and grace to humbly obey the authorities without sacrificing my obedience to You.

Numbers 8:5–9:23 / Mark 12:28–44 / Psalm 50:16–23

HOLLOW LOVE

*"And you must love the L*ORD *your God with all your*
heart, all your soul, all your mind, and all your strength.'
The second is equally important: 'Love your neighbor as
yourself.' No other commandment is greater than these."

MARK 12:30–31 NLT

Many point to today's passage as an excuse for their spiritual laziness. "See?" they say, "All I have to do is love God and others. I already do, so why should I change my ways?"

But what does love mean? If you say you love your spouse but neglect her each day and pretend you don't know her in public, your "love" for her is as genuine as a hollow, cracked eggshell.

So, again. . .what is love? For starters, love isn't a state of mind—it's a verb. Loving someone means volunteering your time, valuing that person above other pursuits, and working hard to make sure that person's needs are met. So when God tells us to love Himself and others, it means far more than just smiling whenever you hear a spiritual song or shedding a tear when you see suffering on the news. It means *action*—action in the form of obedience and servitude. Wherever true biblical love is found, these qualities will follow close behind.

Father God, may my love be more than a word, thought,
or emotion. May it be a lifestyle I choose to live each day,
firmly planted in the love You've always had for me.

Numbers 10–11 / Mark 13:1–8 / Psalm 51:1–9

MEMORY LOSS

*"We remember the fish we ate in Egypt at no cost—also the
cucumbers, melons, leeks, onions and garlic. But now we have
lost our appetite; we never see anything but this manna!"*

NUMBERS 11:5–6 NIV

Wouldn't it be amazing to witness God's power? To watch as an
entire sea is rent in two like an old rag? To watch an entire enemy
army drown in the waters you'd just walked through? To see food fall
from heaven each night, ensuring nobody went hungry? The Israelites
witnessed all these amazing deeds and more. . .and today's passage
gives their response.

The audacity!

But are we any better? When we became Christians, we witnessed
the full power of God. He stepped in, bridging the infinite gap between
us and Him. But the moment a trial comes along—a few scant
paychecks, a strained relationship, a disappointing doctor's visit—how
often do we complain and come dangerously close to throwing it all
away? And for what? A life of temporary sin?

Often, the best way to grow your faith, avoiding the fatal mindset
of the Israelites, is to simply remember. Remembering God's good
deeds in the past will give you the stamina you need to press through
the misfortunes you face in the present. Just as He came through then,
He'll come through again.

> God, fill me with a grateful spirit. May Your blessings
> take root in my memory, shoving out the darkness
> and doubt that threatens to overtake.

Numbers 12–13 / Mark 13:9–37 / Psalm 51:10–19

BLANK CANVAS

*Then Caleb. . .said, "We must go up and take possession
of the land because we can certainly conquer it!"*

NUMBERS 13:30 HCSB

Few people have managed to reach the summit of the mighty Mount Everest. But how many have done it. . .blind? Not many, and Erik Weihenmayer was the first.

Erik says his inspiration to do this impossible task came from a friend named Hugh who lost both his legs on an expedition. Erik explained, "[Hugh] said the greatest breakthrough of his life was when he looked at where his legs were supposed to be and instead of seeing loss, he saw a blank canvas."

In today's verse, Caleb looked at a land full of giants and saw a blank canvas. . .with God as the artist. Unlike the other Israelites, Caleb had been paying attention when God had parted the Red Sea and openly defied the laws of nature. And because of his attentiveness, he knew the extent of God's power. He also knew that the more impossible the task, the louder the noise records make when they're broken.

When you read the Bible, encountering all the amazing deeds God performed for His people, are you looking for ways in which God might be working in your own life? When impossible situations loom ahead, do you see an unscalable mountain. . .or a blank canvas?

*Father, You're the author of impossibilities.
Strengthen my faith by reminding me of Your awesome power.*

Numbers 14 / Mark 14:1-31 / Psalm 52

STRONG WORDS

But Peter said to Him, "Although all shall be
made to stumble, yet I will not."

MARK 14:29 SKJV

Peter confused strong faith with strong words.

Few would doubt that Peter's heart was in the right place. After all, Jesus had earlier told him, "You are Peter, and on this rock I will build my church, and the gates of Hades will not overcome it" (Matthew 16:18 NIV). Clearly, this apostle had the insight he needed to understand Jesus' message and the eagerness to act on it. . .but sometimes his eagerness outpaced his courage. As a result, he ended up committing two sins that day: denying Jesus *and* breaking a promise.

In our walk with Jesus, it's often easy to make rash promises about what we will or won't do—promises that, unbeknownst to us, may be impossible to keep. But God doesn't want to hear our grandiose opinions about how the future will play out; instead, He wants us to simply come to Him with the intention to do His will and the humility to accept His help in carrying it out. And if we fail—as all of us inevitably will at some point—at least we'll only have one sin to bring before God's throne.

Lord, give me a long-term faith that values steady growth over
sudden, impossible leaps. May I fill in the gaps of my weakness
with Your strength instead of my own misplaced confidence.

Numbers 15 / Mark 14:32–72 / Psalm 53

CONSISTENT FAITH

Only fools say in their hearts, "There is no God."
PSALM 53:1 NLT

It's a lot easier to ignore God's existence than it is to acknowledge it and adjust our lives accordingly. Sure, you no doubt agree with the fact that God exists; otherwise, you probably wouldn't be reading this. But when it comes to the small, daily decisions you make, do you *act* like you believe it?

When we're in church and a beautiful song is playing, it's easy to bask in God's glory. . .but the moment God's glory starts stepping on our toes, it's easy to start thinking like a fool and acting like nobody's really watching—boxing up "belief" and "behavior" into different compartments in our minds. It's not hard to see the foolishness in this. If you're crossing a highway and a car is barreling toward you, do you compartmentalize your belief so that it does not affect your behavior? Of course not!

It's not enough to claim you believe something. If your faith is genuine, then your behavior will flow consistently from it. Practicing true faith is hard, of course. But often, *hard* is the only path that'll help us grow. It's time to dig in and start treating faith like the life-changing force it was always meant to be.

If you're a man of God, act like it!

Righteous God, may my faith be more than lip service.
Let there be no separation between my faith and my actions.

Numbers 16 / Mark 15:1–32 / Psalm 54

BETRAYED

So to pacify the crowd, Pilate released Barabbas to them.
MARK 15:15 NLT

We know nearly nothing about Pilate's true opinions about Jesus' identity. All we know is that he recognized that Jesus was innocent, but in the end, his desire for popularity won against his conscience.

Maybe Pilate had no idea that Jesus was the Son of God, and his decision to have Him crucified was merely one choice in a long string of corrupt political actions. Or maybe he *did* know. . .thus adding an infinite amount of gravity to his choice.

Two thousand years later, there's no shortage of "Pontius Pilates"— people who claim to recognize Jesus' lordship but deny Him with their actions.

So how do we avoid becoming like Pilate? Simple: by developing a stronger relationship with Jesus. The more you get to know the Son of God, the less likely you'll be to betray Him. Think of the person you love the most here on earth. Now try to imagine what it would take to make you deny or willfully harm that person. Unthinkable, right? Similarly, if you truly become acquainted with the Savior of mankind and His bottomless love for you, the very thought of betraying Him will become as repugnant as death itself.

Don't try pacifying the crowd by choosing sin; stand up for the one who died for you.

Lord Jesus, I want You to be my closest friend.
May I never betray You for the world's worthless approval.

Numbers 17–18 / Mark 15:33–47 / Psalm 55

INHERITED TREASURE

*And the LORD spoke to Aaron, "You shall have no inheritance
in their land. Nor shall you have any part among them. I am
your part and your inheritance among the children of Israel."*

NUMBERS 18:20 SKJV

Depending on your view of God, Aaron either received the best deal
in history or got the short end of the stick. If you live for worldly,
sinful pursuits, then God's promise in today's verse might sound as
appealing as a pile of rocks in a kid's Christmas stocking. There's just
no use for it. But if you value God's presence, as all true Christians
should, then this is the most beautiful promise of them all. Who
cares about money or land when you have the most valuable treasure
in the universe?

For an example somewhat closer to modern times, consider St.
Patrick—the patron saint of the holiday we celebrate today. His entire
reputation—the whole reason for the holiday's existence—is built on
his missionary work. He didn't build castles or conquer empires. He
simply led pagans to Christ. But if he were alive today, that reputation
would probably bring tears of joy to his eyes, for that's all he really
set out to do!

Where do your priorities lie?

*Lord, I don't care if my name is engraved in stone or scrawled
in sand. In fact, I don't care if it's written anywhere, except for
within Your book of life. May Your name be my inheritance.*

Numbers 19–20 / Mark 16 / Psalm 56:1–7

ROBBING GOD

With that Moses. . .slammed his staff against the rock. . . . God said to Moses and Aaron, "Because you didn't trust me, didn't treat me with holy reverence in front of the People of Israel, you two aren't going to lead this company into the land that I am giving them."

NUMBERS 20:11–12 MSG

At first glance, Moses' actions don't seem like a punishable offense—let alone worthy of the punishment God gave him. But it wasn't Moses' slight departure that angered God so much. Rather, by claiming responsibility for this miracle (verse 10), Moses took the glory that was due to God and tried applying it to himself. His deed was more than a failure to follow instructions to the letter—it was rooted in pride.

In our Christian service, we must always be watchful lest the tiniest fingers of pride slip between the gaps in our obedience, prying it apart and stealing its core—the glory of God.

God's infinite goodness is the wellspring of the small amount of goodness that flows from our lives, so don't try robbing God of the honor that's rightfully His. Instead, train yourself to be humble, always pointing others toward the true source of righteousness and power.

Lord, how foolish it would be for me, a vessel of dust in which You've placed Your Spirit, to take all the credit for the light inside me! Make me humble, God—an eager servant for You.

Numbers 21:1–22:20 / Luke 1:1–25 / Psalm 56:8–13

BOTTLED UP

*You number and record my wanderings; put my tears
into Your bottle—are they not in Your book?*

PSALM 56:8 AMPC

In the mid-nineteenth century, a shocking discovery was made: a glass jar containing a heap of ashes. The shock came with the inscriptions on the jar's lid, claiming that the contents belonged to Joan of Arc, one of Catholicism's famous saints. The jar was taken to a museum and locked away as a holy relic. While the authenticity of these ashes has since then been debated, this isn't the only relic held in high regard by the Catholic Church. The alleged remains of many other martyrs lie scattered throughout the world, locked in glass cases and meticulously preserved by experts.

Part of the reason the Catholics do this is to honor these martyrs' sacrifice. But did you know that God treats our suffering in much the same way? Today's verse says He stores our tears in a bottle. When we cry out in faith that's mixed with pain—when we endure the fires of loss and doubt—our tears are not forgotten. God remembers our perseverance. . .and He will reward accordingly.

While the church can't reverse the deaths of the martyrs it venerates, God can and will for those who serve Him.

*Father, let the knowledge that You care fill me with
a renewed desire to stay faithful to You. Remind me
that my sacrifices for You will never go in vain.*

Numbers 22:21–23:30 / Luke 1:26–56 / Psalm 57

TILL WINTER ENDS

*Have mercy on me, my God, have mercy on me, for
in you I take refuge. I will take refuge in the shadow
of your wings until the disaster has passed.*

PSALM 57:1 NIV

To many people, winter is the most beautiful season. Its glittering snowfalls, frosty mornings, and sparkling icicles all conspire to make it one of the most visually stunning times of the year. But there's no denying that it's also the most unforgiving.

That same delightful coat of snow can topple trees and start avalanches. The same cold that creates the frost can cause frostbite in anyone who stays outside a minute too long. And even brilliant icicles have dangerous tips.

That's why the first day of spring is so welcome—it marks an end to the dangerous cold and the beginning of new life.

Similarly, while this life is filled with beauty, it's also marked by the deadly chill of sin and violence and unfulfilled dreams. But someday, an eternal spring will dawn, ushering in the warmth of God's final reward for His children. Today, all we can do is anticipate this time, dwelling on the brief glimpses found in God's Word and taking shelter in Him for safety. Then, when spring finally comes, we'll be ready to step into His eternal light.

*God, may the warmth of my eternal home with You reach back in time
to warm up my icy soul today. May spring be my song in the winter.*

Numbers 24–25 / Luke 1:57–2:20 / Psalm 58

INQUIRING MINDS

As the angel choir withdrew into heaven, the shepherds talked it over. "Let's get over to Bethlehem as fast as we can."

LUKE 2:15 MSG

As if witnessing a host of angelic beings appear out of thin air wasn't enough, the shepherds faced an even greater surprise when the angels' message finally sunk in: the Son of God had been born! Immediately, the shepherds were overwhelmed with curiosity. They couldn't just sit back and let the news pass over them—they had to see for themselves.

Fast-forward to today, a time in which God has written extensively about Himself in the Bible, uncovering deep mysteries that were once hidden for thousands of years (Colossians 1:26). How many of us are still eager to search the scriptures for these mysteries? Are we just as enamored with God's plan of salvation as those men were two thousand years ago? Or have the winds of familiarity and earthly cares beaten down our enthusiasm, transforming it into a dull, lifeless tribute to truths we no longer explore?

Learning about God should never get old to us—after all, His infinite nature ensures we'll never reach the bottom of His mysteries. So today, if your soul lacks the fire that once drove your devotion, ask God to rekindle it, igniting your curiosity and thirst for His truth.

Eternal God, I want to learn as much about Your unfathomable truth as I can. Grant me an insatiable thirst for Your glory.

HELP!

*Rescue me! Save me, O my God, from my enemies; set me
in a safe place, far above any who come to attack me.*
PSALM 59:1 VOICE

Ever feel like fate itself is against you? Maybe you feel confused and mistreated by everyone—from the government down to even your friends and family. It's almost like the entire world is focusing its efforts on making sure you don't succeed.

If so, don't fret—everyone feels this profound sense of oppression at some point. And David knew that feeling better than anyone. From the time he was a boy, he'd faced enemy after enemy—from giants to mad kings to his own son. Just one failure would've proven fatal, and each near escape inflicted a bevy of emotional scars upon his soul.

So what kept him going each day? Faith. Despite the overwhelming odds, he refused to give in to pessimism. Instead, he regularly spoke of God's mighty power, even before he saw it in action. In many cases, David employed this tactic not to intimidate his enemies but to "encourage himself in the LORD" (1 Samuel 30:6 SKJV). He spoke of God's power not to convince God to help—but to convince himself that He could. And each time, God *did*.

Today, as the world seems to gather its army against you, where will you turn for strength?

*Father, give me the faith to see Your power. Despite how
impossible victory seems now, I know You've already won.*

Numbers 27:12–29:11 / Luke 2:39–52 / Psalm 59:9–17

GARDENERS

*"May the LORD, the God who gives breath to all living things,
appoint someone over this community to go out and come in
before them, one who will lead them out and bring them in,
so the LORD's people will not be like sheep without a shepherd."*

NUMBERS 27:16–17 NIV

Have you ever thought about the fact that God expects each one of us to both be examples to others *and* learn from others? If you do the math, that means there's a lot of teaching and learning being performed by the same people. As guys, we sometimes love fixating on the first part while neglecting or completely ignoring the second. But as today's verse shows, that attitude leads straight to disaster.

While all your instruction should ultimately come from God, you should never be afraid to ask advice from trusted, godly elders as well. In addition, it helps to pay close attention to the sermons you hear each Sunday, searching for ways you can apply the preacher's words to your life. Think of 1 Corinthians 3:6 (SKJV): "[Paul] planted, Apollos watered, but God gave the increase." What would the church have been like if they'd refused the first two steps?

It's often impossible for a Christian to water himself—that's why God sends gardeners.

Lord, it's sometimes hard to accept help from others, especially when I believe I have everything under control. Remind me of the plan You have for Your children to work together as one.

Numbers 29:12–30:16 / Luke 3 / Psalm 60:1–5

BLOODLINES

Bear fruits that are deserving and consistent with [your]
repentance [that is, conduct worthy of a heart changed,
a heart abhorring sin]. And do not begin to say to yourselves,
We have Abraham as our father; for I tell you that God is able
from these stones to raise up descendants for Abraham.

LUKE 3:8 AMPC

The Jews, despite their lofty claims of holiness, were still clinging to Abraham's coattails. Rather than develop their own walk with God, they simply pointed to a man in their ancestral line and used him as an excuse for ignoring the sin that darkened their lives. As long as Abraham remained in their family tree, they could live any way they wanted and still gain God's favor, right?

Little did they realize, God never has cared as much about bloodlines as He does about the heart. You grew up in church? Good! Your parents taught you about Jesus? Great! But if you haven't made the decision to follow Him yourself, what difference exists between you and someone who mocks God's name? A blood relationship to an ancestor should never replace a personal relationship with your Savior.

Don't use your upbringing or your family tree as an excuse to live a shallow existence. Dig deeper by making it personal today.

Lord Jesus, help me rely on Your shed blood instead of the blood
that runs through my veins. Earthly lineage doesn't matter—
all I care about is whether I've been adopted by You.

Numbers 31 / Luke 4 / Psalm 60:6–12

DON'T YOU DARE

Jesus answered, "It is said: 'Do not put the Lord your God to the test.'"
LUKE 4:12 NIV

Standing alongside Jesus atop the pinnacle of the temple, Satan pulled a move straight from a playground bully's handbook: "I dare You to jump." He knew that if Jesus gave in, He'd be using God's power for selfish purposes. . .thus ruining His perfection and making mankind's redemption impossible.

But how many Christians seem to give in to this temptation? How often do we treat God's power like an excuse to do anything we want? Some spend all their money on useless things and then "trust God" to cover their expenses when the bills are due. Others engage in dangerous behaviors such as overeating or drug usage and then expect God to miraculously shield them from sickness and death. Still others plunge headlong into sin, telling themselves God will forgive whatever deeds they commit.

But it doesn't work that way. This perversion of faith imagines God as a mere circus magician, dishing out meaningless miracles for the masses. Our faith should take the form of "give us this day our daily bread," not "let's see how big Your power really is."

Strong faith doesn't dare—it depends.

*Lord, help me rely on You for the things I can't control. . .
and choose responsibly in the situations I can. I want
to be a wise steward of the life You've given me.*

Numbers 32–33 / Luke 5:1-16 / Psalm 61

SUMMIT FAITH

From the ends of the earth I will cry to You; when my heart is overwhelmed, lead me to the rock that is higher than I.

PSALM 61:2 SKJV

Each year, hundreds of people climb Mount Everest, seeking the thrill of reaching the highest point on planet Earth. They know that before they embark on the hardest journey of their lives, they must first undergo at least a year of grueling training.

Today's verse describes God's peace as "the rock that is higher than I." But unlike Everest, it doesn't take near-superhuman strength to reach His summit. Anyone can do it. Why? Because God is the guide. Whenever we want to escape the world's noise by climbing above the clouds, He leads us up with ease. With every swing of the ice pick, God is two steps ahead of us, lifting us with His unlimited power. The more we're willing to lock our rhythm with His—to learn about His ways and seek His guidance each day—the smoother our climb will become.

And in the end, once we've reached the summit, we can look out over the vastness of this life, seeing all our problems and cares like tiny smudges on the earth, barely noticeable against the backdrop of the masterpiece God is painting.

Lord, I'm done camping at the base—I want to start climbing higher toward You. Give me the endurance and faith to keep following You all the way to the top.

Numbers 34–36 / Luke 5:17–32 / Psalm 62:1–6

BREAK THE CEILING

When they could not find a way to do this because of the crowd,
they went up on the roof and lowered him on his mat through
the tiles into the middle of the crowd, right in front of Jesus.

LUKE 5:19 NIV

True faith doesn't care about what's convenient. It recognizes the extreme lengths to which Jesus went to eliminate our sins. . .and it comprehends the inescapable trap that unforgiven sin creates. It knows just how desperate the situation is, and it realizes just how merciful God is to those who diligently seek Him (Hebrews 11:6). It has a firm understanding of the spiritual risks and rewards involved in every choice.

Therefore, true faith is uncompromising in its quest to find the feet of Jesus. Just as the men in today's verse didn't quit when they saw the house was full, so true faith doesn't stop when it gets burnt out or tired. It presses through the pain and the icy fingers of apathy that threaten to chill the soul. And when all conventional avenues are exhausted—when it has tried every method in its comfort zone and found them all lacking—true faith is ready to break the ceiling just to be in Jesus' presence.

Do you have true faith?

Lord Jesus, I'm tired of relying on thoughtless ceremonies and
prayers to access Your presence. Teach me how to break the rut
of convenient living in order to reach Your amazing power.

BUREAUCRATIC TAPE

And Jesus added, "The Son of Man is Lord, even over the Sabbath."
LUKE 6:5 NLT

It's fairly easy to see that the Pharisees were less concerned with actually following the law of Moses than they were with keeping up their appearance. From their position of authority, they reveled in their "duty" of pointing out whenever someone stepped slightly out of line.

But then along came Jesus, exposing their "piety" for the vain game that it was. By criticizing Jesus, the Son of God, for violating their idea of what "keeping the Sabbath" looked like, they'd officially stepped into the realm of absurdity. In their eyes, they'd somehow become holier than God Himself!

But are we any different? How often do we create arbitrary rules for ourselves and then criticize others for not following them? We get so caught up on our own little dos and don'ts that we forget about the commands God actually gave. We wear our obedience on these tiny issues like a badge. . .while neglecting the two most important commandments of all: loving God and loving others as ourselves (Matthew 22:37–39).

Our lives should be about building a deep relationship with the one who loves us, not setting up bureaucratic tape for others to trip over.

Don't be a Pharisee.

> *God, Your laws and ways are just too amazing for me*
> *to waste time enforcing my own imperfect morality on*
> *others. Help me focus on Your holiness, not my own.*

Deuteronomy 2:26–4:14 / Luke 6:12–35 / Psalm 63:1–5

PICKING AND CHOOSING

Do not add to what I command you and do not subtract from it,
but keep the commands of the LORD your God that I give you.
DEUTERONOMY 4:2 NIV

How many Christians treat the Bible like an apple tree, picking the nice, "juicy" verses and tossing all the ones that leave a bitter taste? They love quoting all the passages that talk about God's love. . .but conveniently ignore all the places in which scripture commands us to love Him through obedience. All that's left is a saccharine shell of the gospel, stripped of pesky things like loyalty and endurance and consisting of nothing but hollow emotion.

It's human nature to accept what we want to accept and ignore what we don't. But as John Adams once said, "Facts are stubborn things." If a person leaps off a building, no matter how much he closes his eyes and tries to believe he can fly, gravity will still take over and truth will prevail over foolishness. Similarly, you can either accept truth and grow stronger in your walk with God. . .or reject it and find yourself drifting further away. Facts are facts, and your belief or denial won't change a thing about them. But it can (and will) change you.

Lord, some of the things in Your Word are hard to swallow.
Loving others isn't nearly as easy as I think it should be sometimes.
I need Your strength to accept these commands too.

Deuteronomy 4:15–5:22 / Luke 6:36–49 / Psalm 63:6–11

LESSER GODS

Beware lest you become corrupt by making for yourselves [to worship] a graven image in the form of any figure, the likeness of male or female.
DEUTERONOMY 4:16 AMPC

If you were to make a list of all the gods the ancient Egyptians worshiped—along with a brief description of their attributes—it'd probably be enough to fill a book. One calculation says the Egyptian pantheon included over 1,400 deities, and another places the figure at over 2,000. What is for us a strange collection of mythological tales with no basis in reality was "gospel truth" for these ancient people. Their gods were petty and undeserving of any adoration. . .but the Egyptians served them anyway.

We may laugh at these gods of stone today, but think for a moment about the idolatry that plagues our own culture. Our modern pantheon is filled with celebrities, technology, sports cars, varying degrees of social status, and even expensive brands of clothing. It ranges from high art to the banal. Many people put so much effort into obtaining these tiny, elusive idols that they forget the one who fills the universe with His glory. In order for faith in God to thrive, faith in all these lesser gods must die.

Have you broken down your idols?

Lord, fill my soul with adoration for You alone. Let me never turn anything—not even one of Your blessings—into an idol that drains my devotion to You.

Deuteronomy 5:23–7:26 / Luke 7:1–17 / Psalm 64:1–5

THINKING OUTSIDE THE BOX

*That's why I sent others with my request. Just say the
word, and that will be enough to heal my servant.*

LUKE 7:7 VOICE

At the time in which this account takes place, Judaism had collapsed into a religion of dry, passionless ceremony. The Romans were in charge, and God's promises of a Messiah seemed further than ever.

It's telling that a certain centurion, not one of the religious leaders, was seemingly the only one in the nation who had enough faith to think beyond the confines of his spiritually dead environment. He saw "God" not as three letters on a page but as a living being with infinite power. And when he saw Jesus, he saw that power personified. That's why whenever his servant grew ill, he asked Jesus to do the impossible by healing him from where He stood. He knew Jesus' abilities weren't confined by the easily understood rituals of the priests and leaders but rather reached across time and space, binding everything with the threads of His will.

By spending time with God Himself—going beyond "obligations" and pursuing His truth and power for yourself—you too will begin to see the limitless power He possesses and understand the unique, boundless methods He uses to fulfill His will. Only then can you start thinking outside the box.

*Father, thank You for being an "out of the box" God. Grant me eyes
that can see the invisible, impossible ways in which You work.*

TESTS IN THE WILDERNESS

"He fed you with manna in the wilderness, a food unknown to your ancestors. He did this to humble you and test you for your own good."

DEUTERONOMY 8:16 NLT

The Bible often depicts wilderness as a place of testing—the Israelites post-Egypt, Jesus being tempted by Satan. But really, the entire world is a wilderness of temptation. There is no place, no people, that sin has not infected and impacted. As a Christian, you've been rescued from sin's death grip, but you're still subject to the tendencies of the flesh.

Jesus may have delivered you from an addiction or bad company, but it's easy to forget who God is and what He has done. It's still in your human nature to lose sight of the fact that you are a rescued sheep who tends to wander from your Shepherd. You still have to beware self-centered inclinations—like seeking credit for good behavior or choosing comfort over obeying God.

One way God keeps you on track is testing. It's no longer a question of salvation. You're His son, and nothing can change that. But even a beloved child can go off path, and sometimes a wilderness experience is God's way of checking to see if you're still relying fully on Him.

> *Lord, help me to look to You during the next challenge I face. Thank You for reminding me how much I need You, and that You are with me every step of these rocky paths.*

Deuteronomy 10–11 / Luke 7:36–8:3 / Psalm 65:1–8

THE CALCULUS OF FORGIVENESS

*"I tell you, her many sins have been forgiven—as her great love
has shown. But whoever has been forgiven little loves little."*

LUKE 7:47 NIV

Jesus told the woman who anointed His feet to go in peace because
her faith had saved her. The Pharisees got stuck on Jesus interacting
with a prostitute and offering forgiveness for her sins and missed the
point: those who know they are sinners are closer to God's heart than
those who say they have no sin.

This is "good person" syndrome: someone may be, by all human
accounts, decent, kind, giving, and nice to waiters and dogs. Such a
person figures that being a good person means God will have to bless
him or let him into heaven. In other words, behaving well gives him
power over God. But from God's perspective, that guy's a zombie,
the walking dead.

Unless you embrace your real need for Jesus, your faith will always
be transactional—and, by definition, that's not faith. That's religion,
not relationship. Your relationship with God should always be based
on God condescending to seek you and let you know that He loves
you despite your sin—especially the sin of being a good person as a
way of saving yourself.

*Father, Your math is different than mine. Your love for me doesn't
add up—I could never earn it, but You give it freely. Thank You.*

A TEACHABLE HEART

Be careful therefore how you listen. For to him who has [spiritual knowledge] will more be given; and from him who does not have [spiritual knowledge], even what he thinks and guesses and supposes that he has will be taken away from him.

LUKE 8:18 AMPC

One of the greatest compliments a high-level athlete can receive is that he's coachable. Imagine that—you're at the top of your profession, but you're aware that there's always more to learn. The same is true for faith. The day you think you've got it all figured out is the day you start sliding.

For context, Jesus was discussing putting your light under a bushel. Eventually, though, the full truth about everyone will come out—good and bad. Bad would be hiding your relationship with Jesus, playing down the gifts He has graciously given you in order to maintain your rep.

If you stop longing for truth, even what you think you know will fade. Christians must always be in learning mode, teachable, willing to admit something they don't know. That kind of humility is genuine, and it opens people to hearing what you do know.

Everything you can earn or win in this life will fade over time, or at the end of time, until only God's glory is left. Focus on that now by seeking truth and righteousness is all you do.

Teach me, Lord, more about You and how You want me to live this life You've given me.

Deuteronomy 14:1–16:8 / Luke 8:22–39 / Psalm 66:1–7

WHEN THE WATER IS HIGH

Getting to his feet, he told the wind, "Silence!" and the waves, "Quiet down!" They did it. The lake became smooth as glass. Then he said to his disciples, "Why can't you trust me?"

LUKE 8:24–25 MSG

When storms arise, the question is always, *Where is your confidence that God is who He says He is?* He's right there, isn't He—chilling in the stern of your almost-capsized boat. It's been said that God rules the world with His feet up—nothing fazes Him.

We get fazed regularly. Hard things are, after all, hard. But with God, the hard times are always worked into something good, something we have no right to expect but every right as His children to count on. Sometimes we're not even looking for God in a situation that cries out for Him. And each time He does something, we're right to be amazed—even the wind and waves obey Him!

Trust is essential, though. The Bible doesn't guarantee that God will answer every prayer the way we want or expect. But whatever His response, He is still God. He is always good, faithful, just, and true to His nature. Your faith in the bad times shows you trust Him to be who He is, and that His grace is enough for you.

God, my Lord and my King, You are enough for me in every season and situation. Help me to trust You more and more.

ASSUMED OMNISCIENCE

He said, "Stop the weeping! She isn't dead; she's only asleep."
But the crowd laughed at him because they all knew she had died.

LUKE 8:52–53 NLT

Once we've read the story of Jairus' daughter, we can chuckle at those laughing at Jesus—*Oh, they don't know what we know. Watch this!* We're in the loop, though, only because of our vantage point.

Jesus calling the girl's death "sleep" foreshadowed the resurrection—but how could any of the people present have guessed at that? They thought they knew what dead looked like, but Jesus shocked them. He stopped their wailing—which was expected but superficial—in favor of something unforeseeable but genuine.

Only God knows how our trials and challenges will pan out. As Christians, we know who Jesus is and what He *can* do. But in the moment, we don't know what He *will* do.

Human expectations can be a huge barrier to what God can do. Assuming you know how a situation should go doesn't allow for God's ability to do the impossible, to break through where no one else could. Faithlessness is thinking you know more about it than He does. In every trial, ask whether you will let Him use you for His work instead of trying to put Him to work for you.

Lord Jesus, forgive me for the times I've assumed how
You should act. You alone are God, and You alone
always do what is right, in every situation.

Deuteronomy 19:1–21:9 / Luke 9:1–22 / Psalm 66:16–20

CONFESSION AND PRAISE

I cried out to him for help, praising him as I spoke. If I had not confessed the sin in my heart, the Lord would not have listened.

Psalm 66:17–18 nlt

God's love does not fail. But one of the most misunderstood things about God's love is that it goes hand in hand with His holiness. Only because God is holy—one of a kind, unlike us or anyone else, unique in His qualities and character—can He love the way He does, without limits or conditions.

That unique combination is clear in the psalmist's words, "I cried out. . .praising him as I spoke." We're quick to bring our complaints or requests to God but often slow to confess or praise. We're slow to admit we've messed up, but our self-preservation does a disservice to God's sacrificial love. Jesus' blood means God no longer condemns us. We've been permanently cleansed. We just need to keep our feet clean from daily sins. Doesn't God deserve thanks and praise for that alone?

Only when we praise Him can we fully appreciate His desire to hear and help us. Even better is Psalm 66:16 (voice), telling others what God did: "Come and listen, everyone who reveres the True God, and I will tell you what He has done for me."

Holy and merciful Father, thank You for all You have done so I can know You. May Your praise and my confession always be on my lips.

DON'T TURN AWAY

*If you see your fellow's donkey or ox injured along the road,
don't look the other way. Help him get it up and on its way.*
DEUTERONOMY 22:4 MSG

You don't have to look far to find someone in need. Few things can make a greater positive impression than stopping to help. Often, though, the thought of getting involved is daunting, the prospect, dangerous. For most of us, lending a hand is often a matter of convenience— although if you're rushing to the hospital or to help someone else, your path is clear.

The idea here is more than guilt-giving a few bucks to the homeless guy on the corner. You're not trying to clear your conscience but looking to see if God has something for you to do. It might get messy. You might see or hear something that costs you sleep. But when you act on God's behalf, loving others in Jesus' name, God can do all sorts of amazing things, even if you don't see immediate fruit.

Picture Jesus—holy, perfect, seated in majesty on high over all He created. He didn't settle for the view but came down, took on flesh, and got His hands dirty—and ultimately, pierced—to help us. Why? Because He loves us and we needed help. How, then, can we turn away?

*Lord, give me Your heart toward others.
Strengthen me so I don't turn away, because You didn't.*

Deuteronomy 23:9–25:19 / Luke 9:43–62 / Psalm 68:1–6

WITH OR AGAINST

Jesus said, "Don't stop him! Anyone who is not against you is for you."
LUKE 9:50 NLT

We men tend to seek points of division rather than unity. At home, at work, even in ministry, we want to know if we stack up, but more, if we're better than those other guys. Not in an in-your-face way, but we'd still like to know.

It's one thing, however, to do that on the job or golf course, and another when it comes to biblical truth and God's work. We want to be sure we're aligning our efforts with God's will and ways. Jesus' point here in Luke 9 is instructive, especially set alongside His statement in Luke 11:23 (NIV): "Whoever is not with me is against me, and whoever does not gather with me scatters."

The verses seem contradictory, but this is God's Word: both are true. Everyone is either for or against Jesus. There's no neutral ground. The key is faith and practice. If someone doesn't go to your church but is still being fruitful in line with scripture, he's a brother. If someone gives Jesus lip service but isn't obeying His commands, he's not.

Furthermore, someone can be "not against" Jesus, but without faith, they're defaulting into the enemy's work. Be discerning, but also be open to Jesus working through people you wouldn't expect.

*Jesus, You alone know what's in everyone's hearts. Guide me
in Your Word and by Your Spirit to know who is with You.*

Deuteronomy 26:1–28:14 / Luke 10:1–20 / Psalm 68:7–14

REAL AUTHORITY

I have given you authority. . . . Nevertheless, do not
rejoice at this, that the spirits are subject to you,
but rejoice that your names are enrolled in heaven.
LUKE 10:19–20 AMPC

Jesus gave the seventy He sent out His authority over the powers of evil—physical threats like snakes and scorpions and spiritual challenges, demonic oppression, and the threat of stinging rejection and persecution. Jesus equipped those He sent, and they succeeded.

But Jesus' subsequent statement about witnessing Satan's fall suggests something deeper than defeating demons: the authority He gives His followers in heaven. We have permission to ask God to do mighty works. That's something Satan doesn't have.

However, according to Jesus, what's even more amazing is God's grace—that God desires to be with you and in you, and that you are counted among the saved. Evil's everyday presence makes it easy to think that Jesus came primarily to defeat it. But our liberation from sin and death is only the beginning.

God's plan is to restore all things to life—eternal life, that unending quality of living that He wanted for us from the start. The authority Jesus gives you means you can taste that life now, in this broken world, and share it with others. Trampling on scorpions is just a perk.

Jesus, help me embrace fully what it means to be Yours—to live
out the promise of Your life in me now and for eternity.

Deuteronomy 28:15–68 / Luke 10:21–37 / Psalm 68:15–19

SIMPLE FAITH

Jesus rejoiced, exuberant in the Holy Spirit. "I thank you, Father, Master of heaven and earth, that you hid these things from the know-it-alls and showed them to these innocent newcomers. Yes, Father, it pleased you to do it this way."

LUKE 10:21–22 MSG

Why did Jesus choose the followers He did? These guys, though diverse among themselves, were all regular guys—no academic all-stars, country club movers, or political influencers. In other words, no one who had any real power themselves. An education, network, or influence aren't bad things, but people who have them tend to rely on themselves first and foremost.

Jesus was thrilled that God chose a group that would be able to look at God with fresh eyes and open hearts. That's so much harder when you must first look past your accomplishments, connections, or wealth. God can and does use those things, but He is looking for those who are looking to Him out of sheer need.

In Jesus' day, most of the religious leaders were know-it-alls. Most of the politicians feared Caesar as the only god they knew. But Jesus' rescue mission required those who would receive a radical message of a seemingly upside-down kingdom: those who lived under worldly oppression, whose minds were uncluttered by worldly priorities. He chose those whose faith would be simple and heartfelt, and He seeks them today too.

Father, help me keep my trust in You simple and honest, uncluttered by all the things around me.

Deuteronomy 29–30 / Luke 10:38–11:23 / Psalm 68:20–27

LET GOD HANDLE THE OUTCOMES

*"The LORD our God has secrets known to no one. We are
not accountable for them, but we and our children are
accountable forever for all that he has revealed to us,
so that we may obey all the terms of these instructions."*

DEUTERONOMY 29:29 NLT

Whatever the Bible says about God is all we need to know. God alone is all-powerful, all-knowing, and present everywhere, but more than that, God is also holy, just, and good, full of grace and mercy. Do you live by that?

Faith involves returning to these basic truths over and over, especially when times are hard. We seldom understand the full scope of what God does. His credit is good when things are going well, but what about when they aren't? When we pray the best we can and He doesn't answer, we're dealing with the secret things only God knows.

When God disappoints you, do you still trust Him? Human secrets are mostly negative things you'd be embarrassed if people knew. But God's secrets include things like the mystery of salvation and His redemptive plan for the entire world—knowledge that, as Psalm 139:6 says, is too high for us.

You either accept God's secrets or you don't. Your part is to obey. He will handle the results.

*Lord God, I put my trust in You today. You are good and You do good.
Help me to obey You when I don't have all the information I want.*

FLOODED WITH LIGHT

"If you are filled with light, with no dark corners, then your whole life will be radiant, as though a floodlight were filling you with light."

LUKE 11:36 NLT

What's intriguing about the famous parable of the light is that Jesus shared it in the context of warnings about the power and nature of evil. Luke 11 opens with Him teaching His disciples about prayer and praying persistently. He spoke of God's good gifts and answered the accusation that He was using demonic power to drive out demons.

Jesus promised blessing for those who heard the Word and put it into practice, then rebuked the crowds for demanding a miraculous sign as proof of His identity. He also called out the Pharisees on following the letter of the law but not its heart.

In the middle of these admonitions, Jesus warned against hiding the light of God's truth—not letting it shine in every part of you, revealing everything you need to address and confess. The world is a dark place, but God has not left us without hope.

Once we see evil for what it is, we're responsible to shine God's light on it—both into the depths of our own hearts, and then on a world in desperate need. Let the wonder of God's light inspire you to hope-fueled living.

Father, open my eyes, both to receive Your light and to reflect it. Help me live in wonder and trust, not self-interest and suspicion.

Deuteronomy 32:23–33:29 / Luke 11:37–54 / Psalm 69:1–9

DIG DEEPER

"Frauds! You're just like unmarked graves:
People walk over that nice, grassy surface, never suspecting
the rot and corruption that is six feet under."

LUKE 11:44 MSG

Jesus is all about liberation. His method is simple, though not easy: He sets free each person who puts his trust in Him, and then He calls each to play a role in setting others free. He always does the heavy lifting—the soul saving—but He lets us participate in getting the word out.

That's always been God's way, starting with Israel. He freed the Israelites from Egypt so they could be His own people, following His ways so they could be His light to the world—so everyone would say, "Those Israelites are different. They really must believe in their God—so He must be different from all other gods."

Instead, they fluctuated between extremes—being spiritual cheaters and super religious. Both approaches miss the mark: God wants our hearts, not our apathy or piety. Faith isn't executing a series of commands and proving your worth by your obedience. It's trusting God enough to let His love change you—so that you can care like He cares, abandoning any superior attitudes and getting into the street-level dirt with everyone who needs Jesus as much as you do.

God, by Your Spirit weed my corrupt, self-serving thoughts
and ways out of me. Give me Your heart, broken by
what breaks Yours, fueled by what powers Yours.

Deuteronomy 34–Joshua 2 / Luke 12:1–15 / Psalm 69:10–17

SWIM SMART

*Don't let the floods overwhelm me, or the deep waters
swallow me, or the pit of death devour me.*

PSALM 69:15 NLT

Rip currents exist close to the shoreline, many only knee deep, but they pull you out to deeper water. Most swimmers ignorantly try to swim against the current, exhausting their strength as they get dragged further out to sea. Ironically, rip currents present as still water, hiding their underlying strength.

While swimming against the current is a good metaphor for being a Christian in an increasingly anti-God culture, the key to getting out of a rip current is not to swim against it but parallel to the shore till you break free and can swim back.

Psalm 69 describes a similar approach. When the culture threatens to drag you away from shore, sapping your stamina with overwhelming negativity, panic can set in. But if you know what to do, you can swim away from danger and return to a place of peace and strength.

More than ever, Christians risk being mocked and shunned for standing with God. But check out David's response in Psalm 69: He didn't deny that the insults hurt, but he expressed his expectation that God would pull him out of that pit. He counted on God's "unfailing love," His "sure salvation" and "plentiful" mercy.

Father of wisdom and light, I can always return to You by way of taking Your words to heart. Help me to walk wisely in this dangerous world.

Joshua 3:1–5:12 / Luke 12:16–40 / Psalm 69:18–28

SET A REMINDER

*"These stones will stand as a memorial among
the people of Israel forever."*
Joshua 4:7 NLT

A new generation of Israelites had just crossed the miraculously dried riverbed of the Jordan into the promised land. God, knowing their memory would be short, told Joshua to have them build a monument to their passage. The memorial of twelve stones would remind their children—and everyone else passing by—of what God had done for them there.

The Bible is full of reminders not to forget. Why? Because we tend to, even with the moments and resolutions that we have prayed for fervently. God knows us, but rather than just roll His eyes at our flakiness, He tells us, "Build a monument. Tell yourself regularly what I have done, and that you are Mine."

You set reminders for important events, appointments, and dates. But do you give yourself a way to recall what God has done? Some journal their prayers and God's responses, and that's great. But if writing isn't your thing, find a way that resonates with you. Good with your hands? Build something that points to God's actions. Musical? Write a song. When that day rolls around, gather your friends and family and celebrate: "On this day, God did this. We won't forget."

*Father, thank You for Your faithfulness in every season of
life. I resolve to keep mementos, to remind myself and let
others know that You are my God, and You are good.*

Joshua 5:13–7:26 / Luke 12:41–48 / Psalm 69:29–36

GREAT EXPECTATIONS

For everyone to whom much is given, of him shall much
be required; and of him to whom men entrust much,
they will require and demand all the more.

LUKE 12:48 AMPC

The ethic of the well-off having responsibility to help the needy comes from the Bible. God wants His people to operate on the same principle as He does. He has all wealth and power, but His entire history with humankind can be described as giving. He breathed life into our nostrils, gave us paradise for a home, and then engaged in a sacrificial rescue operation when we screwed it all up.

Adam and Eve fell for the lie that God was holding out on something even better than what He had already provided. They didn't give God their trust, and everything went to pieces. Jesus' life was the cost to set things right, to resuscitate our spiritual selves and begin God's ongoing work of restoration.

In Luke 12, when Jesus laid out the accountability required for those given such blessings, He was fully aware of the price He would have to pay. And He paid it. What He wants in return is what He first gave us: everything. The least we can do is be about His business until He returns to finish His good work.

Jesus, let the weight of what You did settle on me—
the eternal stakes for which You bled and died and resurrected.
Make me ready at any moment for Your return.

Joshua 8–9 / Luke 12:49–59 / Psalm 70

THE DIVIDING LINE

*Do you suppose that I have come to give peace on
earth? No, I say to you, but rather division].*
LUKE 12:51 AMPC

Faith begins with salvation and ends with redemption and restoration,
but the full scope of Jesus' work includes the marathon of the middle—
all the daily ways you put confidence in Him. That includes living
with the tension of Jesus' hard teachings.

The tendency is to see Jesus during His first coming as tender,
meek, and mild—which He was. But He also alluded to the nature
of His return as Holy God and King of kings. In His birth was the
seed of His death, and His death carried the root of salvation.

But salvation implies the need to be saved. Faith requires
acknowledging that every single person deserves God's righteous
judgment. Jesus took on sin, allowing Himself to be separated from
the Father so we wouldn't have to be. That's how desperate the human
condition is.

Such desperation divides loyalties, but the gospel preaches that
Jesus is the dividing line. Choosing Him liberates us from conformity
to the world. He literally died to bring us into His family, and He
demands the same commitment from us as we join His mission: to
lead as many as possible out of the fire.

*Lord Jesus, Your sacrifice required commitment to
the Father's will above all else. Fill me with Your Spirit
so I can commit to Your bigger view of life.*

Joshua 10:1–11:15 / Luke 13:1–21 / Psalm 71:1–6

REALITY CHECK

Jesus answered, "Do you think that these Galileans were worse
sinners than all the other Galileans because they suffered this way?
I tell you, no! But unless you repent, you too will all perish."
LUKE 13:2–3 NIV

We know better than to think tragedies only befall the deserving. Unexpected bad things have been happening to people since the fall. The daily toll is depressing because it echoes the age-old question: if there's a God, why won't He do anything about all this?

This is the good news: He has.

Jesus' resurrection broke sin's grasp on the world, but death still has a foothold until He returns. Each day's disasters aren't God's judgment on sinners. They are the results of living in a world broken by sin—and the blame falls on humankind and the devil. God will judge our sin, but first, at the cross, He made a way out.

God hasn't abandoned us. The way of the world results from us rejecting Him. In addressing recent tragedies, Jesus didn't emphasize levels of sin but repentance. He put heartbreak squarely in the target of His redemptive work. The world will remain a mess till He returns to fix it, but the process begins now, with each heart that turns from sin and toward God.

God, when tragedies occur, help me move past blaming and
toward Your good news: that You can transform everything bad
to something good if we will just turn to You and believe.

Joshua 11:16–13:33 / Luke 13:22–35 / Psalm 71:7–16

A WONDER AND A WITNESS

I have become a sign to many; you are my strong refuge.
PSALM 71:7 NIV

Getting old is definitely not for wimps. All Christians long to hear Jesus one day tell them, "Well done, good and faithful servant," but once you hit middle age, doing everything you're used to doing takes so much more effort and you start wondering how to stay useful. You need God's help more than ever. By His grace, you've earned some wisdom along the way and learned a few things about grace.

That seems to be where the psalmist was, looking back and recalling God's faithfulness, even though the threats to peace and well-being hadn't diminished. Along the way, he had become a "sign to many."

Psalm 71 is an old man's prayer to finish strong. If you're young, being a sign is a goal. *Sign* is a nuanced word in Hebrew, meaning both a miracle and a warning. The context—continuing to seek and serve God in old age—suggests that consistent obedience reflects God's faithfulness and holiness. Your steady, lifelong witness is a warning: God will bless those who stay true and reject those who write Him off.

Father, I ask that many would be surprised, as both a blessing
and a warning, when I finish my race with You strongly.
Glorify Yourself in me in whatever time I have left.

Joshua 14–16 / Luke 14:1–15 / Psalm 71:17–21

BOWED DOWN, LIFTED UP

"Everyone who exalts himself will be humbled,
and the one who humbles himself will be exalted."

LUKE 14:11 HCSB

Dying to self happens every day, especially when we are justified in being upset. Our frustrated response doesn't match with Jesus' humility—giving up all His rights as God to come be questioned and beaten and killed by His creation. He let go of His reputation so He could be lifted up—on the cross and then to heaven—and lift us with Him.

You don't get humble by trying to be humble. That just ends up feeling like false modesty or humblebragging point. Humility comes not from thinking less of yourself, but of yourself less. When you see yourself as the reason (both individually and corporately) Jesus had to die, you learn to value the new life He has given you—and you want others to know Him too.

Sharing your God story is a powerful witness—but keep the focus on Jesus. Your past may have been really messed up, but what He did overcomes everyone's messed up behavior over the past two thousand years. Embrace your part in the mind-staggering work He is doing in, around, and through you, and watch Him go!

Lord Jesus, Your sacrifice for me pulls me down to the grave as I think
about my sin, but then it lifts me up to heaven with You as I consider
the unmatchable gift of Your righteousness in me. Thank You.

RECKONING

*"Don't begin until you count the cost. . . . You cannot become
my disciple without giving up everything you own."*
LUKE 14:28, 33 NLT

Jesus wasn't the first teacher to tell people to give up their wealth, to live simply, with minimal material desires or obligations. But His reasons were different: to gain everything that truly matters, you must give up the world's view of success. Roman oppression eventually ended, but God's kingdom never will. Choose wisely.

That's what it means to take up your cross (Luke 14:27). Suffering will pay dividends in God's calculations. What will you undergo to follow Him? Humiliation? Pain? Everything Jesus endured was to purchase eternal life for you. He is your reward—worth everything you go through.

You are Christ's project, to build as He pleases. You are His soldier, to send wherever He deems necessary. Search your heart today and make a reckoning: give up whatever is getting between you and the one who loves you best.

Jesus isn't calling you to health and wealth, but to glory. Identify with His choice: to leave the splendor of heaven and suffer as a man, so that He could end eternal suffering. We're already hurting in this life, this broken world. Trusting Jesus, we can face it with courage, knowing He is redeeming all things.

*Lord, show me anything in my heart that is keeping me from knowing
You better. Nothing this world offers is worth more than You are.*

Joshua 19:17–21:42 / Luke 15:1–10 / Psalm 72:1–11

GODLY LEADERSHIP

*Give the gift of wise rule to the king, O God, the gift of
just rule to the crown prince. May he judge your people
rightly, be honorable to your meek and lowly.*

PSALM 72:1–2 MSG

You are a leader. Whatever roles you play, at the very least, you're leading
yourself. Start there. How well do you know yourself? What are your
tendencies, especially when challenged? Do you seek the best for the
people you're leading, or are you constantly trying to preserve your
reputation or standing? What's it like to be on the other side of you?

These are hard questions, but without seeking answers, you'll
never be the leader God calls you to be.

Psalm 72 recognizes that leadership requires one essential
ingredient: seeking and following God.

None of Solomon's goals here are self-focused. He asked God
to help him judge fairly and wisely, to bring prosperity to all his
people, to defend those most in need. He wanted his leadership to
be refreshing, like spring rain, a haven for godly people. Yes, he spoke
of other nations bringing gifts and having an enduring name, but he
knew that without God, it wouldn't be possible or worth achieving.

Godly leadership is always others-oriented, trusting that God
will look out for you as you look out for others.

*Father, mold me into a leader more like Jesus,
the perfect mix of righteousness and compassion,
wisdom and strength. Do it for Your glory.*

Joshua 21:43–22:34 / Luke 15:11–32 / Psalm 72:12–20

LOST AND FOUND

"You have always stayed by me, and everything I have is yours.
We had to celebrate this happy day. For your brother was dead
and has come back to life! He was lost, but now he is found!"

LUKE 15:31–32 NLT

Luke 15 features a trio of parables about lost things—a sheep, a coin, a son—and their recovery. The religious leaders saw the behavior in each as ridiculous—leaving ninety-nine to find one, turning over a house for a single coin, glorifying the return of a child whose entitlement decimated a household.

But each story features a call to celebrate the recovery of what was lost. The Pharisees would've scorned the poverty of those searching for their lost pittances, but God's heart is to leave no one behind—regardless of status or what they deserve.

For example, the prodigal's tale is actually about two lost sons. One embraces the world and ends up in the gutter, while the other takes care of business at home and ends up in a snit. But both were driven by what their father could give them rather than relationship with him for its own sake. God clearly wants the latter, and every story of restoration is worth applauding.

Father, You never lost sight of me, never gave up on me, and
You never will. Let me carry that in my heart so I always
rejoice when another child comes home to You.

Joshua 23–24 / Luke 16:1–18 / Psalm 73:1–9

THE PROMISE KEEPER

"Know this with all your heart, with everything in you, that not one detail has failed of all the good things GOD, your God, promised you. It has all happened. Nothing's left undone—not so much as a word."

JOSHUA 23:14 MSG

For all the miracles Joshua had seen—the deliverance from Egypt, the survival in the wilderness, the crossing of the Jordan, the glorious victories and hard, lesson-loaded losses in battle—at the end, he focused on God's trustworthiness. His trust wasn't in God's power or what God had done for Israel and for him, but in God Himself.

If you trust God only because of what He has done, you're operating on a purely human level. That's how trust works with everyone else—trusting them until they give you a reason not to. It's practical. But your word is only as good as the promises you keep. God's Word is as good as done.

We can still care about people we no longer trust, because God knows our changing hearts and chose to save us. But God is God. He deserves your belief because He is always Himself. He will always do what He says He will. You don't have to continually vet His words or actions. Familiarize yourself with God's promises. They are the surest things you'll ever know.

God, thank You for letting me know You. I will trust You no matter what because there is no one like You.

HONEST DOUBT

Did I keep my heart pure for nothing?
Did I keep myself innocent for no reason?
PSALM 73:13 NLT

When David doubted that God's way was working, he went to the temple. When trying to grasp God's will proved frustrating, he sought God Himself. There, among God's people, he worshipped, recognizing God's worthiness to be praised no matter what. He heard God's Word and remembered that God sees it all and will eventually judge those who reject Him.

It's easy to be thankful when we consider God's loving ways—His tender care, His incredible patience, His sacrifice to restore relationship. But when we're suffering, doubts creep in. His love seems far away. At those moments, David regained his faith by focusing on God's justness. "I went into your sanctuary, O God, and I finally understood the destiny of the wicked" (verse 17 NLT). God knows the world is screwed up. He knows when people have done you wrong, when you're suffering while godless people are living their best lives. But that's only for now.

Ultimately, we all answer to God for where we put our faith—in Him or elsewhere. Only in God can we have an end to injustice. Only through Him can we suffer with purpose. Only by Him can we see that the best the world can offer is garbage compared to the simple joy of knowing Him.

Lord, forgive me when I forget who You are—
my strength and shield, my oxygen and my deliverer.

Judges 3–4 / Luke 17:11–37 / Psalm 73:21–28

LIFE ON GOD'S TERMS

"If you grasp and cling to life on your terms, you'll lose it,
but if you let that life go, you'll get life on God's terms."
LUKE 17:33 MSG

Life on God's terms can be challenging. It's hard to let go of basic ways we see the world and how it works. We read about needing only a mustard seed's worth of faith to do great things, and we wonder what faith really is. We haven't moved many mountains lately. Jesus seems to be saying, however, that it's not about the mountain.

It's not a matter of having *more* faith or *less* faith. Apparently, faith isn't quantifiable in the way stamina or determination is. Faith either is or isn't, because God either is or isn't who you say you believe He is. If He is, you're trusting a God who can do anything, who can break through with anyone, who knows all hearts, all beginnings and ends, and will always do what is just and right.

Faith recognizes God for who He is. As a result, you pray boldly, knowing you are heard. You live freely because He has set you free from the world's priorities. Your hands are open, channels of receiving and giving, because this life is temporary and greater things await.

Father, increase my belief in You so that my faith will be simple
and real, that I'll live like I believe You are who You say You are.

KINGDOM LIVING

You can depend on this: if you don't receive the Kingdom
as a child would, you won't enter it at all.

LUKE 18:17 VOICE

In passages like Luke 18, the phrase "childlike faith" (or "faith like a child") isn't about *saving* faith but about receiving the kingdom of God. Jesus indicated a humble perspective is needed to see God's kingdom. So, what is the kingdom? It's not heaven, because humility can't save you. Context suggests it's the current reign of Jesus in your life—His will being done on earth as it is in heaven.

Childlike faith in God isn't blind or naive. A faith that asks no questions makes no sense. Children ask tons of questions. While they believe what their parents and teachers tell them, they still engage, follow up, and sometimes doubt.

Jesus modeled this way of living. His awe of God and sense of wonder about life and people inspired others to move past cynicism and habit to a higher view of God. Experiencing His life requires the same attitude—one that takes for granted God's trustworthiness and goodness.

If you're hungry to learn and grow, to forgive and move on, to think the best about others, to marvel at good and beautiful things, to laugh and have God-guided adventures, you're living the kingdom life.

Father, let Your will be done in and through me.
Help me keep my eyes on You, not on my problems and
disappointments. May Your kingdom live in me today.

POWER TO LIVE

"What is impossible for people is possible with God."
LUKE 18:27 NLT

The rich young ruler went away sad because he valued his wealth above God's wealth in Christ. Jesus sympathized, commenting how hard it is for the wealthy to live God's kingdom life. In fact, it's camel-through-a-needle's-eye hard. When we have more than our daily bread—when we have material security—we tend to lose sight of our need for God.

How could anyone possibly be saved, then? If those who have everything valued in this life—money, respect, influence—can't live for God, who could? And Jesus' response in Luke 18:27 implies that they were right: without God, no one has a chance of living by God's will and ways. This is not about salvation but what to do once you're saved—how to live with godly humility, joy, and a loose grip on the world's things.

Jesus reminded Peter that everyone who sacrifices what is dear to follow Him "will be repaid many times over in this life, and will have eternal life in the world to come" (verse 30). Jesus' life showed the path to true riches, a wealth of joy and peace that will survive this world—treasures stored in heaven.

Jesus, forgive me for the times I've put more trust in stuff or status than in You. Living with and for You is worth more than anything I could ever achieve on my own.

Judges 8:1–9:23 / Luke 19:1–28 / Psalm 74:12–17

SKIN IN THE GAME

*"Risk your life and get more than you ever dreamed
of. Play it safe and end up holding the bag."*
LUKE 19:26 MSG

Heading into His coronation upon entering Jerusalem—one which
would quickly turn to His rejection and execution—Jesus told a story
about a soon-to-be-crowned nobleman who gave three servants funds
to invest on his behalf before he left on a trip. Two servants risked
the investment and were rewarded upon his return, while the third
didn't and was punished.

The point of the parable is for Jesus' followers to work toward
God's goals, with His purposes in mind. We will be held accountable
for what we do with what He gives us—both our natural gifts and
our resources.

How we live our lives now matters. It's all about stewardship.
God owns everything and loans you everything you have. He wants
you to invest in His kingdom. He has given you a ministry—some
way of loving others as Jesus does, of being productive in building His
kingdom. Whatever you do for God's kingdom, do it the best you can,
looking to multiply it through others who have learned from you what
you've learned from God. God put skin in the game—literally—to
bring His kingdom to earth, and He wants us to do the same.

*God, You invested Your best to bring Your kingdom
to earth. Help me to do the same.*

Judges 9:24–10:18 / Luke 19:29–48 / Psalm 74:18–23

RECOGNIZING THE MASTER

"I tell you," he replied, "if they keep quiet, the stones will cry out."
LUKE 19:40 NIV

As Jesus entered Jerusalem to roaring praise, the Pharisees told Him to rebuke His disciples. But this was His time, fulfilling prophecy and bringing to a head His first coming, and there was no stopping the celebration. Even if just for a moment, everyone recognized their King—the people with joy and the Pharisees with fear.

The triumphal entry was both joyous and heartbreaking. Jesus knew that most of the gathered crowd didn't recognize Him for who He was—their hearts hard as stone—and He wept over them (Luke 19:41–44). But as He rode in, the joy was real, the praise was ordained, and if the people had managed to keep quiet, the rest of creation would have exploded with due reverence—maybe not literally, but Jesus made His point: the moment creation longed for, the beginning of its redemption and restoration, was underway.

Romans 8:20–21 (NLT) describes this longing: "With eager hope, the creation looks forward to the day when it will join God's children in glorious freedom from death and decay." Colossians 1:16 (HCSB) says, "All things have been created through Him and for Him." All of God's creation praises Him, but since humans are made in His image, we should praise Him first and most.

Lord Jesus, Creator and King, I join Your creation in praise and hope. Come soon and complete Your liberating work.

BEWARE

Watching for their opportunity, the leaders sent spies pretending to be honest men. They tried to get Jesus to say something that could be reported to the Roman governor so he would arrest Jesus.

Luke 20:20 nlt

Growing up, we were taught to be cautious around strangers. Not everyone was dangerous, of course, but we needed to realize that some people hid evil intentions behind offers of friendship and help.

Today, though the dangers differ for Christian men, caution is still appropriate.

Luke 20 records Jesus' interactions with His primary antagonists, the chief priests, scribes, and elders of the Jews (verse 1). After publicly confronting Jesus (verses 1–19), they turned to stealth, trying to get Him in trouble with the Roman authorities. Certain individuals "pretending to be honest men" posed the question, "Is it right for us to pay taxes to Caesar or not?" (verse 22 nlt). Jesus immediately saw through the ruse, providing an answer that stunned even His enemies (verses 23–26).

The same animosity that drove Jesus' enemies then drives His (and, by extension, *our*) enemies today. Beware those people who pretend to be honest—even some professing Christians—who are really trying to stir up trouble. Jesus called us to be "shrewd as snakes and harmless as doves" (Matthew 10:16 nlt) and promised us guidance through His Holy Spirit (John 14:26).

Beware, and pray:

Heavenly Father, please give me "the mind of Christ" (1 Corinthians 2:16 nlt) so I can recognize and deal with falsehood.

FAITH TO BELIEVE

Then Manoah asked, "When Your words come true,
what will the boy's responsibilities and mission be?"

JUDGES 13:12 HCSB

Samson's parents are among several biblical couples whose infertility was overcome by an act of God. Like John the Baptist's parents centuries later, Manoah and his wife received their good news from an angel.

But Manoah and Zechariah differed in one important way. The man who would father Samson immediately believed the angel's message, asking him about the boy's mission "*when* your words come true." John's father, on the other hand, was struck dumb for several months after his doubtful musing, "How can I know this? . . . For I am an old man, and my wife is well along in years" (Luke 1:18 HCSB).

Zechariah's lack of faith is the more surprising and disappointing when you consider that he was a priest serving in God's temple. Scripture describes Manoah as simply "a certain man from Zorah" (Judges 13:2 HCSB), a town mentioned only a handful of times.

But Manoah had faith to believe what the angel told him. It seems that Samson's father was a man of prayer, because he went to God immediately after his wife described her experience with the angel (Judges 13:6–8).

Not every guy will be a full-time, professional minister. But all of us can pray and exercise faith in God.

When You speak, Lord, I want to believe—completely and
immediately. Help me to exercise my faith day by day.

Judges 15–16 / Luke 21:1–19 / Psalm 76:1–7

GOD IS IN CONTROL

The valiant lie plundered, they sleep their last sleep; not one of the warriors can lift his hands. At your rebuke, God of Jacob, both horse and chariot lie still. It is you alone who are to be feared. Who can stand before you when you are angry?

PSALM 76:5–7 NIV

Our spiritual growth includes an increasing recognition of God's perfect power and justice. Thankfully, as members of His family through faith in Jesus Christ, we need not fear that power and justice coming against us. But we trust they will be applied—fairly and faithfully—to those people who steadfastly oppose God, often by oppressing His children.

To answer the psalmist's question, *no one* can stand before our angry God—unless that anger was pacified by Jesus' ultimate sacrifice for sin. We who follow Him with a true heart, even though we occasionally fail, are protected from divine wrath. Those who refuse the generous gift of salvation will be wiped away, never again to trouble God or His people.

In a world increasingly hostile to real Christian faith, this is an encouraging truth. God knows what we're up against, and He is preparing justice for His enemies. The flipside of that coin is that He is also preparing a beautiful rest for His own (see Hebrews 4).

Father in heaven, I praise You for Your sovereign control of all things. Strengthen my faith as I await Your ultimate resolution of all things.

Judges 17–18 / Luke 21:20–22:6 / Psalm 76:8–12

PREPPING

So you have to stay alert, praying that you'll be able to escape the coming trials so you can stand tall in the presence of the Son of Man.

LUKE 21:36 VOICE

When some guys look at the state of society today—and imagine it next year—they prepare for the worst. Anticipating political and economic upheavals, they stockpile water, food, and other essentials to make sure they're covered if (or when) things go south.

Committed Christians may differ on the necessity or urgency of this kind of "prepping." But every believer should prep for the cultural and spiritual upheavals of our world. They've been intensifying for several years now and promise to continue.

In Luke 21, Jesus warned His disciples about the coming destruction of Jerusalem, accomplished by the armies of Rome in AD 70. But Jesus' words also described an end-of-the-world scenario that features His return to earth to reward His followers and punish His enemies. That day, as both Peter and Paul said, would arrive "like a thief in the night" (1 Thessalonians 5:2; 2 Peter 3:10 VOICE). So Jesus urged every one of us to be ready.

We don't want to be caught unaware, mired in lazy or sinful behaviors (Luke 21:34). Our prepping includes staying alert and praying so God can cover us with His essentials as things go south for everyone else.

Lord, please strengthen me to stand firm for You as this world crumbles. I trust You to provide and protect.

Judges 19:1–20:23 / Luke 22:7–30 / Psalm 77:1–11

OUR VULNERABILITIES

*Then they began to argue among themselves about
who would be the greatest among them.*

LUKE 22:24 NLT

No matter how old we are, no matter how long we've followed Jesus, we have spiritual vulnerabilities in this life. One aspect of our growth, strangely enough, is recognizing how weak we are.

Today's scripture is a fascinating glimpse into fallen human nature. After three years of daily interaction with Jesus, after hearing His teaching and observing His example and feeling His touch both literal and spiritual, the disciples fell flat on their faces—but not in worship.

First, they argued among themselves over which one would fulfill Jesus' prediction of betrayal. But then that argument morphed into a "dispute" over who was the best, most important member of the group. It seems that the initial finger-pointing—"I bet it's him. . . I bet it's *you*"—quickly turned into "Well, I would never do such a thing. . .I'm Jesus' favorite, you know."

And that's typical of our old, sinful nature. Even with God's Holy Spirit in our lives, an advantage the disciples didn't yet enjoy, we are still susceptible to pride, envy, judging, and every other imaginable sin. Maturity demands that we recognize this weakness and defend against it.

How? Well, "put on all of God's armor" (Ephesians 6:11 NLT), starting with the "belt of truth" (verse 14 NLT). God's Word identifies our vulnerabilities and our pathway to safety.

May I never boast of myself, Lord, but only of You.

Judges 20:24–21:25 / Luke 22:31–54 / Psalm 77:12–20

ENGAGE YOUR MEMORY

But then I recall all you have done, O LORD;
I remember your wonderful deeds of long ago.
PSALM 77:11 NLT

Perhaps you've noticed how often the Psalms begin with sadness but end with a celebration of God's goodness and power. Psalm 77 is no exception.

The song is credited to Asaph, King David's musical director, though famed Bible commentator Matthew Henry (1662–1714) mentions a rabbinic belief that the language hints of the Babylonian exile centuries later. Whatever its origin, Psalm 77 provides a way out of the frustrating, depressing, despairing times of our own lives.

Whenever we feel like God's not listening to us (verse 1), when our souls are in turmoil (verse 2), when we sigh and long for deliverance (verse 3), there is an answer. Whenever we can't sleep or even pray (verse 4), when the "good old days" seem ancient (verse 5), when we realize there's no longer a song in our hearts (verse 6), happiness is still possible. But we'll need to make a conscious change of mind, an intentional effort to remember all the good things God has already done.

Why? Because that will encourage our hearts with what He will still do. And our "God of great wonders" (verse 14 NLT) has given us a whole Bible full of promises of better days to come.

Lord, You've done incredible things in my own life and throughout the world. May I trust You to fulfill every good promise You've made.

Ruth 1–2 / Luke 22:55–23:25 / Psalm 78:1–4

BE READY

The men who were guarding Jesus began mocking and beating
him. They blindfolded him and demanded, "Prophesy! Who hit
you?" And they said many other insulting things to him.

Luke 22:63–65 niv

Why would anyone hate Jesus? The perfect Man, who never lied or
cheated, who served others to His own exhaustion, would seem to be
someone everyone could love. While some did rally to Him, many
despised Jesus, wanting Him dead.

But Jesus knew the reaction He'd get, which is the same response
we'll receive as we follow Him faithfully:

> *"If the world hates you, keep in mind that it hated me first.*
> *If you belonged to the world, it would love you as its own.*
> *As it is, you do not belong to the world, but I have chosen*
> *you out of the world. That is why the world hates you.*
> *Remember what I told you: 'A servant is not greater than*
> *his master.' If they persecuted me, they will persecute you*
> *also. If they obeyed my teaching, they will obey yours also.*
> *They will treat you this way because of my name, for they*
> *do not know the one who sent me."*
> John 15:18–21 niv

As a follower of Jesus, don't be surprised by this world's animosity.
Spend more time in prayer and God's Word so you'll be ready when
the crisis comes.

Lord, I don't ask for persecution, but I want to be ready
when it happens. Strengthen me by Your Spirit.

Ruth 3–4 / Luke 23:26–24:12 / Psalm 78:5–8

BY THE RULES

*Then Boaz added, "You realize, don't you, that when you buy
the field from Naomi, you also get Ruth the Moabite, the widow
of our dead relative, along with the redeemer responsibility to
have children with her to carry on the family inheritance."*

RUTH 4:5 MSG

In literary terms, the book of Ruth has it all—drama, tragedy, romance. . .
even the touch of comedy above.

Boaz, a wealthy farmer and "family redeemer" for his relative
Naomi, was clearly interested in her widowed daughter-in-law, Ruth.
Naomi had urged Ruth to nudge Boaz toward marriage, and he was
pleased: "You could have had your pick of any of the young men around.
And now, my dear daughter, don't you worry about a thing; I'll do all
you could want or ask. Everybody in town knows what a courageous
woman you are—a real prize!" (Ruth 3:10–11 MSG).

But Boaz knew of a closer relative, a man who by law had the
first opportunity to purchase Naomi's land. He was interested in
the property. . .but said "no, thanks" when Boaz reminded him that
marriage to Ruth came with the deal: "Oh, I can't do that—I'd
jeopardize my own family's inheritance" (Ruth 4:6 MSG).

Boaz pursued what he wanted, but by the rules. If something's
meant to be, God will make it happen. If it isn't God's will, you really
don't want it anyway.

May I never skirt Your rules, Lord, in pursuit of my own interests.

1 Samuel 1:1–2:21 / Luke 24:13–53 / Psalm 78:9–16

ELI'S BAD EXAMPLE

It so happened that as she continued in prayer before GOD, Eli was watching her closely. Hannah was praying in her heart, silently. Her lips moved, but no sound was heard. Eli jumped to the conclusion that she was drunk. He approached her and said, "You're drunk! How long do you plan to keep this up? Sober up, woman!"

1 SAMUEL 1:12–14 MSG

Why are human beings so quick to judge? Why do we Christians often fall into that trap?

The story of Hannah—of her longing for a son and her readiness to ask God for one—is well known. So is the priest Eli's rude, unhelpful assumption that her passionate praying was the effect of too much wine. Guys, our side looks bad in this encounter.

Eli was God's representative over the entire nation of Israel. He was supposed to teach people about the Lord, intercede for them, and conduct sacrifices for their sins. Though he was quick to accept Hannah's tearful defense, sending her away with a blessing (verses 15–17), the rest of Eli's story indicates that he didn't follow God as carefully as he should have. That's when bad things—like harsh, unfair judgment of others—often crop up.

Today, let's turn Eli's example around. Be sure to cultivate a deep, respectful relationship with God that leads to loving, encouraging interactions with others.

It's so easy to judge and speak harshly, Lord.
Help me instead to speak with grace and truth.

1 Samuel 2:22–4:22 / John 1:1–28 / Psalm 78:17–24

DIMINISHING GOD

They said, "Can God really spread a table in the wilderness? True,
he struck the rock, and water gushed out, streams flowed abundantly,
but can he also give us bread? Can he supply meat for his people?"

PSALM 78:19–20 NIV

We can only diminish God in our own thinking. In reality, He *is* reality, filling all of heaven and earth (Jeremiah 23:24).

But our finite minds struggle with His immensity, and our sin blinds us to God's awesome goodness and power. How often we resemble the ancient Israelites who whined about food and water so soon after the miraculous parting of the Red Sea.

Psalm 78 hits the highlights (actually, lowlights) of the exodus. And today's scripture encapsulates the often schizophrenic way we humans view God: "True, he struck the rock, and water gushed out, streams flowed abundantly, but can he also give us bread? Can he supply meat for his people?"

"Yes, buts" kill—literally, in the case of the Israelites, who infuriated God with their complaining disbelief (Psalm 78:21–31). They're spiritually deadly to us. The New Testament teaches that when anyone asks of God, "you must believe and not doubt, because the one who doubts is like a wave of the sea, blown and tossed by the wind. That person should not expect to receive anything from the Lord" (James 1:6–7 NIV).

Father in heaven, I want You to hear and answer my prayers.
Strengthen my faith so that I never diminish You.

1 Samuel 5–7 / John 1:29–51 / Psalm 78:25–33

DARKNESS AND LIGHT

*Andrew, Simon Peter's brother, was one of these men who
heard what John said and then followed Jesus. Andrew
went to find his brother, Simon, and told him, "We have
found the Messiah" (which means "Christ").*

JOHN 1:40–41 NLT

We live in a very dark world. But we serve "the light of the world"
(John 8:12 NLT).

The only answer for human problems is Jesus Christ. No amount
of education or prosperity or lawmaking will ever correct people's
separation from God due to sin. Only Jesus can do that, and we who
know Him have both the privilege and responsibility of sharing His
good news.

In John 1, as Jesus began His public ministry, John the Baptist
started the ball rolling. Standing with two of his own disciples, John
saw Jesus walking by and declared, "Look! There is the Lamb of God!"
(John 1:36 NLT). John's followers immediately pursued Jesus.

Soon, as you read in today's scripture, Andrew tracked down his
brother Peter to inform him about Jesus. Another guy from their
town, Philip, met Jesus and promptly told his friend Nathanael (John
1:43–45). All four of these men were among Jesus' twelve disciples,
whose gospel-sharing ministry comes down through time to each of
us who believe.

Now it's our turn. Let's never simply curse the darkness when
we know the Light.

*Lord Jesus, give me the opportunities and the courage to share
Your good news with others. Shine Your light through me, I pray.*

1 Samuel 8:1–9:26 / John 2 / Psalm 78:34–41

DO WHAT JESUS SAYS

His mother said to the servants, "Do whatever he tells you."

JOHN 2:5 NIV

A popular Christmas song asks, "Mary, did you know?" Did Jesus' mother imagine all the incredible things her newborn Son would go on to accomplish?

She certainly knew, from the angel Gabriel's words, that Jesus was the Son of God who would rule eternity. But the specifics of His life were details yet to unfold, glimpses of His love and power that would literally change history.

In John 2, Mary helped unveil Jesus' public ministry. She knew He could solve a problem for the host of a wedding banquet—a shortage of wine for the guests. You may know what happened: Mary urged Jesus to help, He told servants to fill large stone jars with water, and the water miraculously became wine. Our focus is Mary's comment, "Do whatever he tells you."

She encouraged the staff to hear and obey Jesus to solve a problem and make things better for others. "Do whatever he tells you" wasn't a theological pronouncement—but could we do better than to view it that way?

If we do what Jesus tells us—through His Word and through our conscience, informed by His Word—we'll solve our problems and make things better for others. It probably won't be as quick or dramatic, but any situation that Jesus addresses is guaranteed to improve.

Lord, lead me to Your Word, then empower me to live out what I find.

1 Samuel 9:27–11:15 / John 3:1–22 / Psalm 78:42–55

A GOOD START. . .

Samuel: The Eternal One of Israel has anointed you as
ruler over His possession, over all Israel. [You will be king
over the people of the Eternal One, and you will deliver
them from the enemies that surround them now.]

1 SAMUEL 10:1 VOICE

When John Paciorek got every young ballplayer's dream opportunity, he took full advantage. On the final day of their 1963 season, the Houston Colt .45's (later known as the Astros) gave the eighteen-year-old a shot at major league play. He performed flawlessly, reaching base in all five at bats, scoring four runs, and driving in three. Strangely, though, a back injury kept Paciorek from ever playing another big league game. His superb start didn't guarantee long-term success.

That's true of our spiritual lives too. Consider King Saul's experience—chosen by God and anointed by the prophet Samuel, Saul quickly led Israel to a smashing military victory over the Ammonites. But careless, selfish choices ultimately caused him to stumble—badly. Saul developed a murderous jealousy of young David, usurped the priest's duty by offering a sacrifice, and refused to follow God's command to completely destroy the Amalekites. . .failures that cost him dearly.

Our Christian lives always start well because Jesus does the work of salvation. But then we need to join Him in the process of sanctification. Let's be sure our finish is as good as our start.

Please give me the desire and strength to follow You fully, Lord.

1 Samuel 12–13 / John 3:23–4:10 / Psalm 78:56–66

JESUS > ME

*"The bride belongs to the bridegroom. The friend who attends
the bridegroom waits and listens for him, and is full of joy when
he hears the bridegroom's voice. That joy is mine, and it is now
complete. He must become greater; I must become less."*

JOHN 3:29–30 NIV

Had Jesus used social media, He might have responded to John the Baptist's statement above with a single word: "This!"

This is the attitude every maturing Christian man must have. *This* is the mindset that honors our Lord and makes us better people. *This* is the countercultural, self-diminishing perspective that sets Christians apart—positively—from the world around us.

Will John's words make you a greater success in your career, your finances, your public notoriety? Though God *could* bless your humility like He did Solomon's (1 Kings 3:1–15), chances are you'll be relatively poor and obscure in this world. But the one person who truly matters, God, will definitely see and ultimately reward your deference to His Son.

Jesus said there wasn't "anyone greater" than John (Matthew 11:11 NIV)—and he was arrested, imprisoned, and beheaded. His humility toward Jesus was repaid by the "well done" he heard when entering heaven.

And let's keep our eyes on heaven. This life is passing quickly, but the eternal Jesus invites us to enjoy His presence and provision forever. That's totally worth "becoming less" now.

I want to give You all the glory, Jesus—only You deserve to be praised.

1 Samuel 14 / John 4:11–38 / Psalm 78:67–72

YOU ꓕND GOD

"Nothing can keep the LORD from saving, whether by many or by few."
1 SAMUEL 14:6 HCSB

Mention the biblical Jonathan, and many think of his deep friendship with David. After Jonathan died in battle beside his father, King Saul, David sang, "Your love for me was more wonderful than the love of women" (2 Samuel 1:26 HCSB).

But there was nothing effeminate about Jonathan—he was a courageous warrior and leader of men. In today's passage, Jonathan and his armor bearer attacked a Philistine garrison by themselves, leaving twenty enemies dead in the space of half an acre (1 Samuel 14:14). God followed up with an earthquake that terrified the larger Philistine army (verse 15), and Israel's powerful enemy was reduced to confusion, with soldiers fighting among themselves (verse 20).

The experience confirmed Jonathan's faith in God, his belief that the Lord could save Israel "by many or by few." This battle at Michmash Pass validates an old saying: "You and God constitute a majority."

Of course, in that "you and God" equation, *you* don't add anything to His power. . .you just allow God to work through you. Then great things happen. As the angel Gabriel said to Mary, "For nothing will be impossible with God" (Luke 1:37 HCSB).

In this crazy world, be a Jonathan. Fight the good fight and trust God to save—by many or by few.

Lord, I ask for courage and Your strength to fight the battles of this life.

1 Samuel 15–16 / John 4:39–54 / Psalm 79:1–7

OVERRUN

*O God, the nations have come into [the land of Your
people] Your inheritance; Your sacred temple have they
defiled; they have made Jerusalem heaps of ruins.*

PSALM 79:1 AMPC

Do you ever feel this way about your own country? Not that the United States or any other western democracy was ever "God's chosen people". . .but that rampant sin has defiled and ruined what was once a place that, to some extent, honored God and His Word.

Psalm 79 seems to reference the destruction of Jerusalem by the Babylonians in 586 BC. God's people became a reproach to their neighbors (verse 4) after their blood was spilled (verse 3) and their bodies were picked over by birds (verse 2). As many prophets had warned, God's wrath was turning toward His own people for their terrible sins, including idol worship.

The psalm writer begged God to forget His people's sin and remember His mercy and compassion for them (verse 8). The psalmist urged God to help His people "for the glory of Your name!" (verse 9 AMPC).

Today, God's people are a spiritual nation, found in every country on earth. Our "land" is under increasing attack from the forces of Satan, who knows "that he has [only] a short time [left]!" (Revelation 12:12 AMPC). Like the psalm writer, let's admit our own failures, beg God's mercy, and then "give [Him] thanks forever" (Psalm 79:13 AMPC).

*Thank You, Father, for Your faithfulness,
even when I am faithless (2 Timothy 2:13).*

AVOID A LIFE OF SIN

*Jesus: Take a look at your body; it has been made whole
and strong. So avoid a life of sin, or else a calamity
greater than any disability may befall you.*

JOHN 5:14 VOICE

These days, many people view Jesus' universal *welcome* as a universal *acceptance.* "He hung out with prostitutes" is a common refrain, implying that Jesus was fine with people just as they are. That's a dangerous half-truth.

Certainly, Jesus welcomes all people, just as they are, to come to Him. We can't do anything to earn His salvation. But once we're "in," once He's healed us of our soul's great disability, we must "avoid a life of sin" as Jesus told the formerly lame man of John 5.

All of us will fail from time to time. We react in sinful ways and sometimes consciously pursue the wrong things. When that happens, we should go directly to God's throne of grace (Hebrews 4:16), claiming the confession-forgiveness promise of 1 John 1:9. What we dare never do is assume that salvation allows us to "persist in a life of sin" (Romans 6:1 VOICE).

We only grow deeper in faith by knowing Jesus as His Word presents Him. As we study scripture, we'll see the Lord welcoming everyone to come as they are. . .then expecting them to become like Himself. "You are to be holy, for I am holy" (1 Peter 1:16 VOICE).

Lord, please give me a passion for Your purity.

1 Samuel 18–19 / John 5:25–47 / Psalm 80:1–7

MAKE WAY

Jonathan made a covenant with David because he loved him as himself.
Jonathan took off the robe he was wearing and gave it to David,
along with his tunic, and even his sword, his bow and his belt.

1 SAMUEL 18:3–4 NIV

Jonathan should have become the second king of Israel. His father, Saul, was the man God chose in response to the people's demand for a human ruler. Sadly, Saul's selfishness and folly caused God to declare an end to his royal house (1 Samuel 15). But he would remain on the throne for several years while God raised David from the obscurity of watching his father's sheep.

When David defeated the Philistine giant Goliath, Jonathan quickly recognized the young man's qualities and "became one in spirit with David" (1 Samuel 18:1 NIV). Today's scripture, describing the handing over of royal clothing and military equipment, indicates Jonathan realized David was destined for leadership. Jonathan would protect his beloved friend against his own father's murderous intentions and suffer Saul's emotional abuse for doing so (see 1 Samuel 20:30–31).

What about us? Can we admit that others may surpass us in wisdom and ability, and make way for them to accomplish their God-given objectives? It's always better to support God's plan than resist it—to quote a thoughtful Pharisee from a millennium later, "You will only find yourselves fighting against God" (Acts 5:39 NIV).

Lord, keep me humble and ready to serve at whatever level You choose.

1 Samuel 20–21 / John 6:1–21 / Psalm 80:8–19

GOD ALREADY KNOWS

When Jesus looked up and noticed a huge crowd coming toward Him,
He asked Philip, "Where will we buy bread so these people can eat?" He
asked this to test him, for He Himself knew what He was going to do.

JOHN 6:5–6 HCSB

This scene precedes Jesus' feeding of the five thousand. Large crowds, drawn by His miraculous healing ability, had followed Jesus up a mountainside near the Sea of Galilee.

Though the average people recognized Jesus' power, His disciples were somehow blind to it. The Lord "tested" Philip with the question above—sadly, he flunked. "It would take more than half a year's wages," Philip sputtered, "to buy enough bread for each one to have a bite!" (John 6:7 NIV). Andrew fared slightly better by bringing the boy with the five-loaves-and-two-fish lunch to Jesus. "But how far will they go among so many?" he wondered (John 6:9 NIV).

Jesus, the all-knowing God, already had a plan for feeding these people, perhaps twenty thousand including women and children. It's no strain on the Creator of the universe to multiply one little lunch into food for a city's worth of people.

And it's no problem for Jesus to solve whatever problems *we* face. He may test us first, as with Philip, but He already has a plan. And though we may not always understand what He's doing, we can be sure His plan is good.

Thank You, Lord, for knowing my needs and providing for me.

1 Samuel 22–23 / John 6:22–42 / Psalm 81:1–10

HONOR YOUR FATHER AND MOTHER

*David went to Mizpeh of Moab where he said to the
king of Moab, "Please let my father and mother stay
with you until I know what God will do for me."*

1 Samuel 22:3 hcsb

Today's scripture is a snapshot of David's flight from King Saul, a
stressful episode made worse by the young man's concern for his
parents. Prophetically anointed to succeed Saul but running for dear
life from the insanely jealous king, David made a cave near Adullam
his base of operations. His entire family joined him there (1 Samuel
22:1), but David soon escorted his parents to Moab, asking its king
to shelter them temporarily. (David and his father were descended
from a Moabite woman who had married an Israelite.)

From the very beginning, God instituted a cycle of care that
applies in all times and cultures: moms and dads care for their young
children, then those grown-up kids care for their aging parents. At every
age, children should honor their parents, as the fifth commandment
decrees. Granted, that's easier to do if mom and dad are loving, wise,
generous, and good. Yet the rule applies to guys whose parents aren't
great—or even terrible.

Today, what can you do to honor your father and mother? Is there
a physical, financial, or relational need you can meet? Or if they're
gone, can you serve someone else in their memory?

May I honor You, Lord, by honoring the parents You gave me.

A DEAD DOG

"Against whom has the king of Israel come out?
Who are you pursuing? A dead dog?"

1 SAMUEL 24:14 NIV

This wouldn't happen today: when the Soviet Union launched *Sputnik 2* in November 1957, space officials sent a stray dog along. Laika became the first living creature in orbit but soon expired in the capsule, which stayed aloft another five months.

Dogs were expendable in Old Testament Israel too, more pests than pets—so when David called himself "a dead dog" before King Saul, he was really being humble. Of course, everyone is deferential to royalty, but David had already been anointed by the prophet Samuel to replace Saul on the throne.

A man of many passions, not all of them good, David's humility helped him greatly. In 1 Samuel 24, he rejected an opportunity to hasten his own coronation by violence. When his men urged the assassination of an unsuspecting Saul, David replied, "The LORD forbid that I should do such a thing to my master, the LORD's anointed" (verse 6 NIV). Later, as king himself, he marveled at God's blessing: "Who am I, Sovereign LORD, and what is my family, that you have brought me this far?" (2 Samuel 7:18 NIV).

This is the attitude God wants from us. As Jesus said, in a promise captured three times in scripture, "those who humble themselves will be exalted" (Matthew 23:12; Luke 14:11, 18:14 NIV).

I'm just a dead dog made alive in Christ. Thank You, Lord!

1 Samuel 25:32–27:12 / John 7:1–24 / Psalm 82

COMING AROUND

His brothers were pushing him like this because
they didn't believe in him either.

JOHN 7:5 MSG

Ever been frustrated with someone who just couldn't "get" your faith?
Ever been frustrated with yourself for struggling to live up to it?

We've all felt such disappointment. But that's not strange.
Even Jesus' brothers initially rejected who He really was. And they
had actually lived with Him for years, seeing Jesus, hearing Him,
experiencing His perfection every day. (Come to think of it, though,
that would undoubtedly stir up some insecurity and resentment among
the less than perfect.)

After his miraculous conversion, the apostle Paul, of all people,
still wrestled with sinful desires. "The moment I decide to do good, sin
is there to trip me up," he wrote. "I truly delight in God's commands,
but it's pretty obvious that not all of me joins in that delight. Parts
of me covertly rebel, and just when I least expect it, they take charge"
(Romans 7:21–23 MSG).

The good news for Paul was that "Jesus Christ. . .acted to set
things right in this life of contradictions" (Romans 7:25 MSG). And
among Jesus' brothers, at least two came around to faith and Christian
leadership.

Not everyone will accept God's offer of salvation or fully live up to
it. But many will. If someone you care about hasn't yet, keep praying.
Give God time to do His work in human hearts.

I do believe, Lord. Grow my faith, and help me share it.

1 Samuel 28–29 / John 7:25–8:11 / Psalm 83

PAST PERFORMANCE. . .

*Do to them as you did to Midian, as you did to Sisera and
Jabin at the river Kishon, who perished at Endor and became
like dung on the ground. Make their nobles like Oreb and
Zeeb, all their princes like Zebah and Zalmunna, who said,
"Let us take possession of the pasturelands of God."*

PSALM 83:9–12 NIV

You've probably heard investment fund ads that end with the disclaimer, "Past performance does not indicate future results." It arises from a federal securities law prohibiting "portrayals of past performance, made in a manner which would imply that gains or income realized in the past would be repeated in the future."

No such limitations apply to God.

Psalm 83 laments the threats of Israel's enemies, who said, "Let us destroy them as a nation, so that Israel's name is remembered no more" (verse 4 NIV). But the psalmist called on God to reprise His annihilation of foes like the Canaanite leaders Sisera and Jabin (Judges 4), the army of Midian (Judges 7), and the Midianite rulers Oreb, Zeeb, Zebah, and Zalmunna (Judges 7–8).

God has vanquished His enemies before. He will do it again. "God is just," the apostle Paul wrote. "He will pay back trouble to those who trouble you and give relief to you who are troubled" (2 Thessalonians 1:6–7 NIV). With God, past performance simply guarantees the future result of His promises.

Lord, I know You'll come through for us. Thank You.

1 Samuel 30–31 / John 8:12–47 / Psalm 84:1–4

ALL FOR ONE, ONE FOR ALL

"As his part is who goes down to the battle, so shall his part be who stays by the belongings; they shall share alike."

1 SAMUEL 30:24 SKJV

This chapter is famed for David's reaction to extreme hardship: he "encouraged himself in the LORD his God" (1 Samuel 30:6 SKJV). Where else could he turn? Running for his life, David found it safer among the enemy Philistines than with King Saul, who was bent on killing him. Then, while David and his men were away from their home base, Amalekite raiders captured all their women and children. Distraught, the men talked of stoning David.

As was typical, David prayed. God told him to pursue the Amalekites. David obeyed, rescuing all the women and children and even gaining the livestock of his enemies. But then more trouble arose.

Some of David's fighting men—described as wicked and worthless—declared they wouldn't share the spoils with the exhausted men who'd stayed behind. David scotched that idea by saying, "You shall not do so, my brothers, with what the LORD has given us" (verse 23 SKJV). And he laid down the rule of today's scripture.

It's a good reminder for us as Christian men today. We're all part of the Lord's army, and whatever our role, we serve a larger cause. Work hard, look out for your fellow soldiers. . .and trust God to provide everything you need.

Lord, make me generous and compassionate with all other believers.

2 Samuel 1–2 / John 8:48–9:12 / Psalm 84:5–12

THE REAL JESUS

Jews: We were right when we called You a demon-possessed Samaritan.
JOHN 8:48 VOICE

If you intend to follow the Jesus of the Bible—as opposed to the "anything goes" Jesus today's culture prefers—you'll get blowback.

As the tradition-bound Jews of Jesus' time called Him names (notice the ethnic insult in today's scripture), so people today will throw every name in the book at us. For carefully following His Word—as the vast majority of Christian churches have for centuries—we'll be called "hateful," "divisive," "phobic," even "murderous."

But why should we expect anything else? Jesus told His twelve disciples (and, by extension, all of us) that trouble was coming. "If you find that the world despises you, remember that before it despised you, it first despised Me," He said. "If you were a product of the world order, then it would love you. But you are not a product of the world because I have taken you out of it, and it despises you for that very reason" (John 15:18–19 VOICE).

Many people say they want Christians to "be more like Jesus." That's a great idea, though not even that will result in acceptance. Never forget that Jesus Himself was hated, arrested, and crucified.

Even so, stay faithful to the real Jesus as presented in scripture. He promised, "Whoever acknowledges me before others, I will also acknowledge before my Father in heaven" (Matthew 10:32 NIV).

Give me boldness, Lord, to live completely for You.

2 Samuel 3–4 / John 9:13–34 / Psalm 85:1–7

PLEASING EVERYBODY?

This pleased the people very much. In fact,
everything the king did pleased them!
2 SAMUEL 3:36 NLT

Here is a true miracle: an entire nation happily agreed on something. Actually, they happily agreed on some*one*—their new king, David. The storyline is complex for a brief devotional, but suffice it to say that David responded wisely to infighting between his military leaders and the late King Saul's commander, who had recently joined David. All of his subjects were pleased.

That was a unique outcome in a specific time and place. Christians today should never expect to please everyone.

Certainly, we should treat people kindly, helpfully, and respectfully. But Jesus told His apostles that "all nations will hate you because you are my followers" (Matthew 10:22 NLT). Another time, He said, "Do you think I have come to bring peace to the earth? No, I have come to divide people against each other!" (Luke 12:51 NLT). As the perfect human being, God in the flesh, Jesus was despised by many—so much so that He was ultimately crucified.

True Christians will never please this world. But be a true Christian anyway. "Be careful to live properly among your unbelieving neighbors," the apostle Peter wrote. "Then even if they accuse you of doing wrong, they will see your honorable behavior, and they will give honor to God when he judges the world" (1 Peter 2:12 NLT).

Lord Jesus, may I always demonstrate Your
grace and truth in this world.

2 Samuel 5:1–7:17 / John 9:35–10:10 / Psalm 85:8–13

DO IT GOD'S WAY

David was grieved and offended because the Lord had
broken forth upon Uzzah, and that place is called
Perez-uzzah [the breaking forth upon Uzzah] to this day.
2 SAMUEL 6:8 AMPC

Poor Uzzah, struck dead for trying to do good.

Of course, there's more to the story than just that.

David, recently crowned king of all Israel, had made the newly-conquered Jerusalem his capital. In a celebratory mood, he decided to bring the ark of the covenant to the city from its resting place several miles north. Along the way, David and his subjects "played before the Lord with all their might, with songs, lyres, harps, tambourines, castanets, and cymbals" (2 Samuel 6:5 AMPC). The man after God's own heart was leading God's people in a rousing time of praise and worship. What could possibly be better?

Well, it would have helped for the ark to be transported properly. This gold-plated box, where God manifested Himself to Israel, was supposed to be carried by poles inserted through solid gold rings. When David moved it, the ark was simply set on an oxcart—and when the animals stumbled and Uzzah reached out to steady the load, tragedy followed.

Perhaps that seems extreme. But God sets the rules, and we are wise to follow them exactly. Don't ever do your own thing and assume God will bless you. Do everything *His* way.

Lord, thanks for Your grace—but help me to honor
You by following Your rules precisely.

2 Samuel 7:18–10:19 / John 10:11–30 / Psalm 86:1–10

LOWER-CASE "GODS"

Among the gods there is none like you,
Lord; no deeds can compare with yours.

PSALM 86:8 NIV

That there is only one true God is a key element of Christian belief. Yes, He's a trinity of Father, Son, and Holy Spirit, but the three "persons" constitute one all-powerful, all-knowing, everywhere-present God.

That same three-letter word—lower-cased—has been applied to any number of lesser things. Some are actual physical beings, whether people or objects. Some are simply ideas or figments of the human imagination. None of these "gods" are eternally self-existent like the God of scripture. None of them could create a universe from nothing, sustain it day by day, or manage the affairs of literally trillions of living things. This is David's point in Psalm 86.

As God's hand-picked king of God's hand-picked people, David was important. But he was still very human—"poor and needy" (Psalm 86:1 NIV), hoping for mercy (verses 3 and 6), longing for joy (verse 4), in distress (verse 7). And only one of all the gods—the capital-*G* God—could help: "You are great and do marvelous deeds; you alone are God" (verse 10 NIV).

No Philistine or Ammonite idol could ever help David. No amount of money, no politician or celebrity, no clever philosophy will ever ultimately benefit us. The utterly unparalleled God upholds every person who humbly follows Jesus Christ. Don't ever be distracted by a lower-case alternative.

Help me, Lord, to recognize and honor Your absolute uniqueness.

NO MIRACLES REQUIRED

*And many came to Him and said, "John did no
miracle, but all things that John spoke of this man
were true." And many believed in Him there.*

JOHN 10:41–42 SKJV

Are you a leader or a follower? Do you prefer to be in front of people
or in the background? There's no "right" answer to these questions,
since God has made every man different. The important thing is that
you're faithful to God with the personality and skills He's given you.

John the Baptist was a powerful preacher who drew large crowds
as he prepared the way for the Lord (see Matthew 3:3). When
Jesus arrived on the scene, though, John immediately stepped aside,
introducing "the Lamb of God" to all who would look to the one
"who takes away the sin of the world" (John 1:29 SKJV). Due to John's
influence, many did.

People who had heard John's preaching later came to Jesus,
praising the Baptist's truthful, accurate words. "John did no miracle,"
they said, "but all things that John spoke of this man were true." Even
more people put their faith in Jesus.

Every one of us, whatever our level of intelligence, talent, or
success, can speak truthful, accurate words about Jesus. There's no
need for us to perform miracles, literal or figurative, to serve our Lord
and help our fellow man. We just have to be willing and obedient to
the Spirit's leading.

Lord, I'm willing. Please speak Your truth through me.

2 Samuel 12:26–13:39 / John 11:17–54 / Psalm 87

DEAL WITH PROBLEMS, NOW

King David heard the whole story and was enraged, but he didn't
discipline Amnon. David doted on him because he was his firstborn.

2 SAMUEL 13:21 MSG

David's family tragedies grew out of his sin with Bathsheba (see 2
Samuel 12:7–10). Having lots of kids by multiple wives didn't help
things, either. But there are still lessons for all of us in his story.

Today's passage is rated R: David's son Amnon became infatuated
with his half sister, Tamar. Amnon feigned sickness to gain her
sympathy—then raped her when she brought him food. Tamar's full
brother Absalom took her home and seethed, plotting revenge.

The king, father to all involved, was furious. . .but did nothing.
Maybe guilt over his own sexual sin kept him from dealing decisively
with the situation. Because he didn't, Absalom took matters into his
own hands, killing Amnon two years later. Then Absalom attempted
a coup against his father.

Our small, everyday irritations should be disregarded and allowed
to dwindle away. But big problems need to be dealt with quickly.
Favoritism must never color our response to difficult issues. And
prayer should cover our every thought and action. Sadly, for a man
who prayed so deeply and often, David is never described in 2 Samuel
13 as going to God.

Finally, stay on guard, all the time. It helps if we avoid the sins
that set off a spiritual avalanche.

Lord, may I never create the situations David did.

SIN IS ILLOGICAL

A large crowd of the Jews learned He was there. They came not only because of Jesus, but also to see Lazarus the one He had raised from the dead. Therefore the chief priests decided to kill Lazarus also because he was the reason many of the Jews were deserting them and believing in Jesus.

JOHN 12:9–11 HCSB

Does it make any sense for the Jewish chief priests to plot to kill a guy Jesus had already brought back from the dead? This odd vignette in the book of John illustrates how illogical sin is—and makes us.

We've all been tempted to do things we clearly know are wrong, foolish, dumb. And yet, at times, we've all given in. This is a sad reality of life in a broken world, even though we've been saved and changed by Jesus.

The apostle Paul also felt that crazy internal tug-of-war. "I do not understand what I am doing," he wrote, "because I do not practice what I want to do, but I do what I hate" (Romans 7:15 HCSB).

Paul recognized the only answer to his problem was God's grace through Jesus Christ. Though his body craved wrong, Paul's mind could pursue a deeper, more loving and obedient relationship with his Lord (Romans 7:24–25).

That was something the Jewish leaders of Jesus' day steadfastly refused. May we never allow ourselves to wander down that illogical path.

Lord, make me wise and keep me true to You.

2 Samuel 15:13–16:23 / John 12:20–43 / Psalm 88:10–18

NOT ASHAMED!

Yet at the same time many even among the leaders believed in him.
But because of the Pharisees they would not openly acknowledge
their faith for fear they would be put out of the synagogue;
for they loved human praise more than praise from God.

JOHN 12:42–43 NIV

Jesus made quite the impression on some of the Jewish religious leaders, so much so that they believed in Him. The problem? These leaders failed to openly profess their faith for fear of losing their positions of power and influence. Today's scripture verse said that "they loved human praise more than praise from God."

Ouch!

Contrast these men with Paul, a former Jewish religious leader whom God tasked with taking the message of salvation to the Gentile world, who wrote, "For I am not ashamed of the gospel, because it is the power of God that brings salvation to everyone who believes: first to the Jew, then to the Gentile" (Romans 1:16 NIV).

What's more important to you—acceptance from other people or pleasing God with your every word and action? God wants you to be bold and courageous enough to openly proclaim your faith in Jesus to those around you—even when it feels uncomfortable to do so.

Jesus, please embolden me to courageously stand up for You, even
when I fear opposition or persecution. May I always put You and
my relationship with You ahead of what other people think of me.

TRUST JESUS!

Jesus shouted to the crowds, "If you trust me, you are trusting not only me, but also God who sent me. For when you see me, you are seeing the one who sent me. I have come as a light to shine in this dark world, so that all who put their trust in me will no longer remain in the dark."

JOHN 12:44–46 NLT

If you want to know how God feels about you and other people, how He wants you to treat other people, how you are to relate to Him. . . closely watch and listen to Jesus as you read His earthly story in the four gospel accounts.

In today's scripture verses, Jesus told a crowd of His followers that trusting Him was the same as trusting the heavenly Father. Earlier in the Gospel of John, He stated, "My teaching is not my own. It comes from the one who sent me. Anyone who chooses to do the will of God will find out whether my teaching comes from God or whether I speak on my own" (John 7:16–17 NIV).

You can trust Jesus and build your life of faith around His every word and action.

Loving Father, thank You for sending Your only Son to earth, where He would teach and heal many before dying a sacrificial death so that I could be saved. Thank You, Jesus, for revealing the heart and mind of God during Your time here on earth.

2 Samuel 18:19–19:39 / John 13:21–38 / Psalm 89:7–13

BE LIKE BARZILLAI THE GILEADITE

Barzillai the Gileadite also came down from Rogelim
to cross the Jordan with the king and to send him on his
way from there. Now Barzillai was very old, eighty
years of age. He had provided for the king during his
stay in Mahanaim, for he was a very wealthy man.

2 SAMUEL 19:31–32 NIV

Barzillai was an obscure Old Testament character who earned his place in the pages of scripture through his faithfulness, loyalty, and generosity. Today's scripture verse tells us that he was a wealthy man who provided for David in a time of dire need.

Barzillai was a real-life illustration of the words of James: "Show me your faith without deeds, and I will show you my faith by my deeds" (James 2:18 NIV). The Bible clearly teaches that we are saved by God's grace through faith in Jesus Christ (Ephesians 2:8–9). But James pointed out that good works would always be a by-product of true faith.

If you want to demonstrate your faith in a tangible way, you could follow the example of Barzillai, who saw his brother's need and did what it took to meet it.

Lord God, may I have the kind of faith that motivates me
to wholeheartedly serve You in whatever way You choose.
May my service be done without regard to personal recognition
or accolades. I choose to believe that You recognize the
things I do for You—and that's enough for me.

2 Samuel 19:40–21:22 / John 14:1–17 / Psalm 89:14–18

GREATER THINGS?

*"Very truly I tell you, whoever believes in me will do the works I
have been doing, and they will do even greater things than these,
because I am going to the Father. And I will do whatever you
ask in my name, so that the Father may be glorified in the Son.
You may ask me for anything in my name, and I will do it."*

JOHN 14:12–14 NIV

What an amazing promise straight from the mouth of Jesus! His
disciples had seen Him perform spectacular miracles and heard Him
deliver teaching the likes of which no man had ever heard—and now
He told them they would "do the works I have been doing, and they
will do even greater things than these."

How could these mere mortals do greater works than Jesus, the
Son of God? Simply because Jesus would soon return to heaven, where
He would be seated at the right hand of the Father, *and* because of
His promise that they He would do anything they asked for in His
name so that the Father would be glorified.

Jesus changed these men and empowered them so that they could
later go out and change the world with His wonderful message of
salvation.

And He'll do the same thing for you today!

*Jesus, I ask that You bless me and empower me through
Your Holy Spirit so that You can use me in mighty ways to
bless others and do great things for Your kingdom.*

2 Samuel 22:1–23:7 / John 14:18–15:27 / Psalm 89:19–29

ABIDING IN THE VINE

"Abide in Me, and I in you. As the branch cannot bear fruit by itself, unless it abides in the vine, no more can you, unless you abide in Me. I am the vine; you are the branches. He who abides in Me, and I in him, the same brings forth much fruit. For without Me you can do nothing."

JOHN 15:4–5 SKJV

You don't need to be an accredited botanist to know that a vine that has been separated from a plant's main branch cannot produce flowers or fruit. On the contrary, that branch quicky wilts and dies, never to produce anything again.

Jesus used the beautiful word picture in today's scripture verses to illustrate just how desperately we need to cling to Him—to abide in Him—if we desire to grow in our faith and produce good "fruit" for Him. There truly is no other way!

Jesus truly is our True Vine. Everything we need to live a life that pleases God and to perform good works for Him flows outward from Jesus—and *only* from Jesus. No amount of self-effort or religious practices can take the place of doing what Jesus commanded His disciples to do: "Abide in Me."

Jesus, I truly cannot produce the kind of spiritual fruit You call me to produce on my own. I need You, the Vine that nourishes and waters me so that I can do the things You call me to do.

2 Samuel 23:8–24:25 / John 16:1–22 / Psalm 89:30–37

SORROW TURNED TO JOY

*"So you have sorrow now, but I will see you again;
then you will rejoice, and no one can rob you of that joy."*

JOHN 16:22 NLT

Jesus' disciples were disturbed and confused over what Jesus had told them would happen in the coming hours. They would suffer deep sadness when their Master was arrested, tried, and condemned to die the death of a common criminal.

But before these things would come to pass, Jesus made them one of His final promises, namely that they would soon be reunited with Him and that their sorrow would be turned into a joy that no one could take away. The disciples didn't fully understand Jesus' words, but they would just a few days later.

Jesus' promise to the disciples applies to us today. One day, "the throne of God and of the Lamb will be in the city, and his servants will serve him. They will see his face, and his name will be on their foreheads" (Revelation 22:3–4 NIV).

No matter what kinds of sorrows we face in this life, we can take comfort and joy in knowing that we will one day see our precious Savior face-to-face.

*Jesus, thank You for giving Your all so that I could be
brought into Your eternal kingdom. Help me to focus not
on the sorrows of this life but on the indescribable joy I will
experience when I one day see You face-to-face in heaven.*

1 Kings 1 / John 16:23–17:5 / Psalm 89:38–52

A SAVIOR WHO COMFORTS

*"I have told you all this so that you may have peace in me.
Here on earth you will have many trials and sorrows.
But take heart, because I have overcome the world."*

JOHN 16:33 NLT

Before facing His ultimate destiny here on earth—a horrific, excruciating death on a Roman cross—Jesus spoke words of comfort to His confused and fearful disciples. The following hours would be more difficult, more heartbreaking than they dared imagine, but Jesus spoke to them words of peace and comfort.

As God in the flesh, Jesus was and is "the God of all comfort" (2 Corinthians 1:3 NIV). Jesus has saved you and given you eternal life. He has given you the Holy Spirit to teach you and empower you to live a God-pleasing life. And He remains for you your source of comfort as you make your way through life in this fallen world.

You will likely suffer through difficult times in this world, times of crushing heartache and loss. But no matter how dark things may get, you can take comfort in these words from the mouth of the Lord Jesus: "But take heart, because I have overcome the world."

*God of comfort, thank You for calming my soul and easing
my mind when I am going through my own personal
dark valleys. May I always rely on Jesus and His perfect
peace to sustain me as I face life's difficulties.*

1 Kings 2 / John 17:6–26 / Psalm 90:1–12

A LIFE OF FAITH

When the time drew near for David to die, he gave a charge to Solomon his son. "I am about to go the way of all the earth," he said. "So be strong, act like a man, and observe what the LORD your God requires: Walk in obedience to him, and keep his decrees and commands, his laws and regulations, as written in the Law of Moses. Do this so that you may prosper in all you do and wherever you go."

I KINGS 2:1–3 NIV

King David knew his time was short, so he took the time to instruct his son and successor, Solomon, on the life he was to lead as Israel's new king. David instructed Solomon to be strong in the Lord and do all that God required of him, namely obeying all the decrees and statutes written in the Law of Moses.

That was to be the look of Solomon's life of faith.

As Christians living under the New Covenant, we are no longer bound by the rules and regulations in the Mosaic Law. Now we live under grace and are guided by the "law" of life in the Spirit in Jesus, which God has given us in the New Testament.

That is the look of *our* life of faith.

Father in heaven, help me to live in true faith and to walk in obedience to the commandments and directives You've provided in Your Word.

1 Kings 3–4 / John 18:1–27 / Psalm 90:13–17

ASKING IN FAITH

*"Now, LORD my God, you have made your servant king in place
of my father David. But I am only a little child and do not know
how to carry out my duties. . . . So give your servant a discerning
heart to govern your people and to distinguish between right and
wrong. For who is able to govern this great people of yours?"*

1 KINGS 3:7, 9 NIV

Solomon knew he had some huge shoes to fill as he began his reign
as Israel's third monarch. Solomon was a young man who wasn't so
sure he was prepared to replace his father David as king. So instead
of adopting a "come-what-may" attitude, Solomon went proactive,
asking God for an "an understanding heart"—another way of saying
"wisdom."

The Lord was happy to give Solomon what he had asked for,
simply because the young king had so audaciously prayed a prayer of
faith in asking for it.

God still hears and answers those kinds of prayers today. The
apostle John affirmed this truth: "This is the confidence we have in
approaching God: that if we ask anything according to his will, he
hears us" (1 John 5:14 NIV).

What do you need to live the life of faith today? Ask God for
it! He delights in answering those prayers and meeting your needs.

*Heavenly Father, thank You for Your willingness to provide
for me everything I need to live a victorious life of faith.*

SEEKING SHELTER

Whoever dwells in the shelter of the Most High will rest in the shadow of the Almighty. I will say of the LORD, "He is my refuge and my fortress, my God, in whom I trust."

PSALM 91:1–2 NIV

If you live in a region prone to severe winter storms, you know that it's unwise and unsafe to venture outside, even for a short time, when the snow is falling, the ice is forming, and the wind is howling. Common sense should guide you to the best decision that day: stay sheltered indoors where it's dry and warm.

The writer of Psalm 91 understood well the importance of remaining sheltered in the Lord, especially in times of difficulty and danger. He knew that God never promised him a trouble-free life (verse 15), but he also was convinced that his best hope was to dwell "in the shelter of the Almighty."

God hasn't changed one iota since Psalm 91 was penned all those centuries ago. Today, we still have the privilege of resting in the shelter the Lord provides. When we purposefully take shelter in our loving heavenly Father's shadow, we put ourselves in the place to receive an amazing blessing: God's protection and comfort.

Lord Jesus, thank You that because I belong to You, I can take refuge under the Father's shadow today and every day. May I never stray, for even one moment, from that shadow.

1 Kings 7 / John 19:6–25 / Psalm 91:11–16

TRUE INTIMACY

The LORD says, "I will rescue those who love me. I will protect those who trust in my name. When they call on me, I will answer; I will be with them in trouble. I will rescue and honor them."

PSALM 91:14–15 NLT

A married couple who enjoys a truly intimate relationship is a couple who will not only hang together for life but will also do so *happily*. Doing that successfully means growing together in a mutual relationship of love and trust.

That's very much what our relationship with our God should look like.

Today's scripture verses offer an excellent summary of what it really means to have an intimate relationship with the Lord. It's a relationship based on love and trust.

It's an incredible thought: almighty God, the Creator of the universe is also a loving heavenly Father who wants you to dwell in and enjoy an intimate relationship with Himself, a relationship based on ever-growing love and faith.

Our relationship with God is to be rooted in love. As we open ourselves to His love, our hearts are filled with love for Him—and as we grow in our love for Him, we learn to trust Him more and more each day.

What a privilege it is to not just know God's name, but to know Him intimately!

Father in heaven, I want to follow You more closely and know You more intimately. That means both loving and trusting You more deeply each day.

1 Kings 8:1–53 / John 19:26–42 / Psalm 92:1–9

LAYING HOLD OF GOD'S PROMISES

"O LORD, God of Israel, there is no God like you in all of heaven above or on the earth below. You keep your covenant and show unfailing love to all who walk before you in wholehearted devotion. You have kept your promise to your servant David, my father. You made that promise with your own mouth, and with your own hands you have fulfilled it today."

1 KINGS 8:23–24 NLT

The words from today's scripture verses are a prelude to Solomon's prayer at the dedication of the just-finished temple. The king began by thanking God for keeping His promises to King David, Solomon's father, and then recounted His other promises.

This prayer stands as an example of praying in faith—believing God's promises and then humbly asking Him to keep those promises. This is the prayer He delights in answering.

The great nineteenth-century preacher Charles Spurgeon put it like this: "Nothing pleases God better than to see his promises put in circulation; he loves to see his children bring them up to him, and say, 'Lord, do as thou hast said.' And let me tell you that it glorifies God to use his promises."

Don't just read God's promises—lay hold of them and believe God for the answer!

Lord, thank You for the many, many promises You've made to me in Your written Word. Remind me often to lay hold of those promises for myself as I come to You in prayer.

1 Kings 8:54–10:13 / John 20:1–18 / Psalm 92:10–15

A BLESSING TO ALL

"How happy your people must be! How happy your officials, who continually stand before you and hear your wisdom! Praise be to the LORD your God, who has delighted in you and placed you on the throne of Israel. Because of the LORD's eternal love for Israel, he has made you king to maintain justice and righteousness."

1 KINGS 10:8–9 NIV

Out of context, the words of today's scripture verses seem like a profession of faith by someone who knew and walked with the Lord. But these are the words of the Queen of Sheba, who had traveled some 1,500 miles to see for herself if the things she'd heard about Solomon's kingdom were true.

Indeed they were, and she was moved to glorify the Lord, the one true God. The queen even acknowledged that the Lord had appointed Solomon as king because He loved Israel so deeply.

How do you think the friend of a friend would respond after observing you—how you live, how you speak, how you treat others—for some time? Would they see the Lord at work in you and through you? Would you be a blessing to that person?

Lord Jesus, I will never possess the extraordinary wealth of a man like Solomon. But I still want to bless others just by being an example of the blessedness of a life of faith and obedience. Make me a blessing to all, especially to those who desperately need You.

1 Kings 10:14–11:43 / John 20:19–31 / Psalm 93

NOT SEEING BUT STILL BELIEVING

Then Jesus told him, "Because you have seen me, you have believed;
blessed are those who have not seen and yet have believed."

JOHN 20:29 NIV

Thomas was a disciple of Jesus whose faith was obscured by doubt—temporarily. Thomas had followed Jesus throughout His earthly ministry. He had heard Him deliver life-changing teaching and perform miracles that proved He was who He said He was.

Thomas was there when Jesus said that He would die but would be raised from the dead three days later. Yet after Jesus had died so horribly on a wooden cross, Thomas went on, his heart heavy with crushing grief, as though he hadn't heard a word Jesus said. When the other disciples told him that Jesus was alive, his response was essentially, "I won't believe it until I see it!"

Paul once wrote, "For we live by faith, not by sight" (2 Corinthians 5:7 NIV). Nobody today has seen Jesus in the flesh, but we know by faith that He is our Lord and Savior. Because we believe, Jesus calls us "blessed"—and we call Him "My Lord and my God" (John 20:28).

Jesus, thank You for opening my spiritual eyes of faith to see You as who You really are—my Lord and God. I have never physically seen You, but I still believe. I look forward with great anticipation to seeing You face-to-face as I begin eternity in my forever home in heaven.

1 Kings 12:1–13:10 / John 21 / Psalm 94:1–11

PARTIAL OBEDIENCE?

But the man of God answered the king, "Even if you were to
give me half your possessions, I would not go with you, nor
would I eat bread or drink water here. For I was commanded
by the word of the LORD: 'You must not eat bread or drink
water or return by the way you came.'" So he took another
road and did not return by the way he had come to Bethel.

1 KINGS 13:8–10 NIV

Today's scripture verses recount the words of an unnamed man of God who had traveled from Judah to Israel to speak out against King Jeroboam. He courageously preached God's Word and obeyed His instructions. Sadly, however, 1 Kings 13:21–22 tells us that he paid a steep price because he didn't finish his God-ordained mission without falling into disobedience.

This man's story is a stark reminder to avoid "partial obedience." Any man can be tempted to partially obey. For example, we know that we are to avoid sexual immorality and that we are to avoid looking lustfully at women. Yet too many men act as though staying away from "the act" is good enough.

God wants us to obey Him in all things 100 percent of the time. That's why it's so important to regularly examine our hearts in light of the Word of God.

Lord, help me to examine my heart and my actions to see if there
are areas in my life where I engage in partial obedience.

1 Kings 13:11–14:31 / Acts 1:1–11 / Psalm 94:12–23

LOVING DISCIPLINE

*Blessed is the man whom You chasten, O LORD, and teach
out of Your law, that You may give him rest from the days
of adversity, until the pit is dug for the wicked.*

PSALM 94:12–13 SKJV

A loving earthly father—or a coach or teacher—understands well that discipline is important to the growth, personal behavior, and success of the object of that discipline. If you've ever had the misfortune of spending time around children who haven't been properly disciplined, then you have some understanding of just how important firm, loving, consistent discipline really is.

Psalm 94:12–13 calls the man who is the object of the Lord's hand of discipline "blessed" because it later prevents him from suffering unnecessary adversity later on. The writer of Hebrews 12:11 (NIV) expands that thought: "No discipline seems pleasant at the time, but painful. Later on, however, it produces a harvest of righteousness and peace for those who have been trained by it."

Being disciplined isn't fun. It can sometimes be uncomfortable and downright painful. But a man of faith can endure it when he understands that it comes from the God who does all things out of love.

*Loving Father, I fully identify with the statement "No discipline
seems pleasant at the time, but painful." But I understand that
when You lay Your hand of discipline upon me, it is an act
of love intended to teach me, mold me, and protect me.*

1 Kings 15:1–16:20 / Acts 1:12–26 / Psalm 95

OUR SHEPHERD-GOD

*Come, let us bow down in worship, let us kneel before
the LORD our Maker; for he is our God and we are the
people of his pasture, the flock under his care.*
PSALM 95:6–7 NIV

Many of the psalms paint beautiful word pictures depicting the mutual
love relationship between God and His people. Psalm 95 is one of
those psalms. The writer of this psalm, particularly in today's scripture
verse, likens that relationship to that between a flock of sheep and the
shepherds charged with caring for them.

Psalm 95:6–7 points to just how worthy the Lord is of His people's
praise. . .and love. Yes, He is our almighty Creator, but He didn't just
design everything about us and then just send us on our way to fend
for ourselves. No, the Lord is our Shepherd-God who cares for us,
provides for us, protects us, and loves us on a deeply personal level.

We truly are the people of his pasture, the flock under His loving,
tender care. Our response to Him and who He is should be nothing
less than total trust.

*Lord God, You are both my Creator and my God. You are my
loving, caring, protective Shepherd, and I am Your sheep—helpless
and wholly dependent on You in every way. So please protect,
provide, and guide me by Your grace for Your glory today.*

1 Kings 16:21–18:19 / Acts 2:1–21 / Psalm 96:1–8

NEW SONGS

Sing to the LORD a new song; sing to the LORD, all the earth.
Sing to the LORD, praise his name; proclaim his salvation day after day.
PSALM 96:1–2 NIV

If we're not careful, our worship time can start to feel stale or monotonous. But you can fight those "same old, same old" feelings by stopping and closely focusing on the many ways God demonstrates His goodness to you each day.

God loves you more than you can truly comprehend, and He loves it when you dwell in that love by opening your mouth and speaking words of praise and thanksgiving. When You do that, He can bring to your mind blessings you may not have considered before, giving you the opportunity to sing that "new song."

Though he was looking at the horrific aftermath of Babylon's sacking of the once-great city of Jerusalem, the prophet Jeremiah offered these hopeful words of praise: "Because of the LORD's great love we are not consumed, for his compassions never fail. They are new every morning; great is your faithfulness" (Lamentations 3:22–23 NIV).

If you pay attention, you can find different reasons every day to sing a "new" song of praise and adoration to the Lord. Just open your mouth and sing!

In heaven, I lift my voice in praise and gratitude for the
many wonderful things You do for me each and every day.
Put a new song of praise in my mouth each morning.

1 Kings 18:20–19:21 / Acts 2:22–41 / Psalm 96:9–13

FEELING DISCOURAGED?

After the earthquake came a fire, but the LORD was not in the fire.
And after the fire came a gentle whisper. When Elijah heard it,
he pulled his cloak over his face and went out and stood at the mouth of
the cave. Then a voice said to him, "What are you doing here, Elijah?"

1 KINGS 19:12–13 NIV

There may be no starker example of discouragement in the Bible than that of the prophet Elijah as he hid in a cave, knowing there was a price on his head.

Elijah desperately needed to hear from his God. As he listened, there came a wind so powerful that it tore mountains apart. Then came a powerful earthquake, then a fire. But God was not in any of these things Finally, the Lord spoke. . .*in a gentle whisper*.

"What are you doing here, Elijah?" God asked, and then Elijah poured out his complaints (verse 14).

Why did the Lord speak so gently and quietly? Perhaps because He knew what Elijah needed in the moment. Whatever the reason, this account teaches us an important lesson about hearing from God: sometimes we need to find a way to tune out the world's noise. . .and just be quiet and listen.

Father God, when I feel discouraged and alone, may I never withdraw
into a cave of self-pity. Instead, remind me to come to You and pour
out my heart and talk to You openly and honestly about my problems.

1 Kings 20 / Acts 2:42–3:26 / Psalm 97:1-6

A FITTING RESPONSE

Then Peter took the lame man by the right hand and helped him up.
And as he did, the man's feet and ankles were instantly healed and
strengthened. He jumped up, stood on his feet, and began to walk! Then,
walking, leaping, and praising God, he went into the Temple with them.

ACTS 3:7–8 NLT

Imagine the joyous excitement the crippled man at the temple gate
felt when he heard Peter exclaim, "In the name of Jesus Christ of
Nazareth. . .walk" (Acts 3:6 NIV), and then helped him to his feet.
He had been bound to a damaged, dysfunctional body for more than
forty years, and now, for the first time in his life, he could stand and
walk under his own power. Filled with joyous gratitude, this formerly
disabled man began "walking, leaping, and praising God."

God did a spectacular miracle when He healed the crippled
man at the temple gate. But He did an even greater one when He
saved you by His grace through your faith. You were lost in your sin
and completely unable to do anything to heal or save yourself. But
God was able. . .and willing.

The man God healed through Peter had a great reason to leap
and praise God. You have an even greater one.

Lord Jesus, thank You for forgiving me and saving me from
eternal punishment for my sins. May I never lose the sense of
awe and gratitude for all You have so freely given me.

1 Kings 21:1–22:28 / Acts 4:1–22 / Psalm 97:7–12

BE LIKE PETER AND JOHN

The members of the council were amazed when they saw
the boldness of Peter and John, for they could see that they
were ordinary men with no special training in the Scriptures.
They also recognized them as men who had been with Jesus.

ACTS 4:13 NLT

The members of the Jewish religious leadership during the days of the
apostles had brought Peter and John before them for questioning after
their preaching had resulted in thousands of conversions in Jerusalem.

The council members were impressed with the two apostles'
boldness in preaching their message, especially since they were ordinary,
uneducated men with no special training. But what really got their
attention was the fact that Peter and John, men who had been toiling
as simple fishermen before Jesus called them to follow Him, "had
been with Jesus."

What do you think people who meet you see first? Your gifts
and intellect? Your educational credentials? Your professional
accomplishments? Or. . .do they see that you've been with Jesus?

Each of us should pray that God helps us to be like Peter and
John—men others could plainly see had been with Jesus.

Lord Jesus, I don't want others to see me first as anything
extraordinary in and of myself or as a learned or intelligent man.
Instead, I want people to see me as a man who has been with You.
Help me to reflect You to a world who desperately needs to see You.

JOYFUL SINGING

*Shout for joy to the LORD, all the earth, burst into jubilant song
with music; make music to the LORD with the harp, with the
harp and the sound of singing, with trumpets and the blast of
the ram's horn—shout for joy before the LORD, the King.*

PSALM 98:4–6 NIV

Where are some of your favorite places or settings to sing? In church?
In the shower? In your car on the way to work? While doing household
chores? Life gives us men countless opportunities to sing if we'll just
pay attention for them. And the Bible, including today's verses, tells
us that God loves hearing us singing songs of love and praise to Him.

As you go through each day, sing songs about God's goodness
and love. Sing songs that remind you of His greatness. Sing songs that
glorify Jesus and remind you to share His love with others.

If God has given you the ability to sing, then sing! Sing with
a joyful heart. God doesn't care whether you sound like the second
coming of Frank Sinatra or whether you can't carry a tune in a bucket.
He just takes great delight when you open your mouth and sing of
your love and devotion for Him.

*Loving Father, thank You for giving me the ability to sing.
Your Word tells me that You love hearing Your people sing songs
of praise to You. I will sing to You whenever I have the chance.*

2 Kings 2–3 / Acts 5:12–28 / Psalm 99

AWESOMELY MERCIFUL

The LORD reigns, let the nations tremble; he sits enthroned between the cherubim, let the earth shake. Great is the LORD in Zion; he is exalted over all the nations.

PSALM 99:1–2 NIV

Psalm 99 is a poem of praise for an awesome God who reigns and rules over all things and for whom mere men's only fitting response is to shake and tremble. Every man on earth is a rebel, a sinner worthy of this great God's eternal wrath. But because this awesome and great God is also a good and merciful God, He reaches down to us and invites us to fellowship with Him.

The fourth verse of this psalm tells us that "the King is mighty, he loves justice." When you consider the fact that *justice* for a sinner like you means eternal separation from this holy God, but that He has *chosen* to save you to Himself, your only response is to lift your voice and praise Him for His justice, His might, and His amazing grace and mercy.

You were once hopelessly lost in your own sin and completely separated from God. But through faith in Jesus Christ, you have been brought into His own family and are now an object of His love and mercy, not His wrath and judgment.

Lord God, I praise You for Your greatness and holiness and justice, and I praise and thank You for Your grace and compassion and mercy. You are an awesome God in every way.

2 Kings 4 / Acts 5:29–6:15 / Psalm 100

WORTHY OF SUFFERING

The apostles left the Sanhedrin, rejoicing because they had been counted worthy of suffering disgrace for the Name. Day after day, in the temple courts and from house to house, they never stopped teaching and proclaiming the good news that Jesus is the Messiah.

ACTS 5:41–42 NIV

Peter and the other apostles were deeply committed to preaching the name of Jesus in the city of Jerusalem, and their zeal got them in hot water with the Jewish leadership of the day. They were arrested—twice—and beaten and ordered to stop preaching the name of Jesus.

But these men's suffering only served to make them more tenacious for their message. Instead of keeping their mouths shut, they rejoiced that they were counted worthy to suffer for Jesus and kept preaching His name.

While it's easy to look back with admiration at the apostles' response to their suffering, it begs the question: Would we stop preaching the truth if we were threatened with violence? Or would we respond with joy for the privilege of suffering for Jesus?

In modern-day America, we Christians don't presently face the kind of opposition the apostles faced. But how would you respond when those things happen in your lifetime—fearfully or joyfully?

Lord Jesus, I confess that I would prefer a life free of suffering, hardship, or persecution. But should those things come—and I know they may in my lifetime—I want to continue glorifying You in everything I do and say.

2 Kings 5:1–6:23 / Acts 7:1–16 / Psalm 101

A BLAMELESS LIFE

I will be careful to lead a blameless life—when will you come to me? I will conduct the affairs of my house with a blameless heart. I will not look with approval on anything that is vile.

PSALM 101:2–3 NIV

Early in Psalm 101, David expresses his desire to live a "blameless" life. David loved his God and believed all His promises, so he wanted his life to reflect who he was as a man of faith in the living God.

The Lord calls each of us to live lives that reflect our love for and faith in Him, not lives marked by selfishness, self-will, and sinful choices.

The good news is that He empowers you to live in a way that pleases Him in every way.

When Jesus saved You, He made you a "new creation" (2 Corinthians 5:17). That means that even though you still battle against your sin nature, you are a person with a new nature, one that makes a way to live the life that pleases the Lord, a life befitting one who professes faith in Christ. Your desire is no longer for sin but for a blameless life in which you desire integrity of heart.

Dear God, I want to glorify You by living a life of integrity. It's impossible for me to do that without Your help, but with the power of Your Spirit working in me, I can walk in a way that pleases You.

2 Kings 6:24–8:15 / Acts 7:17–36 / Psalm 102:1–7

CRYING OUT TO GOD

Hear my prayer, LORD; let my cry for help come to you.
Do not hide your face from me when I am in distress.
Turn your ear to me; when I call, answer me quickly.

PSALM 102:1–2 NIV

The first eleven verses of Psalm 102 make it clear that the writer is a man going through some serious difficulties. He is a man so afflicted and stressed out that he can't sleep or eat. He needs to hear from his God—and he needs His God to hear Him. . .and act quicky on his behalf.

A life of faith isn't always easy, is it?

As we progress through this psalm, we see that the writer is a man of great faith who knows he can rely on his God and on His promises.

The writer of Psalm 102, even though he spends the early part of the psalm crying out his complaints to God, sets for us a great example of utter dependency on the Lord, especially during times of difficulty and anxiety. He knows how much he needs his God, and he is supremely confident in His willingness to hear him, comfort him, and deliver him.

When you feel afflicted, stressed, or anxious, re-read Psalm 102—and then take encouragement in knowing that God wants to hear from you.

Father in heaven, thank You for hearing me and for caring
about me when I call out to You in my time of need.

2 Kings 8:16–9:37 / Acts 7:37–53 / Psalm 102:8–17

SPIRITUAL CIRCUMCISION

"You stiff-necked people! Your hearts and ears are still uncircumcised.
You are just like your ancestors: You always resist the Holy Spirit!"

ACTS 7:51 NIV

The Jewish religious leaders in the days of the apostles had the traditions and rites of their religion down. They had all been circumcised in the physical sense, but they had missed the bigger point of circumcision, namely that it was an outward expression of the inward influence of the Holy Spirit. These proud, self-righteous men failed to allow the Spirit of God to change them inwardly, so they couldn't recognize their Messiah when He arrived.

Jesus sent the Holy Spirit to convict unsaved people of sin so that they might repent and turn to Him for forgiveness and eternal salvation. In the life of believers, the Spirit teaches, convicts, and guides us toward a deeper, more personal knowledge of our Lord and Savior.

We Christian men should always be careful not to resist the Holy Spirit. We can do that by remaining humble, by listening to Him, and by allowing Him to lead us where He wants us to go. These things mark the life of a man who avoids a religious spirit and who is circumcised in heart and ear.

Father in heaven, may I never allow religion to take the place
of the leading and teaching of Your Holy Spirit in my life.
Keep me humble so that I can live a life of faith in You.

RADICAL FORGIVENESS

While they were stoning him, Stephen prayed, "Lord Jesus, receive my spirit." Then he fell on his knees and cried out, "Lord, do not hold this sin against them." When he had said this, he fell asleep.

Acts 7:59–60 NIV

The Bible makes it abundantly clear that the Christian man's life should be marked by radical forgiveness for those who have done him wrong—even when the offender shows no remorse for what he has done.

Stephen, a man the Bible called "a man full of faith and of the Holy Spirit" (Acts 6:5 NIV), set an amazing example of radical forgiveness. As he was being stoned to death for preaching the gospel of Jesus, Stephen spoke forgiveness for his attackers—not anger, not hatred, not vengeance, but unconditional, complete forgiveness.

Stephen's words—"Lord, do not hold this sin against them"—are astonishing when we consider the horrible agony inflicted on him that day. But they are well worth remembering.

God wants His people to make forgiveness a hallmark of our life of faith. It can be excruciatingly difficult to forgive those who have wronged us. But Stephen was an example of how it can be done. When we allow the Holy Spirit to guide us and help us control our emotions, we too can forgive and set ourselves free to live in faith, peace, healing, and reconciliation.

Dear Lord, thank You for Stephen's example of radical forgiveness.

2 Kings 12–13 / Acts 8:9–40 / Psalm 103:1–9

MAKE A LIST

Let all that I am praise the Lord; may I never forget the good things
he does for me. He forgives all my sins and heals all my diseases. He
redeems me from death and crowns me with love and tender mercies.
He fills my life with good things. My youth is renewed like the eagle's!

PSALM 103:2–5 NLT

In today's scripture verses, David declares that he wants to praise the Lord with everything he is—from the very depths of his soul. David never wants to forget all that God does for him. Today, let's share in David's words of gratitude to our God because:

He forgives all our sins. Through our faith in Jesus Christ, God offers forgiveness and eternal life, which no one can ever take away (Romans 6:23).

He heals all our diseases. In this life we may face sickness and disease, but one day, He will do away with all sickness and death (Revelation 21:1–4).

He covers us with unfailing love and mercy. God loves us deeply and has made a way to extend to us His mercy (Romans 8:38–39).

He blesses us with good things. God desires to bless us (James 1:17).

What benefits of belonging to the Lord can you think of today? Make a list and then thank and praise Him for each and every one!

My precious Lord, I praise Your wonderful name and thank You
for all the benefits I enjoy simply because I belong to You.

HUMAN PERSPECTIVE VS. GOD'S PERSPECTIVE

"But Lord," exclaimed Ananias, "I've heard many people talk about the terrible things this man has done to the believers in Jerusalem!" . . . But the Lord said, "Go, for Saul is my chosen instrument to take my message to the Gentiles and to kings, as well as to the people of Israel."

ACTS 9:13, 15 NLT

From a purely human perspective, the protests of Ananias, a man of God who lived in Damascus, seem completely rational and logical. God had commanded Ananias to welcome and minister to Saul of Tarsus (later the apostle Paul), the man who had angrily and violently persecuted Christians in Jerusalem. Ananias must have wondered if he'd heard God correctly.

But God knew something Ananias didn't. The Lord saw Saul from an eternal perspective—past and future—while Ananias was limited by what had been happening in the here and now. God saw in Saul a faithful servant who would change the world through his preaching and writing, while Ananias saw a murderous persecutor.

To his credit, Ananias did as God had directed him. The rest, as the saying goes, is history. . .the history of how God used such an unlikely vessel to accomplish great things for God's eternal kingdom.

Because Ananias obeyed the Lord, he held a position of importance in history.

Lord, help me to remember that You often do things in ways that might not make human sense and that I should always make sure I follow Your leading.

2 Kings 16–17 / Acts 9:17–31 / Psalm 103:15–22

YOU ARE WHAT YOU PURSUE

They followed worthless idols and themselves became worthless.

2 KINGS 17:15 NIV

Today's verse is a poetic description of how far Israel—God's chosen nation—had fallen. Instead of pursuing their infinite God, they chased after small, lifeless statues of wood and stone, becoming just as hollow as the figurines they knelt before.

Whatever your heart craves the most, that's what you start to resemble. If you crave worthless pleasures and unfulfilling dreams, your life begins to lose all purpose. The tools that God has given you to glorify His name—money, influence, talents, etc.—suddenly become little gods themselves, and before you realize it, you've lain aside their rightful usage and enshrined these now-worthless trinkets in your heart. You become little more than a fleshy shell—a cruel parody of the image of God that lives dormant inside you.

But if you crave the truth and the righteousness that comes with it, then because of Jesus' sacrifice that bridges the gap between you and God, you will become true and righteous yourself. When you chase not after fleeting shadows of happiness but after the infinite well of joy, you will find your life imbued with the purpose it was always meant to have.

When you chase after Christ, you will become Christlike.

Lord God, may the foolish inclinations of my heart never become so strong that they define who I am. Teach me to resist these fallen urges and keep chasing Your holiness.

2 Kings 18:1–19:7 / Acts 9:32–10:16 / Psalm 104:1–9

ARGUING WITH GOD

Then a voice said to him, "Get up, Peter; kill and eat them."
ACTS 10:13 NLT

Peter had been a "good Jew" all his life, always careful to eat only the things permitted in the Law of Moses. But then came God, shattering his legalistic observation with spiritual revelation. But Peter, always eager to share his thoughts, brazenly declared, "No, Lord" (verse 14 NLT). Yet God persisted. He sent the vision three times, making sure Peter understood the lesson: God was the one who'd made the Law, so He could change the Law whenever He liked.

By testing Peter in this way, God was ensuring that Peter's loyalties lay not in a series of rules and regulations but in a relationship with the divine Lawgiver.

If we're not careful, we can become just like Peter, valuing the unique rules of our denominations or upbringings—some of which may or may not be biblical—over the God who died to reconcile all His children to Him. But when God shatters our opinions with His truth, how willing are we to accept His ways over our own?

Learn about Your Savior today by studying Him in His Word, and develop a relationship with Him through prayer. It's the only way to avoid finding yourself arguing with God.

> *Lord, help me follow Your commands to the best of*
> *my ability. But if it turns out I'm mistaken, may I be*
> *willing to accept Your truth over my error.*

DEFLECTED PRAISE

*When Peter entered, Cornelius met him, fell at his
feet, and worshiped him. But Peter helped him up
and said, "Stand up! I myself am also a man."*
ACTS 10:25–26 HCSB

Gemstones are arguably the most interesting rocks in the world. When they are found, most of them look like smooth, shiny rocks—unique enough to be singled out in a pile of pebbles but not brilliant enough to be placed on a necklace. But when they are faceted—meticulously cut and chipped by the hand of a skilled expert—they glow and glimmer like kaleidoscopes in the light.

Similarly, on our own, we're far from spectacular, even less so than a gemstone in its natural state. We arise from the dust, covered in the sins and imperfections of our fallen nature. The image of God that dwells inside us is hidden by mud and grime. But whenever we allow God to clean us, cut away our imperfections, and shine His holy light on our souls, we suddenly transform into spectacular displays.

Peter understood this—that's why he deflected Cornelius' worship toward God. By accepting God's process at chipping away his natural self, and by reflecting His light instead of absorbing it, Peter was able to glow brighter than any mortal could on his own, pointing thousands of souls to Christ.

*Lord, help my faith grow brighter each day—not because of my
own efforts but because of my strengthening reliance on You.*

2 Kings 21:1–22:20 / Acts 10:34–11:18 / Psalm 104: 24–30

INDEPENDENCE

*And the believers from among the circumcised [the Jews] who came
with Peter were surprised and amazed, because the free gift of the Holy
Spirit had been bestowed and poured out largely even on the Gentiles.*

ACTS 10:45 AMPC

This Independence Day, we celebrate the freedom that was gained
through the blood and tears of our forefathers. Without their sacrifice,
America as we know it may have never come to fruition, and the
unique form of liberation we enjoy today would've remained a dream.

But today's verse describes another type of freedom. In it, the
cage that locked the world away and prevented it from reaching God
was suddenly shattered, opening the floodgates for a global spiritual
awakening. The Holy Spirit had fallen not just on the Jews but on
the Gentiles—people who were once believed to be outside the reach
of God's salvation.

On this day, Peter realized that the gospel wasn't a message for
the elite—it was freedom for the masses. All who heard it could
leave behind sin's shackles and pursue a relationship with God. The
phrase "God's people" suddenly became synonymous with "everyone
who believes."

Today, as you dwell on the sacrifices of our forefathers that set
this nation free, meditate also on Jesus' sacrifice that brought freedom
to our souls.

*Lord God, please strengthen my understanding of just how
revolutionary Your grace is. Teach me to appreciate Your salvation
more each day. May I never squander this amazing freedom.*

2 Kings 23 / Acts 11:19–12:17 / Psalm 104:31–35

NO HESITATION

The king read to them the entire Book of the Covenant that had been found in the LORD's Temple. . . . Then the king instructed Hilkiah the high priest. . .to remove from the LORD's Temple all the articles that were used to worship Baal, Asherah, and all the powers of the heavens.

2 KINGS 23:2, 4 NLT

When King Josiah read the law of God and saw how badly Israel had failed to follow it, he went straight to work. Every altar to Baal he could find, he smashed. Every pagan priest, he deposed. Every idol, he ground to dust.

He knew that if he failed to act on the truth right now, complacency would set in and he and his nation would find some irrational excuse to let these abominations exist side by side with God's righteous commands. And he wasn't about to let that happen.

Whenever we become aware of sin in our lives, how often do we shrug and tell ourselves, "Hm. I'll have to work on that someday"? When it comes to sin, complacency is our worst enemy, for it whittles away at our convictions until we lose all sight of right or wrong. The only remedy for this disease is immediate action.

Why put off repentance for tomorrow when you can start today?

Father, help me bring all sin before Your throne the moment I spot it in my life. Replace my apathy with the urgency You want me to feel.

2 Kings 24–25 / Acts 12:18–13:13 / Psalm 105:1–7

REPULSIVE PRIDE

They shouted, "This is the voice of a god, not of a man." Immediately,
because Herod did not give praise to God, an angel of the Lord
struck him down, and he was eaten by worms and died.

ACTS 12:22–23 NIV

If the story of Peter and Cornelius shows what we should do when others praise us, then today's passage shows us what we *shouldn't* do.

Instead of merely reflecting these praises toward God—and thereby becoming a radiant, splendid gemstone—Herod absorbed these lofty words...and so became little more than an ugly rock. The judgment was swift and severe—historical records say he was dead within five days of contracting the disease—and the glory that he once accepted with pride was now transformed into an ugly, repulsive display. Why? Because being made in the image of God was no longer enough for him—He wanted to *be* God.

But the moment a vessel tries to expand its size beyond the potter's influence is the moment it becomes ugly and disfigured, fit only for breaking. A Christian man is only as strong as his faith, and the only way to grow your faith is to surrender yourself to the one who made you. Taking the glory for yourself will only leave you like Herod—disgraced and devoured by the worms of pride and self-importance.

Father, help use my talents wisely, always eager to
point any praise I may receive back to You.

SPARK OF CURIOSITY

*As they [Paul and Barnabas] went out [of the synagogue],
the people earnestly begged that these things might
be told to them [further] the next Sabbath.*

ACTS 13:42 AMPC

When the people in Antioch's synagogue heard that Paul would be speaking that day, they never could've imagined how revolutionary his message would be. They came expecting a "message of encouragement" (verse 15 HCSB), but here's what they received: "Through [Jesus] forgiveness of sins is being proclaimed to you, and everyone who believes in Him is justified from everything that you could not be justified from through the law of Moses" (verses 38–39 HCSB).

Talk about a surprise!

Paul's audience couldn't get enough of this exciting new message. It offered a stern warning yet gave indescribable hope. It both grieved and delighted. Why? Because it was the truth, and the truth will always capture the imagination of the pure at heart. That's why studying the truths found in God's Word will strengthen not only your walk with God but every aspect of your being—your character, thought life, passions, and dreams. Like the most profound stories, the gospel enthralls all who are willing to accept it. . .but unlike these stories, the gospel is 100 percent true.

Are you as eager as Paul's audience to learn the truth?

*Father, teach me how to soak up Your truth like a tree soaks
up water. I want to grow in my knowledge of You.*

1 Chronicles 3:1–5:10 / Acts 13:44–14:10 / Psalm 105:16–28

THE CURE

Some of the Jews, however, spurned God's message and poisoned the minds of the Gentiles against Paul and Barnabas.

Acts 14:2 nlt

It shouldn't surprise you to learn that we live in a toxic culture. Constant social media use is driving up depression and anxiety, and steady, doom-laden news feeds are snatching away the hope that keeps us going. The background noise, once a mere static that could be easily ignored, has become something far more sinister—a soul-sucking, vampiric force that preys on the spiritual well-being of all those careless enough to pay it too much heed. It's poison of the most insidious sort. So what's the cure? What could possibly cut through such a thick fog of despair and hostility?

Frequent meditation on the truth in God's Word.

The Bible doesn't exist simply to fill a slot on your shelf or to provide good reading material for when you can't sleep. No, it's less a book than it is a weapon—a force that can cut down the enemies' temptations and unlock enduring power in the hearts of those who meditate on its words. It's also an antidote—a well of life-bringing promises that can cleanse our hearts and minds of the stale, toxic air to which we've become so accustomed.

Don't succumb to the poison of this world; use God's cure.

I feel so worn down and defeated by the toxicity all around me, God. Please strengthen my soul with Your love and reassurance.

1 Chronicles 5:11–6:81 / Acts 14:11–28 / Psalm 105:29–36

TESTIMONY

"Yet he has not left himself without testimony."
ACTS 14:17 NIV

This marvelous universe is so familiar to us that we take it for granted. How often do you notice the gravity that keeps you glued to the earth? The oxygen that fills your lungs? The steady stream of light that enters your eyes and finds its way to the supercomputer that is your brain?

Scientists are gradually discovering just how fine-tuned this physical reality is for sustaining life. Existence as we know it balances on a knife's edge of just-right natural laws and conditions. If only one of them was altered by the tiniest sliver of the smallest fraction imaginable (physicists estimate that one of these conditions is finely tuned to an order of one part in 10 to the 120th power), life would become impossible and reality would collapse into unstructured chaos. Such extreme levels of design led one atheist to say, "A common sense interpretation of the facts suggests that a super-intellect has monkeyed with physics."

God built this reality as a well-oiled machine, and the more we discover the innumerable gears that keep it running, the more gratitude we ought to show to the Creator. Meditating on this amazing but fragile world is one way to grow our faith in the one who made and now sustains it.

Thank You, God, for giving us a small glimpse of Your infinite power in the form of Your creation. I want to study this amazing testimony You've left for us.

SHADOWS OF THE FUTURE

For he remembered his sacred promise to his servant Abraham.

PSALM 105:42 NLT

This psalm serves as a memorial for the good things God has done for Israel. It's a "greatest hits" compilation of God's miraculous deeds. Beginning with the covenant with Abraham, it moves on to God's work in Joseph's life, Israel's period of Egyptian slavery, and their ultimate deliverance at the Red Sea.

As you can probably tell by now, the Bible isn't content to simply tell these great stories once: it repeats them over and over again, adding new blessings whenever they occur. In a sense, God's Word is a song, and the miracles He's performed for His people form the lyrics of its chorus. Even though this song is rooted firmly in the past, its purpose always lies in the future. By reminding themselves of God's miracles throughout history, the writers of scripture anticipated the next step in God's amazing plan of salvation.

When you look back upon your own life, what blessings do you see? Look beyond the superficial, focusing instead on the tiny events and choices that culminated in the walk with God you currently enjoy. And then, once you've chronicled the past, look to the blank canvas that is the future and ask yourself, *What might God do next?*

> *Sometimes, Lord, the things I see strengthen my faith*
> *in the things I don't. May I always see shadows of my*
> *amazing future with You scattered across my past.*

1 Chronicles 9:10–11:9 / Acts 15:19–41 / Psalm 106:1–12

FORBIDDEN KNOWLEDGE

*So Saul died because he was unfaithful to the LORD. He failed
to obey the LORD's command, and he even consulted a medium
instead of asking the LORD for guidance. So the LORD killed
him and turned the kingdom over to David son of Jesse.*

1 CHRONICLES 10:13–14 NLT

As king over God's chosen nation, Saul should've realized his potential
for spiritual growth. He was God's anointed, and before him stretched
a vast plain of nutrient-rich soil in which he could plant his spiritual
roots. All he needed to do was keep himself in God's will, and God
would make him grow higher than any king in history.

But power tends to corrupt, and by the end of his life, Saul had
drifted so far from God's will that he sought wisdom in places he
had once prohibited in his kingdom: the prophet Samuel had died,
and Saul wanted to bring him back. For anyone who knows just how
dangerous such misplaced trust can be, the end of Saul's story is
painfully unsurprising. This séance backfired horribly, and the very thing
he'd hoped would save him pronounced his ultimate doom instead.

Just like a starving tree with shallow roots falls in the slightest
windstorm, so Saul toppled under the weight of his disobedience.
God's truth is the only soil in which we can truly grow. Where have
you planted your trust?

*Father, may I never seek knowledge in places You've
forbidden. Your truth is more than enough.*

ANSWER THE CALL

During the night a vision appeared to Paul: A Macedonian man was standing and pleading with him, "Cross over to Macedonia and help us!" After he had seen the vision, we immediately made efforts to set out for Macedonia, concluding that God had called us to evangelize them.

ACTS 16:9–10 HCSB

As Christians, we serve a Savior who sacrificed Himself so that we could gain eternal life. Consequently, we ourselves should be willing to offer help to any struggling soul we find.

And in this culture, there's no shortage of struggling souls. Every school shooting, every drug overdose, every relationship-shattering curse, every scar on the wrists of the youth is a cry for the kind of help that only God can offer. And whose responsibility is it to bring this help? *Ours.*

Strengthening our relationship with God—growing in His truth and righteousness—is of no use to anyone if we keep to ourselves and ignore the Macedonian call echoing through the halls of this broken nation. God has given each of us—including you—talents and gifts for the advancement of His kingdom, but what use are these gifts if we keep them locked away or exploit them for selfish gain? It's time we shake off our complacency, pack our bags, and prepare for a journey through this desolate land, planting seeds wherever we can.

God, help me feel the pain of the hurting so that I'll be eager to offer the cure—Your truth.

BE PREPARED

Then [the jailer] brought them out and asked, "Sirs, what must I do to be saved?" They replied, "Believe in the Lord Jesus and you will be saved."

ACTS 16:30–31 NLT

Chances are, you'll probably never face a situation as dramatic as Paul and Silas did in today's passage.

But who knows? Maybe you will. Maybe you'll meet someone today who's on the verge of taking his life. Maybe he'll see something in you that he's never seen—a joy that reaches deeper than the false smile he's worn all these years. Maybe he'll strike up a conversation about God, hoping beyond hope that you'll have an answer to save him from the death he's planned for tonight. And maybe you'll never know this person's struggles. Maybe all you'll see is a casual conversation with a seeker—a small incident you might even forget in the following weeks.

But the most important question is this: will you know what to say? Has your relationship with Jesus given you the answers you claim to possess, or have you kept God at arm's length, finding yourself at a loss for words when confronted by someone who's searching for something beyond the superficial?

There's only way to prepare for such an encounter: regularly submerging yourself in the truth of God's Word.

Father, give me the words to speak to those who need to hear Your message. I'm willing to be Your vessel of truth and encouragement.

1 Chronicles 16–17 / Acts 17:1–14 / Psalm 106:34–43

BAFFLING LOVE

Then King David went in, sat in the LORD's presence, and said, Who am I, LORD God, and what is my house that You have brought me this far?

1 CHRONICLES 17:16 HCSB

David's humility wasn't just a string of pious words. He wasn't pretending to abase himself while secretly basking in the glow of false modesty. No, he was genuinely baffled that God had chosen *him*, a small shepherd boy, as king over Israel—one whose offspring would impact the course of history! What did he do to deserve this?

As a Christian, it might be easy to take your status as God's child for granted. You've heard it ever since you were saved, so the meaning behind these words might've lost its initial force. But think: Why would God choose *you* to be His child? Were you born into a line of nobility? Are you gifted with superhuman abilities? Probably not.

God didn't choose us because of our position. In fact, He chose us *in spite* of it. We were all sinful little creatures wallowing in the mud of our dirty passions. . .but God reached down, cleaned us up, and placed crowns on our heads. When we truly dwell on the love our Father has displayed, we will join the baffled king in his cry: "Who am I?"

Father, guide my thoughts today as I meditate on the depths of Your love. Help me comprehend just how incomprehensible Your grace truly is.

SPIRITUALLY CONFUSED

While Paul was waiting for them in Athens, he was greatly distressed to see that the city was full of idols.

ACTS 17:16 NIV

Does your faith in Jesus cause you to be disturbed when you see people flagrantly disobeying Him? It should.

When Paul arrived in Athens, nothing could've prepared him for the level of debauchery and spiritual confusion he saw all around him. He'd visited some pretty ungodly cities, but the sheer number of idols in Athens struck his soul to the core. He couldn't just let these people stumble blindly in sin and ignorance—He had to tell them the glorious truth!

In our "post-Christian" society, modern idols can be spotted everywhere you look. People are more enslaved than ever, yet they've convinced themselves that this slavery is actually freedom. Confusion and chaos are the new norm, and anyone who sees through the lies is discounted as a lunatic.

But despite how hopeless that sounds, it simply means the soil is ripe for planting the seeds of the gospel. People need to hear it, and we should be driven by our love for God to proclaim it. It's not enough to wall ourselves in and just pray—we need to put feet on our prayers, boldly announcing our faith in this faithless generation.

Whenever I'm discouraged by the sinfulness all around me, Lord, help me use this disappointment to fuel my passion for outreach. Help me build the world I want to see.

DEVASTATING MISTAKE

Then David said to God, "I have sinned greatly by taking this census. Please forgive my guilt for doing this foolish thing."
1 CHRONICLES 21:8 NLT

Have the mistakes you've made in the past ever left you paralyzed in the present? Perhaps you truly want to move forward in your relationship with God, but memories of failure freeze up your legs, leaving you in a place of spiritual stagnation. *What if it happens again?* you wonder. *How could God forgive—let alone use—such a broken mess?*

But as David's plea in today's verse illustrates, the process of strengthening your faith never starts with perfection. It's precisely *because* we're broken, fallen messes that we have room to grow in the first place.

David wasn't content to let his sin derail the well-being of his nation. He knew that in order to move forward, he needed to dig up the ugly, rotten transgressions he'd buried in his past and lay them at God's feet, begging for forgiveness. And even though his mistakes had physical consequences, as seen in the following passage, God was willing to ultimately forgive his error, allowing David to move into the future as a wiser man.

Are you stewing in your past mistakes, or are you handing them to God so that He can repurpose them for good?

Forgive me, God, for stepping out of line. Help me learn from this misstep so that I can walk Your path better tomorrow.

1 Chronicles 23–25 / Acts 18:24–19:10 / Psalm 107:10–16

LAW AND ORDER

*They rebelled against God's commands and despised the plans
of the Most High. So he subjected them to bitter labor; they
stumbled, and there was no one to help. Then they cried to the
LORD in their trouble, and he saved them from their distress.*

PSALM 107:11–13 NIV

One thing that separates God's laws from the laws of man is that
God's system is much more interested in reforming sinners than in
punishing them. Sure, sin often incurs severe consequences, but these
consequences are never dished out for spite or simply because God
likes it. Instead, He wants His wayward children to learn from their
mistakes. . .and sometimes that requires a bit of discomfort. Just as
a loving father would never let his child get away with dangerous
activities, so God will never let us stray too far from Him without
letting us feel the heat of our own decisions.

So if you ever find yourself straying from God and experiencing
the painful weight of guilt, don't use it as an excuse to distance
yourself even further. Learn from the Israelites and cry out to God for
forgiveness, drinking deeply from His wellspring of mercy. Repentance
will strengthen your walk with Him, transforming your mistakes into
stepping stones toward His righteousness.

*Father, may I never let my regrets become so strong that I
forget the hope You provide. Thank You for always leading
me home, even when the path is sometimes hard to bear.*

1 Chronicles 26–27 / Acts 19:11–22 / Psalm 107:17–32

LINKS TO THE PAST

And many of those who had practiced curious, magical arts collected
their books and [throwing them, book after book, on the pile]
burned them in the sight of everybody. When they counted the
value of them, they found it amounted to 50,000 pieces of silver.

ACTS 19:19 AMPC

As trees grow upward toward the sunlight, their old layer of bark peels off, revealing a brand-new layer underneath. Soon, the tree you were looking at just a short time ago has become entirely different, its old exterior replaced by the new.

That's the stage of growth in which the Christians in Ephesus found themselves. Having accepted Christ as Savior, they suddenly found their old possessions—books filled with magic arts—as useless as a crumbling layer of bark. So what did they do with these vestiges of their former life? The same thing we often do with dried-up pieces of bark—they used them as kindling. As the flames flickered across the dusty pages of their secret, sinful practices, it burned the last thread that connected these Christians to their past. There was no turning back now—their eyes were now exclusively fixed on Jesus.

What links to the past might you need to start throwing on the fire today?

Lord, may I never treat my past sins like nostalgic relics.
I'm not content with simply putting them down—I want rid of
them for good. Help me burn these sins and rise closer to You.

1 Chronicles 28–29 / Acts 19:23–41 / Psalm 107:33–38

IRRIGATING DESERTS

He turns the wilderness into a standing water
and dry ground into water springs.
PSALM 107:35 SKJV

C. S. Lewis once said, "The task of the modern educator is not to cut down jungles but to irrigate deserts." In other words, a teacher should focus less on tearing down students' preconceived notions, leaving them in a state of cynicism and confusion, and more on producing passion in disinterested minds, transforming dried-up apathy into insatiable curiosity. If the growth of new ideas succeeds, the weeding out of faulty ones will naturally follow.

This is exactly what God does in the life of a Christian. Before you accepted Jesus, your spiritual life was a barren wasteland, filled with the tumbleweeds of doubt and hostility. Perhaps you didn't understand the point of Christian living. . .and had no desire to learn. But thankfully, God wasn't finished with you. He never stopped planting the seeds of curiosity in your heart. And the moment you gave in to His flowing love, He began to irrigate your desert with spiritual knowledge and zeal for His truth. This process is still underway, and as long as you are willing, it will continue until you wake up on the shores of the eternal garden of paradise.

Are you drinking in this life-giving water today?

Thank You, Jesus, for Your life-saving water of truth.
Make my heart into a garden of spiritual curiosity, filled with
the fruits of the Spirit and always growing closer to You.

GRONER'S CHOICE

That night God appeared to Solomon and said to him:
"Ask. What should I give you?" And Solomon said to God:
"You have shown great and faithful love to my father David,
and You have made me king in his place. . . . Now grant me
wisdom and knowledge so that I may lead these people."

2 CHRONICLES 1:7–8, 10 HCSB

In 1935, a woman by the name of Grace Groner made a 180-dollar stock investment. That may not sound like much, but after years of patience, decades of wise spending, and a lifetime of increasingly profitable investments, she managed to transform this small sum into seven million dollars.

Many people, upon the first sign that their money had multiplied to a comfortable amount, would've blown it on whatever distraction held their attention at the time. But Grace chose a different route. Over the years, she anonymously distributed pieces of her wealth to the needy and lived as if she had barely enough to get by. And what did she do when her life came to an end? She donated most of the sum to Lake Forest College, her alma mater.

Grace's story proves that true contentment comes not through greed and impulsive spending but through a quiet, consistent life spent with Jesus, storing up His blessings and using them to bless others in return.

Father, give me a wise and patient heart, willing to wait for
the opportune time to benefit others with Your blessings.

SHRINKING

Be exalted, O God, above the heavens,
and Your glory above all the earth,
PSALM 108:5 SKJV

What does it take to ensure God's name is exalted through your actions? First, you must have the desire to see righteousness prevail over unrighteousness. This is hard, since by default, all humans are unrighteous. We naturally want our own ways to prevail, and only God's Spirit can change our desires.

Second, you must be willing—eager, even—to cause your own presence to shrink, allowing God's presence to attract every eye in the room. When people see you, they will no longer see you but the God who lives inside you. Like a glass case holding a valuable diamond, your exterior simply becomes a transparent substance through which the glory of the treasure within can be displayed.

John the Baptist understood this truth when he proclaimed, "He must increase, but I must decrease" (John 3:30 SKJV). Until that point, John had enjoyed immense success as a traveling preacher, attracting attention from crowds of people who flocked to hear his messages. But it was never about the fame for John—it was all about the one of whom his preaching spoke, Jesus Christ. So when Jesus came onto the scene, John was happy to fade into the background, content knowing that his purpose had been achieved.

What's your purpose?

Father, help me grow in You by shrinking my own image.
I want to value Your plan over my own faulty desires.

2 Chronicles 6:12–7:10 / Acts 21:1–14 / Psalm 109:1–20

COME WHAT MAY

When it was clear that we couldn't persuade him,
we gave up and said, "The Lord's will be done."

ACTS 21:14 NLT

Today's verse is a perfect illustration of faith in action.

All of Paul's friends agreed about one thing: Paul was in trouble. Everybody could see that traveling to Jerusalem was a suicide mission, and a prophecy from Agabus only reinforced that knowledge. Naturally, they tried their best to dissuade him from going. But when Paul kept insisting, they soon realized all their efforts would be in vain.

So what did they do? Berate Paul for his foolishness? Collapse in despair? No. They said, "The Lord's will be done." They knew the dangers that lay ahead. . .but they also knew that God works in mysterious ways. If the Lord wanted to rescue Paul, great. But if God had a reason for Paul's imprisonment, so be it. Either way, God was in charge. Who were they to get in the way?

Faith isn't blindness. It doesn't ignore the winds of fear and change. Instead, whenever it sees the storm brewing, faith digs its roots down into its one and only source of assurance: God's promises. Because Paul's friends understood God knew what He was doing, they were willing to step back and let Him work—come what may.

Lord, may I never believe I know better than You. Show me the gaps in my knowledge so that I can better trust Your infinite wisdom.

2 Chronicles 7:11–9:28 / Acts 21:15–32 / Psalm 109:21–31

THANKS IN ADVANCE

I will give great praise and thanks to the Lord with my mouth; yes, and I will praise Him among the multitude.
PSALM 109:30 AMPC

In Psalm 109, David goes to great lengths to describe just how abysmal his situation has been. Surrounded by enemies and slowly wasting away, David had every right to give up hope.

But notice something about the way this psalm ends. David never describes an end to his woes: his pain still persists, and his hope remains as of yet unrealized. But David still holds to the one truth he knows about God: that He always comes through, no matter how dire things seem. By being honest with his Creator—explaining his emotions and admitting his need for help—David fulfilled the only obligations he had. . .so he was free to thank God for the answer he knew was coming.

Do you have this kind of faith? Have you planted yourself so deeply within the rhythms of God's mercy that you're able to offer your thanksgiving before His help even arrives? The closer we draw to God, the less relevant the time between our cry for help and God's actual act of helping becomes. We already know it's on the way—it's just a matter of waiting in a state of perpetual thanksgiving.

Father, may my faith be so strong that my thanksgiving comes before Your help. Strengthen my trust in You by helping me understand what You've already done.

FUTILE WARS

" 'What shall I do, Lord?' I asked. 'Get up,' the Lord said, 'and go into Damascus. There you will be told all that you have been assigned to do.' "

ACTS 22:10 NIV

Say what you want about Paul's life, both before and after he became a Christian—one thing is certain: he was always willing to fight for what he saw as the truth. Scriptures seem to indicate that Saul didn't persecute Christians out of a sense of rebellion against God; rather, he simply believed he was doing the right thing (1 Timothy 1:13).

But the moment the light hit his eyes and he heard Jesus' voice from the heavens, he realized his error. So what did he do? Curse God for disrupting his worldview? Curse himself for being too far gone to be of any use? No. He said, "What shall I do, Lord?"

If you truly believe something—especially if it's something as life-changing as the gospel—then you will fight for it. But the only way to know the truth is to keep regular company with the author of all truth, studying the wisdom He's left for you. Otherwise, you'll be stuck fighting futile wars, locked in conflict with the only one who can help.

Lord Jesus, I know mere faith isn't enough—it's what I put my faith in that matters. Please help me have faith in You alone so that I won't waste the time and energy You've given me.

2 Chronicles 13–15 / Acts 22:17–23:11 / Psalm 110:4–7

PAYDAY

*"But as for you, be strong and do not give up,
for your work will be rewarded."*

2 CHRONICLES 15:7 NIV

Sometimes working for God feels fantastic. You revel in the joy that comes with loving your neighbor and living a holy life. The sun is shining, the odds are in your favor, and you feel revitalized, like you could take on the world.

And then you step outside.

Suddenly, that burst of morning optimism vanishes like a huge, freshly popped bubble, leaving behind a bitter spray. You step in a puddle of sloppy mud, ruining your new clothes and bringing a supply of unwholesome words to the forefront of your mind. On the way to work, someone swerves in front of you, tempting you to give him an earful as you pass him. That annoying coworker starts testing your patience, and you want to rudely walk away.

By the end of the day, even if you've made the right decision in each of these tests, you still feel exhausted and maybe a little depressed. Why do you struggle against your human nature each day? Is anyone even watching?

Yes. Today's verse is here to remind you that even when you feel alone, unseen, and worn out, God is smiling down on your obedience. So don't let your hands be weak—your work shall be rewarded.

Thank You, Lord, for promising such an indescribable reward for my flawed but sincere obedience. Help me grow stronger each day.

HOLLOW NOTIONS

The fear of the LORD is the beginning of wisdom;
all who follow His instructions have good insight.

PSALM 111:10 HCSB

In 1818, an American army officer named John Cleves Symmes Jr. had a "brilliant" plan. Fascinated by strange scientific theories and eager to make history with his discoveries, he proclaimed, "I declare the earth is hollow and habitable within; . . . I pledge my life in support of this truth, and am ready to explore the hollow, if the world will support and aid me in the undertaking."

Of course, poor Symmes never found what he was looking for. Because of his lack of knowledge about the earth, his entire scientific purpose was nothing more than a foolish fantasy. He persisted in this delusion until the day of his death, making his life a cautionary tale for any would-be adventurers.

Today, we all know the earth isn't hollow. . .but how many of us spend our lives pursuing hollow notions about God? Such ignorance is as tragic as it is avoidable: God has presented everything we need to know about Him in His Word. The fear of the Lord—gained through studying His Word and learning of His love, power, and grace—is the only way to reach true understanding. . .and thereby avoid wasting our time in silly pursuits.

Father, may my notions about You be filled with the wisdom
Your Spirit brings, not with the pride of willful ignorance.

2 Chronicles 18–19 / Acts 24:22–25:12 / Psalm 112

CONFIRMATION BIAS

And King [Ahab] of Israel said to Jehoshaphat, Did I not tell
you that he would not prophesy good to me, but evil?

2 CHRONICLES 18:17 AMPC

King Ahab was less concerned with the truth than he was with hearing other people agree with his vain and faulty ambitions. So when he asked the prophet Micaiah whether he should go to battle, he was furious when Micaiah broke the farce and told him no.

When we pray, how often are we like Ahab, falling on our knees with our idea of God's answer already firmly in mind? That isn't faith in God—that's confirmation bias. It's having faith in ourselves, using God's name as a way to decorate our plans and desires with illusions of divine approval. When God says yes, we're eager to jump on board. But when He says no, many of us are tempted to shrug it off, plug our ears, and say, "Oh well—God didn't answer this time. Guess I'll just have to do it my way."

Unsurprisingly, this strategy doesn't lead to growth. Instead, it effectively cuts off any chance of honest communication with God. . . leaving us even more in the dark. When you pray, expect an answer, but don't expect the answer to be the same as your own.

Lord, guide me according to the truth, not according to
my understanding. And as I grow, help these two things
become closer and closer to being one and the same.

2 Chronicles 20–21 / Acts 25:13–27 / Psalm 113

GOD-SHAPED VACUUM

*He raises the poor from the dust and lifts the needy from the garbage
pile in order to seat them with nobles—with the nobles of His people.*

PSALM 113:7–8 HCSB

There's not an unbeliever alive who lacks nothing. No matter how
much money or fame he has, he'll always feel incomplete without God
by his side. Why? Because this is a fallen world, one that's separated
from God by sin and hostile to the wants and needs of humanity.

The ungodly man who says he has everything he needs is lying—
either to others or to himself. Death and disease and shame will visit
him just as they visit every creature under the sun. In God's eyes,
the unrepentant sinner—even if he's the richest man alive—is just
as poor as the lowly beggar, desperate for someone to meet his basic
needs. As Pascal allegedly said, "There is a God-shaped vacuum in
the heart of each man."

But for the man who recognizes his desperate situation and raises
his hand toward heaven for help, there's no longer such a thing as
unfulfilled need. The poorest among us become unfathomably rich,
and the rich-but-unfulfilled are gifted with purpose and limitless
satisfaction.

Our journey upward begins with our recognition of how far we've
fallen. Have you started this voyage?

*Father, thank You for creating within me a void that
can only be filled with Your presence. May I never
try filling this void with useless pursuits.*

2 Chronicles 22–23 / Acts 26 / Psalm 114

YOUR LIFE'S DREAM

"I am fortunate, King Agrippa, that you are the one hearing my defense today against all these accusations made by the Jewish leaders."

ACTS 26:2 NLT

Paul was in a heap of trouble. The prophet Agabus had warned him about going to Jerusalem, he'd gone anyway, and now he was in chains, standing before King Agrippa to plead his case. So what were his first words? "I am fortunate."

Why? What on earth was "fortunate" about this? Simple: he now had the opportunity to spread the gospel to an entirely new crowd of people, some of whom held great influence. His life's dream hadn't been a comfortable mansion or unlimited wealth—it'd been this.

His priorities were planted firmly in the success of God's kingdom, and his years of devotion had produced an unfailing optimism that remained unshaken, even in the face of certain punishment. Nothing else mattered—any petty aspirations he might've had for himself had long been entirely overtaken by zeal for God's plan.

The only way we can share Paul's enthusiasm is if we truly understand how important the gospel is. And the only way to understand that is to immerse ourselves in it each day, asking God to slowly mold our priorities so that they match His own.

> *God, may my life's goal be to spread Your Word—if not before kings then before my friends and family. Fill me with the same spiritual urgency that Paul possessed.*

2 Chronicles 24:1–25:16 / Acts 27:1–20 / Psalm 115:1–10

EYES OF TRUST

*Why do the nations say, "Where is their God?" Our God
is in heaven; he does whatever pleases him. But their
idols are silver and gold, made by human hands.*

PSALM 115:2–4 NIV

What is faith? Is it blind adherence to something we know is wrong,
like so many religious cults and atheists claim? Or is it a rational
decision, grounded firmly in what we know about the nature of God
and seen crystal-clear through eyes of trust?

Today's passage suggests the latter. Faith is the ability to see
through appearances and trust the decisions of an all-knowing God
who lives just beyond the veil of our sight. Faith is ignoring the cynics
who have given up on purpose and meaning in the face of unexplained
mysteries. Faith is knowing that the sun is still shining, even when
the clouds conceal it. Faith is continuing to search for the God who's
walked with you all this way, even when it feels like He's absent.

Faith is optimism grounded in reality. Faith is hope that is surer
than any wish. Faith is our lifeline, our one path toward the God who
will reward us for keeping it. Do you have faith?

*Lord, if all I saw were the lies and half-truths that the world
proclaims so loudly, I'd truly be a hopeless man. Thank You for
offering me faith that's grounded in Your unshakable truth.*

2 Chronicles 25:17–27:9 / Acts 27:21–28:6 / Psalm 115:11–18

UNCONDITIONAL TRUST

"But take courage! None of you will lose your lives,
even though the ship will go down."

ACTS 27:22 NLT

Paul just couldn't catch a break. He'd been persecuted nearly to the point of death, imprisoned, hauled before a king, and shipped off to Rome. And now. . .his ship was sinking!

Most men would've panicked in this situation (or lost their last shred of hope somewhere back in Iconium). But Paul had one thing that most men didn't—a strong relationship with his God. God had revealed Himself to Paul, protected him from angry Jews and mobs, brought him to his feet after he was nearly stoned to death, and worked mighty miracles through him everywhere he went. And now, this same God was telling him, "It's going to be okay."

So what choice did Paul have but to believe? What others saw as irrational optimism was actually a reasonable conclusion he'd reached through years of experience. From the moment Jesus had supernaturally appeared to him, God had flawlessly kept up His end of the bargain by protecting him and using his words for good. So now, on this sinking boat in the middle of a thunderstorm, Paul knew that if God said He would protect, then God would protect. Full stop.

How strong is your relationship with God?

Father, thank You for being so reliable. No one else offers the
degree of assurance You provide as I strive to walk in Your will.

BOUND FOR GLORY

"I am bound with this chain because I believe that the
hope of Israel—the Messiah—has already come."
ACTS 28:20 NLT

Even in chains, Paul saw God's purposes coming to fruition. The hope of knowing Jesus sustained him in his darkest hours and gave him renewed purpose. When would he ever get a chance to share the gospel with Roman guards if he hadn't been chained to them in shifts? In Philippians, Paul mentioned new believers in Caesar's household and that the whole Praetorian Guard knew about Jesus Christ.

In a way, you are chained to the culture, prisoner of your environment, subject to the whims of those who oppose God. Like Paul, you have a choice: to let an oppressive atmosphere hamper your mind and spirit, or to remember that Jesus has overcome the world.

The worst the world can do is take away temporary things: reputation, earthly goods, physical freedom, maybe even your life. But death sets the Christian free.

If all you can ever be is limited to this time on earth, cling to possessions and status, and work with all you are for respect and acclaim. But Paul called all those things rubbish compared to the joy and glory of knowing Jesus and what He has done. He is your legacy.

Jesus, let Your hold on me strengthen and grow. Give me
courage to stand for You, to find that rhythm of truth and
love that breaks through against a godless culture.

2 Chronicles 29:20–30:27 / Romans 1:1–17 / Psalm 116:6–19

FROM FAITH TO FAITH

I am not ashamed of the gospel, because it is God's power for salvation to everyone who believes. . . . For in it God's righteousness is revealed from faith to faith, just as it is written: The righteous will live by faith.

ROMANS 1:16–17 HCSB

Romans is Paul's Magna Carta of Christian faith, and Romans 1:16–17 is its theme: how to live a life defined by Jesus' resurrection power in us. To show us how, he uses familiar terms but goes beyond the obvious meanings.

Here, "God's power for salvation" goes beyond the moment you received Christ. Salvation won't be completed until Jesus returns and breaks you free from your sin-wrecked body, replacing it with a new, resurrected one like His own—no more struggles against your own fleshly desires and habits.

"From faith to faith" underscores the idea. Faith is when you put your trust in God to save you. But that's just the start. Once you're saved, you walk in faith—putting Jesus at the center of your life and letting Him work on you—to prepare you for the salvation to come. You received His gift by faith, but you're working it out in how you think, act, and speak, drawing closer to Jesus in all you do.

Lord Jesus, move me from faith to faith, from being saved to living a redeemed life. Let Your resurrection power change me, day by day, choice by choice, so I can be more like You.

SWIMMING UPSTREAM

Through everything God made, they can clearly see his invisible qualities—his eternal power and divine nature. So they have no excuse for not knowing God.

ROMANS 1:20 NLT

Romans 1:18–32 details the depth and depravity of the fall. It's tough reading. God made us to take care of what He made, to oversee, explore, and manage the natural world. But because of our position as caretakers, our sin impacts all of creation.

Even when we look at the beauty that remains in a sunset, flower, or flock of birds, it's not what God meant it to be. Sinful human nature looks at the world and chooses to see a God who failed, who doesn't care or doesn't have enough power to fix things. Mankind has lost the thread, and things are only getting worse.

Praise God that Paul preceded this depressing account of mankind's appetite for destruction by proclaiming the good news of Jesus. You're part of His plan. God refused to let go, to leave you in the wreckage of your choices. Walking in faith means swimming against every current in this world. But you do so from a position of strength—God's Spirit and might—and hope: Jesus is coming back to make all things new.

The world is heartbreaking, God, but You mend hearts. Your image in us is fractured, but You are fixing it one believer at a time. Start with me. Help me to keep swimming.

EYES ON THE PRIZE

To those who by patient persistence in well-doing [springing from piety] seek [unseen but sure] glory and honor and [the eternal blessedness of] immortality, He will give eternal life.
ROMANS 2:7 AMPC

Good people often trust their goodness more than God, because they don't realize that their good behavior is still bad compared to God's goodness. Many have cried, "Unfair—God is God and I'm just me," but He knows us, knows that such a complaint is driven by our awareness that we come up short even by our own standards.

Because God doesn't play favorites, the same salvation works for all people. Everything that we use to separate ourselves from others— education, wealth, race, influence—means nothing to the God who made and holds power over all of it. God's impartiality works to your benefit. Because you belong to His Son, counted righteous by your trust in Christ's sacrifice, your past has been replaced by a meaningful present and a glorious future.

Each life matters to Him. You matter to Him. Everything He has put in your heart, starting with the desire to follow and serve Him, is worth the hardship it brings in this life. Even now, instead of struggling to make meaning and find purpose on your terms, you have "glory and honor and [heart] peace" (Romans 2:10 AMPC).

Jesus, by Your blood, Your glory and honor are mine. You are continually showing me Your better way, and I choose to walk in it today.

CORNERSTONE

The stone that the builders rejected has now become the cornerstone.
This is the LORD's doing, and it is wonderful to see.

PSALM 118:22–23 NLT

One of God's calling cards is that He likes to do things the hard way. He gave us free will and we made a selfish mess. He built a beautiful world, and we exploited it for our own gain. To fix it, He sent His beloved Son, and we killed Him. That's the prophecy of Psalm 118—the rejected stone who would become the cornerstone for God's redemption plan. The worst thing that ever happened—Christ crucified—became the best.

Doing things the hard way means God's victories are so much more glorious. Only He can do what He does. The wonder is less that He can do the impossible but that He chooses to, over and over.

God is nothing if not faithful. He is true to Himself in every moment, every situation. It's impossible for Him to be anything other than who He is—that's why He is God and you are not. He does not change. Because of that, there's no better foundation to build your life on, to trust your soul to. The refrain of Psalm 118 (NLT) is a chief building block itself: "Give thanks to the LORD, for he is good! His faithful love endures forever."

Father, I praise You for being Yourself. You alone are good,
faithful, holy, and just. I will build my life on Your cornerstone.

2 Chronicles 35:20–36:23 / Romans 3:27–4:25 / Psalm 118:24–29

THE OPENING MOVE

God does not respond to what we do; we respond to what God does.
. . . Our lives get in step with God and all others by letting him set
the pace, not by proudly or anxiously trying to run the parade.

Romans 3:27–28 msg

All chess games start in bad shape, the pawns blocking the movement of the more powerful pieces, which describes the world accurately. After the fall, we were in bad shape—we made a bad opening move.

Spiritually speaking, it was game over. Satan's plan to destroy all that God loves had just gained him control of the board—the entire world. We were demoted from the power players God meant us to be—agents for His glory—to mere pawns.

So, God made the first move of redemption—a countermove to send a Seed to crush the serpent's head and free mankind from sin and death. It was the game within the game, a spiritual battle with physical symptoms and eternal consequences that's been going on ever since.

But that wasn't God's opening move.

God's first play was to create a good world and share the love and harmony that has always existed within the Trinity. Love is always God's first move. It drives His strategy throughout history and His interactions with you, and it will conquer in the endgame.

You are the one and only Master, God. Thank You for
loving me first and wiring me to love You back.

Ezra 1–3 / Romans 5 / Psalm 119:1–8

HARDSHIP PRODUCES HOPE

We also rejoice in our afflictions, because we know that
affliction produces endurance, endurance produces proven
character, and proven character produces hope.

ROMANS 5:3–4 HCSB

Romans 5 demonstrates that all the damage done by sin is nothing compared to the grace God has poured out on those who put their faith in Jesus. He died for us while we were still His enemies, He replaced the universal death resulting from Adam's choice with eternal life, and He redeemed millions of rebellious moments with one act of obedience to the Father.

When people wonder how a good God can let bad things happen, only the Christian can answer, "He is redeeming our pain into something good and beautiful." Without God, hoping good comes out of bad is a shot in the dark. But in Christ, it's a guarantee: God makes straight lines from crooked sticks.

How powerful is the righteousness at work in us? Enough to fill every terrible hardship, every frustrating season of dryness, with the promise of better days ahead. His "hope will not disappoint us" (Romans 5:5 HCSB) because He is using affliction to build His character in us.

God's grace makes death a gardener. Stick a Christian in the dirt and he will rise, because that's the power of Christ's resurrection. It's true in eternity but also every day, in every difficulty we face.

You have justified me by Your blood, Jesus, and because You
defeated death, I will rise through each setback and hardship.

REBORN IN POWER

We died and were buried with Christ by baptism.
And just as Christ was raised from the dead by the glorious
power of the Father, now we also may live new lives.

ROMANS 6:4 NLT

How does the gospel change you? You've heard the message. You understand your need and what Jesus has done for you, but what difference does it make in everyday life? That's Paul's focus in Romans 6.

First, acknowledge the power of sin. You are made to look for something bigger than yourself, to count on it to give your life meaning. God made us to find that meaning in Him, because anything else moves us away from Him.

Sin's dirty trick is making you think you were free and independent. But you were enslaved to gods that seemed good—love, career, influence, integrity. Because those things controlled you, they were your master. Tainted by this sin-stained world, though, they could never ultimately satisfy you.

But Jesus overcame sin's grip. You're united with Jesus in His death and raised with Him to new life. Reborn in Christ, you have His power to overcome the grasp of lesser gods. Now, "you live under the freedom of God's grace" (verse 14 NLT). You are free to do what's right, unbound by the world's standards, and by God's Spirit you also have the power.

Father, You have changed my life for the better,
and I will live for You today and every day.

Ezra 6:1–7:26 / Romans 7:7–25 / Psalm 119:17–32

EVERYDAY DEPENDENCE

I have chosen to be faithful; I have determined to live by your
regulations. I cling to your laws. LORD, don't let me be put to shame!
I will pursue your commands, for you expand my understanding.

PSALM 119:30–32 NLT

Faith is sometimes translated as *truth*, an interesting connection. Hebrews 11:1 (NLT) says, "Faith shows the reality of what we hope for; it is the evidence of things we cannot see." God speaks only truth, so if He says something is true, we must act on it as such—as something we can lean on in hard times, seek clarity from in confusion, and share with confidence that God will stay true to Himself and what He has said.

The psalmist clearly put his faith in God's truth, revealed in God's words and His faithfulness. Because God alone is constantly reliable and good, it makes sense to put faith in Him—to choose to trust Him, to determine to follow His ways, to stand on His words, and to be open to learning from Him.

Christian faith is supported by credible evidence, not superstition or hopeful theory. The more we know of God's truth, the stronger our faith becomes. We cling to God when nothing else makes sense, because we believe He is still working, even when we can't see what He's doing.

God, You are the source of all truth, goodness, and beauty.
I put my faith in You today, in everything I say and do.

Ezra 7:27–9:4 / Romans 8:1–27 / Psalm 119:33–40

PAIN'S PURPOSE

What we suffer now is nothing compared to
the glory he will reveal to us later.
ROMANS 8:18 NLT

Suffering without Jesus has no purpose. Even if we face hardship with courage, our good example ends with us. If all Jesus came to do was provide a good example, He would've been quickly forgotten. His resurrection changed everything.

It's because Jesus defeated conspiracy, mockery, injustice, torture, and execution that your pain has meaning. Car accidents and bankruptcy and cancer are terrible, but they can still build your faith that He is working all things together and making everything new.

Because He rose, you still have reason to believe. You are God's adopted son, heir with Christ to His blessings and glory. The worst the world can do only reveals God's best plans for you: "We must share His suffering if we are to share His glory" (verse 17 AMPC).

Making a habit of "putting to death...the [evil] deeds prompted by the body" (verse 13 AMPC) leads not to less life but more—eternal life, which we can barely imagine because of our ongoing struggles against the flesh and the world. But walking in faith destroys fear. When you're in the daily habit of dying to yourself, you're preparing for anything hard that God might allow—but also for the glory to come.

God, You bring incredible things out of terrible ones, and in
Christ, You've given me reason to trust everything You permit.

Ezra 9:5–10:44 / Romans 8:28–39 / Psalm 119:41–64

NO CONDEMNATION, NO SEPARATION

*For I am persuaded that not even death or life, angels or rulers,
things present or things to come, hostile powers, height or depth,
or any other created thing will have the power to separate us
from the love of God that is in Christ Jesus our Lord!*

Romans 8:38–39 hcsb

Nothing can separate you from the love of God in Jesus. Romans 8 says that's what the Holy Spirit is trying to convince you of—your unity with Christ. He makes His destiny yours—the renewal, restoration, and eternity of glory—and the Spirit persuades you that it's true.

Romans 7 details the Christian's internal struggle: "When I want to do what is right, I inevitably do what is wrong" (Romans 7:21 nlt). Romans 8 clarifies your standing with God. Because God's Spirit is in you, you now love pleasing God. Sure, you fall short. Sin and death are still a reality—but they won't always be. But now and forever, nothing can separate you from His love.

If the Spirit weren't living and at work in you, you would hate God's law, rejecting it in favor of whatever seems best to you. Romans 8:35–39 says nothing can separate you from God's love. Lean into the gospel: you live in this world, but because of Jesus, you cannot be condemned in it or by it.

*God, thank You for Your Holy Spirit,
my guarantee that I belong to You.*

Nehemiah 1:1–3:16 / Romans 9:1–18 / Psalm 119:65–72

THE SHOT CALLER

It is God who decides to show mercy.
We can neither choose it nor work for it.

ROMANS 9:16 NLT

Ever get stuck on the idea of God choosing who will or won't receive His mercy? From our perspective, it can seem random and unprincipled. But consider this: Can God make an unjust decision? Only God knows the measure of each person's heart and whether they'll ever surrender to Him.

No one deserves His grace. No one can earn it, or it wouldn't be grace. So, if fair is defined as everyone getting the same thing, why should God show mercy to anyone? And yet, He does.

You don't know who God has called and whose hearts are hardened. You know that only faith in Jesus can save a soul. Your job is to share the good news and let that person's decision reveal their status before God. At that point, it's between them and God's Spirit.

Because you know what God can do to break through even the hardest heart, you can't give up on anyone. Only God knows whether they will ultimately choose Him. Once you're His, let God be God and do whatever He pleases. Trust that He is always good, just, and right. Let Him be God; you be the messenger.

God, keep me from getting tangled in the weeds of human reason and philosophy. Help me trust You, especially when I don't understand what You're allowing. You are good and You do good.

Nehemiah 3:17–5:13 / Romans 9:19–33 / Psalm 119:73–80

STUMBLING OVER THE ROCK

Gentiles, who did not pursue righteousness, have obtained
righteousness—namely the righteousness that comes from faith.
But Israel, pursuing the law for righteousness, has not achieved the
righteousness of the law. Why is that? Because they did not pursue it by
faith, but as if it were by works. They stumbled over the stumbling stone.

ROMANS 9:30–32 HCSB

Faith in God is not adherence to His laws, which can only reveal our sin, even when we keep them. Just look at the Pharisees, who had all the truth and none of the love. Without love, we can't understand grace. Without grace, we can't have faith in Jesus. He is the stone we can't avoid, the one reminding us that God has done everything to make salvation possible.

God's love is self-sacrificing and humble. We can't leverage God into blessing or saving us. We can only accept His remedy for our brokenness, seeing our deep and dire need for His righteousness, something we can never get on our own.

When we see what Jesus did for us, really see Him doing what we could never do, we are changed. Then, judging others for their lack of righteousness looks as foolish to us as it does to God. Don't stumble over Christ. When you bump against Him, cling to the rock that is higher than you are.

Lord, show me when I miss the heart of what You're about,
that rhythm of truth and love that Jesus demonstrated.

Nehemiah 5:14–7:73 / Romans 10:1–13 / Psalm 119:81–88

WORTH THE WAIT

*I'm homesick—longing for your salvation; I'm waiting for
your word of hope. My eyes grow heavy watching for some sign
of your promise; how long must I wait for your comfort?*
PSALM 119:81–82 MSG

The Psalms show us many requests for God's help against flesh-and-
blood enemies, but here the psalmist is also waiting on a promise. His
request for vindication against his foes is woven with his commitment
to cling to God's words: "I keep a steady gaze on the instructions you
post" (verse 82 MSG).

God's words carry His truth, promises, and hope. Hebrews 4:12
(NLT) reminds us, "The word of God is alive and powerful." In an
increasingly divided and contentious world, the Bible promises days
of peace and glory, and the strength to withstand today's trials.

Proverbs 13:12 (NIV) says, "Hope deferred makes the heart sick,
but a longing fulfilled is a tree of life." Revelation 22:2 (AMPC) speaks
of "the tree of life. . .[and how] the leaves of the tree were for the
healing. . .of the nations." Our world is still under the curse of sin.
We and all of creation long for a restored world, and this is what God
promises to create.

It's hard to wait—we are heartsick and homesick with *waiting*—
but it's coming, and it will be better than we could ever have imagined.

*Lord, I will stand by Your Word through all of life's trials. Your promises
are trustworthy, and You will redeem Your faithful creation.*

Nehemiah 8:1–9:5 / Romans 10:14–11:24 / Psalm 119:89–104

KEEP ON KEEPING ON

The point is: Before you trust, you have to listen. But unless
Christ's Word is preached, there's nothing to listen to.

ROMANS 10:17 MSG

When you've been following Jesus for a while, it's easy to get in a rut. You've heard your pastor's illustrations before, your Bible reading offers little inspiration, and your prayer life feels flat. These things are normal, and they pass.

When you've plateaued, maintain good habits. Keep going to church, and reading your Bible, and praying. Too many Christians use such seasons to justify the thought that God has somehow changed— that He no longer satisfies—and pull away from Him and His people. They lose faith.

Faith comes through hearing the word of God. Some messages stick out more than others, but the cumulative effect of regularly listening to sound Bible teaching is spiritual nourishment. You may not recall every sermon you've heard any more than you do every meal you've eaten. But you haven't starved—physically or spiritually—so they've done you good.

Paul's point is that going back to basics steadies your faith—the gospel, Jesus Himself, and what He has done for you. Trust that hearing and reading the Bible will pull you out of your funk. God doesn't change, and He will see you through.

Father, help me to stay faithful the way You are
faithful, to keep doing what I know builds my faith,
especially when it doesn't feel like it's working.

Nehemiah 9:6–10:27 / Romans 11:25–12:8 / Psalm 119:105–120

UNDERSTAND YOUR STANDING

The only accurate way to understand ourselves is by what God is and
by what he does for us, not by what we are and what we do for him.

ROMANS 12:3 MSG

Most Christians are familiar with Paul's challenge in Romans 12:1–2 to offer our lives to God as living sacrifices—that, because of all Jesus has done for us, it's the only right response. We're familiar with the idea of letting Jesus rule in every aspect of our lives, of offering all we have to Him. It's a key part of growing in faith.

What's interesting, and often left in the corner, is Paul's follow-up admonition in verse 3 (NLT): "Be honest in your evaluation of yourselves." What he's getting at is our tendency to think we're bringing our good behavior to God, showing Him He made a good call in saving us. Paul's warning reminds us to always keep in mind that everything we have is by God's grace.

The biggest sacrifice we can make is to submit ourselves completely to God. That requires embracing the truth that we need Him, that He chooses to love us and wants to lift us to a higher view of ourselves and our purpose. God always makes the first move. Our best response is total trust.

God, You know everything about me and still love me
enough to die for me. Help me to trust You enough to see
myself as You do—worth forgiving and redeeming.

WHAT SACRIFICE LOOKS LIKE

*Never pay back evil with more evil. Do things in such
a way that everyone can see you are honorable. Do all
that you can to live in peace with everyone.*

ROMANS 12:17–18 NLT

We live in a tit-for-tat world—do unto others what they just did to you, but up the ante so they never mess with you again. If this life was all there is, that would make sense. Faith requires taking the high road—but not on a high horse. To imitate Christ is to be meek—to realize God's power is working in and through you, but not for use in dismissing or diminishing others.

Paraphrasing Romans 12:9–16 gives a picture of being a living sacrifice: If you're going to love others, don't fake it. Real love is sacrificial, putting others first. That annoying family member, neighbor, or coworker will only see the difference Jesus makes if you show it to them. Seek what's best for them, even when they haven't done the same for you.

Serve God and His people out of love, not duty. Go through life's ups and downs with empathy, not rolling eyes. Some people don't want peace or reconciliation, but God made peace with you and wants you to try with others. Take heart—God is with you and for you!

*Lord, You have my back, especially when I commit to doing life
Your way. Let me overcome evil the way You do, by doing good.*

Nehemiah 12:27–13:31 / Romans 13:8–14:12 / Psalm 119:129–136

STICKS IN SPOKES

*Each of us will give a personal account to God. So let's stop
condemning each other. Decide instead to live in such a way
that you will not cause another believer to stumble and fall.*

ROMANS 14:12–13 NLT

No Christian should undo God's work in another believer by our
personal convictions. Under God's grace, for example, it no longer
matters what we eat or drink, because those things no longer impact
our relationship with God. Christ's blood covers everything—but it
also obligates us to show others the same grace He showed us.

Grace means being careful in using the freedom God has given
us. We all have our own histories, and God knows what each of us
needs to grow in faith. What's okay for us may bring another believer
down. If we treat every Christian like we should all have the same
freedoms or restrictions, we're jamming a stick in their spokes.

Jesus is "Lord both of the living and of the dead" (verse 9 NLT),
so be careful that what you live for or say you'll die for lines up with
the gospel. We're all going to stand before God—as believers, not
on the count of salvation but for what we've done to share the good
news, and how we live according to God's example of sacrificial love.

*Lord Jesus, give me grace with other believers so I can honor You by
respecting the different ways You're working in each of our lives.*

Esther 1:1–2:18 / Romans 14:13–15:13 / Psalm 119:137–152

JOY UNDER PRESSURE

As pressure and stress bear down on me, I find joy in your commands.
PSALM 119:143 NLT

Trouble is always coming. Today could bring a disheartening headline from across the globe, an unexpected confrontation, or a devastating personal loss. We know the world hates Jesus, and hates us because we follow Him, so that's not news, but it's still hard. Temptations also abound, whether the enemy's work or our own shortcomings. "Pressure and stress" are also translated "trouble and anguish" (AMPC), the weight of pain and uncertainty that threatens to derail us.

Fortunately, in God's Word, you have a shelter and a shield. Whether it's arrows raining down or turmoil bubbling up from inside, the Bible holds God's unchanging truth, His everlasting promises and instructions.

Stress comes in great part because of constantly changing conditions—few of which seem to be improving anything. We wonder if we can get through them all—challenge after challenge, trial after trial. Some love a challenge, but there's always something that knocks us flat. That's where we find the quality of our faith, the depth of our reliance, of our willingness to trust God. Knowing He is with us no matter what brings joy—that certainty that He is always good and trustworthy and will reward us for our faithfulness in these dark hours.

God, guide me in Your words so I can live the life You have for me. In the face of constant troubles, steady me by Your truth.

Esther 2:19–5:14 / Romans 15:14–21 / Psalm 119:153–168

HIS WILL BE DONE

"If you remain silent at this time, relief and deliverance for the Jews will arise from another place, but you and your father's family will perish."

Esther 4:14 niv

What is God's will for your life? It's at the heart of Mordecai's statement to Esther: God's will is going to get done one way or another—will you play the role He has for you here and now, or will He get it done through someone else?

Romans 12:2 tells us that God's will is perfect, and that we will know it if we turn from the world and toward Him for all we need. His Word renews our minds so we can discern what He wants us to do in each situation. Because God knows everything, He knows what we'll do in any circumstances. That's why He can work all things together for our good and His glory. His plans, like His promises, don't fail.

In God's perfect will, we always do what pleases Him. But He has to account for sin's impact. He makes room for all the brokenness in the world and still accomplishes His purposes. As often as we can, we want to let God work His perfect will in us, doing what pleases Him whenever possible.

Lord, Your will and ways are perfect. Align me with them, so that my imperfections don't get in the way of what You want to do in and through me.

Esther 6–8 / Romans 15:22–33 / Psalm 119:169–176

SEARCH ENGINE

*I have wandered away like a lost sheep; come and find
me, for I have not forgotten your commands.*
PSALM 119:176 NLT

That lost feeling all Christians experience at some point isn't about
you going off God's radar. It's because He has gone off yours. You
may feel that distance because of a trial in your life and God doesn't
seem to be responding, or you may be cruising along, seeking Him
and doing fine, and then *bam*! You're off-track. That sudden feeling
of desertion is what this part of Psalm 119 is about.

This section begins, "O LORD, listen to my cry; give me the
discerning mind you promised" (Psalm 119:169 NLT). In *The Message*,
it's a cry to "provide me with insight that only comes from your Word."
This guy hasn't forgotten what he knows about God, but he's afraid
God has forgotten about him. When that happens, the best move is
to return to the Bible. Faith requires certainty where none is apparent.
Return to God's words and you'll find Him, searching for you.

Luke 15:4 assures us that Jesus will search for one lost sheep, even
leaving the rest of the flock to find it. When you feel lost, He still
knows where you are and is working to bring you back to His fold.

*Lord, when I'm feeling far from You, remind me to seek
You where You'll be looking for me—in Your Word.*

Esther 9–10 / Romans 16 / Psalm 120–122

SEEK HIM FIRST

I look up to the mountains; does my strength come
from mountains? No, my strength comes from GOD,
who made heaven, and earth, and mountains.

PSALM 121:1–2 MSG

We trust other people every day, but to rely on them rather than God for our peace and purpose is fruitless. In a moment of greatest need, we should still trust that any human help comes from God. Don't let urgency or expedience or fear keep you from seeking God first. Who else can help like God does?

The enemy wants to keep your focus on your troubles rather than lifting them up to God, who sees and knows everything. Satan is thrilled when you stay stuck in your own head, expecting the worst, avoiding prayer and the counsel of seasoned Christians. The kids call it *dooming*. But if you can put your eternal fate on the line by trusting that Jesus died and rose for you 2,000 years ago, trusting Him with your current situation is a no-brainer.

God is not only able to help, He is willing. If His timing doesn't match yours, trust His bigger picture. It's hard to imagine something more majestic than a mighty mountain range—but for all its majesty, you're looking at God's footstool. Look beyond sky and mountain to the one who made them both. He is your help.

Lord God, my help in times of trouble, thank You for
today's mercies. I will look to You first and always.

Job 1–3 / 1 Corinthians 1:1–25 / Psalm 123

TAKE THE BAD WITH THE GOOD

"Should we accept only good from God and not adversity?"
JOB 2:10 HCSB

Suffering brings what's inside us to the surface. It reveals our true expectations of God. If you can imagine (or have experienced) trials like Job's, you'll see that his wife's response—"Ditch the God who ditched you!"—feels natural, even reasonable. She was grieving too. But her pain revealed her basic belief: she trusted God to the extent that He blessed their lives.

Job, however, devastated as he was, stuck to his core belief: "I came naked from my mother's womb, and I will be naked when I leave. The LORD gave me what I had, and the LORD has taken it away. Praise the name of the LORD!" (Job 1:21 NLT). He was too broken to be taking an arrogant stance. This was what got knocked out of him when Satan was allowed to clobber him: "God is God, and I am not."

That doesn't mean Job didn't wonder why God let it happen or if he would ever get a chance to plead his case. But he didn't let grief and anguish divorce him from his faith. God doesn't owe us good things. He gives them as gifts—and sometimes those gifts are buried in our adversity. Will we trust Him enough to look?

> *God, You are always faithful to me. Even when I can't see what You're doing, I will trust You in good times and bad.*

Job 4–6 / 1 Corinthians 1:26–2:16 / Psalm 124–125

TRUSTING HIS POWER

My speech and my proclamation were not with persuasive words of wisdom but with a powerful demonstration by the Spirit, so that your faith might not be based on men's wisdom but on God's power.

1 CORINTHIANS 2:4–5 HCSB

Paul wanted the Corinthians to understand where the powerful results behind his preaching came from—not his own skills as a speaker but the Holy Spirit. There's something here about sharing our faith, both for those who are born connectors and those for whom it's hard to speak about something so personal and so easily rejected.

For the gifted speaker, it's a reminder to stay humble about results that come from your oratory prowess. Without the Spirit convicting your hearers, your witness might get them fired up, but that fire will fade.

For the introvert, it's an opportunity to trust God. If He is prompting you to talk about Jesus with someone, He will give you the words. Matthew 10:19–20 (HCSB) says, "You will be given what to say at that hour, because you are not speaking, but the Spirit of your Father is speaking through you." The context is persecution—when you get arrested for your faith, God will give you the right response. So He will definitely do so in your everyday life.

In both cases, trusting His power in you will lead to the best possible results.

Father, help me to obey Your call to share Your good news and let You handle the outcomes.

Job 7–9 / 1 Corinthians 3 / Psalm 126–127

WHO'S BUILDING YOUR LIFE?

If GOD doesn't build the house, the builders only build shacks. If GOD doesn't guard the city, the night watchman might as well nap. It's useless to rise early and go to bed late, and work your worried fingers to the bone. Don't you know he enjoys giving rest to those he loves?

PSALM 127:1–2 MSG

It's human nature to worry. It starts as a sign we care. But past that, we need to decide whether we're going to build on fear or faith.

Fear says, "If God were big enough or really cared, He would take care of this right now." Continuous worry tells others that you have a small God who can't help or needs to be leveraged into action.

Faith says, "I can trust that God will do what's right in His perfect time, and that He will give me strength to deal with the in-between moments." People pick up on your steadiness and your belief that, even though you don't know what God will do, or how long He'll take, whatever He does will never change His love or care for you.

If you view today's challenges and trials through the lens of faith, you are building a firm foundation for your life. Hardship is still hard, but it won't threaten to move you off your footing.

Lord, I hand over the keys to this day to You. Guide me to do what's right and help me stand strong when trouble happens.

Job 10–13 / 1 Corinthians 4:1–13 / Psalm 128–129

SOUND JUDGMENT

Don't make judgments about anyone ahead of time—before the Lord returns. For he will bring our darkest secrets to light and will reveal our private motives. Then God will give to each one whatever praise is due.

1 CORINTHIANS 4:5 NLT

Paul addressed the challenges of leadership in 1 Corinthians 4, defining himself as God's servant, put by God in charge of "explaining God's mysteries" (verse 1 NLT). When it comes to being faithful, God is the sole judge. He alone determines whether we've done a good job, whether we've focused on what matters to Him rather than our own ambitions.

There's no point in trying to make yourself out to be someone you're not, or to judge someone else based on a single impression or what others have said. You can measure good work based on fruitfulness, but God alone knows what's really going on in each heart. So, your ultimate responsibility is to Him. With that as a baseline, you can lead with wisdom.

Each day requires you to make sound judgments. Your assessment of yourself and the actions of others should be tempered by grace and the understanding that God should be leading you, and your part is to try and help others as much you can. That's both godly wisdom and effective leadership.

Father, everything I have comes from You, my final authority. Help me to lead myself with wisdom and insight, and then to lead others well.

Job 14–16 / 1 Corinthians 4:14–5:13 / Psalm 130

WAITING FOR THE DAWN

I am counting on the LORD; yes, I am counting on him. I have put my hope in his word. I long for the Lord more than sentries long for the dawn.

PSALM 130:5–6 NLT

In biblical times, standing sentry was a crucial job. Cities had walls and gates because the threat of attack was always real. The job description? Watch and wait. However long your shift lasts, be on your toes. To fall asleep or space out could be all the advantage a foe needed to break through. A soldier's account of World War I was "months of boredom punctuated by moments of terror."

While it's rare nowadays to have to stand watch for the sake of an entire city, we are still called to be on the lookout—not just for enemies but for God. In some ways, watching for God is harder. Bad news is everywhere and always present, but we must trust that God is sovereign, working all things together for our good and His glory. So often, He works behind the scenes, but He is still working.

Vigilance is part of faith, a sense of duty to stay watchful, for God's promises and their fulfillment. What relief we'll have when He finally returns to relieve our watch and completes His redemptive work!

Lord, I will wait and watch for You. You finish what You begin, and Your work continues in me and in the world You love.

Job 17–20 / 1 Corinthians 6 / Psalm 131

WITH MY OWN EYES

*"I know that my Redeemer lives, and he will stand upon the
earth at last. And after my body has decayed, yet in my body
I will see God! I will see him for myself. Yes, I will see him
with my own eyes. I am overwhelmed at the thought!"*

JOB 19:25–27 NLT

One of the most remarkable aspects of Old Testament faith was belief
in God coming to dwell among His people—and what it would take
to make that possible. Abraham believed that if God required him to
follow through with Isaac, God would also raise Isaac from the dead
since He had promised to bring a nation of believers through him.

In Psalm 110, David foresaw he would have a descendent who
would also be his Lord. And Job, during soul-crushing pain, knew
that his Messiah would stand on the earth—that his Redeemer would
make something good and beautiful from all suffering.

In hindsight, we still marvel at such trust, such confidence, that
with nothing to go on but God's promises and His revealed character,
these people never doubted God. They didn't know about Jesus, at least
not the way we do. But they believed God was not going to abandon
His people or His creation, and He would have to satisfy both His
holiness and His love to make things right.

*God, You are always working to fulfill Your good
plan. I can't wait to see You face-to-face!*

Job 21–23 / 1 Corinthians 7:1–16 / Psalm 132

THIS IS THE WAY

"He knows where I am and what I've done. He can cross-examine me all he wants, and I'll pass the test with honors. I've followed him closely, my feet in his footprints, not once swerving from his way. I've obeyed every word he's spoken, and not just obeyed his advice—I've treasured it."

JOB 23:10–12 MSG

If we're honest, we probably wouldn't have Job's confidence in letting God cross-examine us. But we can have that assurance in Jesus—that with His righteousness replacing ours, we'll come through anything—our sins, the world, and the enemy.

Job's statement is loaded with that kind of belief: God knew Job's path, where he was headed and how he would get there. Job knew by keeping God's commands, by treasuring them the way a man in a cave values a lamp, that he would stay on that path.

In the early days of the church, Christianity was often referred to as the Way—perhaps because of Jesus' famous statement in John 14:6 (NLT): "I am the way, the truth, and the life." He didn't come to show us the way to God, which is what every other religion strives to do. He Himself is the way. If you've put your faith in Him to save you and you're living for Him, you're on the way to His kingdom.

Jesus, thank You for showing me who You are—the road,
the truth, the life. Keep me going Your way.

Job 24–27 / 1 Corinthians 7:17–40 / Psalm 133–134

THE JOY OF FELLOWSHIP

*How wonderful and pleasant it is when
brothers live together in harmony!*

PSALM 133:1 NLT

David used the image of Aaron, the high priest, overflowing with anointing oil, more than prepared for God's service. Most images of a priest's duties are more solemn or bloody—tending the temple and offering sacrifices. But here is an image of joy, followed by one of a beautiful, fresh morning on Mount Hermon. It's a picture of how much God values relationship and how good it is when we put His attitude toward fellowship into action.

Harmony with fellow believers is about serving and rejoicing. Consider Aaron's job, to mediate between God and God's people. Since Christ is our mediator, we can stand in the gap, praying for each other, offering support and encouragement. Aaron conducted offerings and sacrifices. We offer our time and attention to go through life's ups and downs with people.

Even if you're an introvert—that is, you recharge by making time for yourself—you still need others. Make the investment. Carve out time to meet with other Christians, to share each other's burdens and joys, to pray for each other. They'll show you Jesus in ways only they can—ways that God has gifted them for—and you'll do the same for them.

*Jesus, You make fellowship with God and with other believers
possible. Help me to serve others with joy, knowing it pleases You.*

Job 28–30 / 1 Corinthians 8 / Psalm 135

LOVE > KNOWLEDGE

Knowledge puffs up while love builds up. Those who think they know something do not yet know as they ought to know. But whoever loves God is known by God.

1 CORINTHIANS 8:1–3 NIV

Knowing God's Word is foundational to our walk with Him. Jesus modeled it, quoting two dozen Old Testament books almost 180 times in the Gospels. Colossians 3:16 (NIV) tells us to "let the message of Christ dwell among you richly." In Romans 12, Paul said to renew our minds by knowing God's will—which we can by reading His words. Psalm 119 says a man can keep his way pure by keeping God's Word. Knowledge of God matters.

But knowledge isn't everything. A humble heart is more valuable than a proud mind. Think of Jesus washing His disciples' feet. The ultimate knowledge of God centers on love—not feeling warm and fuzzy toward God or people but following God's example of sacrificing comfort and status to honor and serve others.

For most guys, knowledge is comforting. We like to be the one who knows the answer or how to fix something. That knowledge is fine, but godly wisdom harnesses it to serve others with humility. You can't touch God when it comes to knowledge and understanding, but you can imitate Him when you love people.

Lord, You know everything, and all Your actions are guided by love, by connecting with people and bringing them into relationship. Help me to follow Your lead.

Job 31–33 / 1 Corinthians 9:1–18 / Psalm 136:1–9

JOB'S EXAMPLE

"Did not he who made me in the womb make them?
Did not the same one form us both within our mothers?"

JOB 31:15 NIV

Job's experience torpedoes any idea that righteous behavior guarantees an easy life. Recall that God Himself called Job "blameless and upright" (Job 1:8 NIV). . .shortly before He allowed Satan to destroy the man's possessions, family, and health.

Job tried to make sense of his trials, losses we can't even imagine touching our lives. Often, he claimed unfairness, considering the positive ways he'd treated God and others. That ultimately wasn't the point (see God's response in chapters 38–42), but Job's story still carries examples for us.

In today's scripture, Job recognized God's handiwork in his own servants, people who deserved justice if they ever had a grievance against Job (verse 13). He observed the same stamp of God even on his enemies (verses 29–30). This is something all of us who follow Jesus should do, as He taught in the Sermon on the Mount (Matthew 5:43–48).

Our enemies may be deceitful coworkers, irritating neighbors, political opponents on social media, or just garden-variety bad drivers. They're *all* made in God's image. . .so treat them all with respect. It really doesn't matter whether they notice or care. God will and does. And, as Job did in the end, trust that God has a far greater perspective than you could ever imagine.

Please love others—friend and enemy alike—through me, Lord.

BE GOOD TO YOURSELF

*I discipline my body like an athlete, training it to do
what it should. Otherwise, I fear that after preaching
to others I myself might be disqualified.*

1 CORINTHIANS 9:27 NLT

Today's devotion title is also the name of a hard-rocking 1986 hit by the San Francisco band Journey. Be good to yourself, the incomparable Steve Perry sang, when nobody else will.

For us as Christian men, being good to yourself looks a lot like controlling yourself. The apostle Paul likened his faith life to an athlete's training, a grueling process of self-denial and hard work that leads to even greater rewards. But *you* have to control yourself because nobody else can do it for you.

It's tough to walk away from the wrong things—kinds and amounts of food, laziness or overwork, the sexual temptations this world and your own mind throw at you. It's much easier, day by day, to binge watch TV shows, sleep in, overdo hobbies, bypass God's Word. But none of these things develop a strong, healthy spirit...and may, in the end, lead to your disqualification as a Christian example.

None of us wants to end up there. Instead, get into the gym—God's gym. With His help, work hard at developing self-control. Be good to yourself, and to everyone else who's watching your life.

Lord Jesus, this world pushes ease and pleasure to people's destruction. Help me to be like You, doing the hard things that bring eternal benefit.

Job 37–39 / 1 Corinthians 10:14–11:1 / Psalm 137

RESENTMENTS

*Happy are those who dash your children against
the rocks so you will know how it feels.*

PSALM 137:9 VOICE

Whew—what do you do with a verse like this?

Psalm 137 clearly arose late in Old Testament times, after Babylonians had destroyed Jerusalem and carried off many of its people captive. "By the rivers of Babylon, we sat and wept," the psalmist lamented, "when we thought of Zion, our home, so far away" (verse 1 VOICE).

Though the prophet Jeremiah had, at God's direction, told the Jews to accept their new home and work for its good (see Jeremiah 29:7), Babylon's demolition of Jerusalem had been cruel and complete. Its people felt a natural resentment, which today's scripture reflects.

But God's people, especially now that His Spirit lives in us, are called to be more than "natural." The wise and still readable old-time Bible commentator Matthew Henry (1662–1714) wrote of Psalm 137:9, "In singing this psalm we must be much affected with the concernments of the church, especially that part of it that is in affliction, laying the sorrows of God's people near our hearts, comforting ourselves in the prospect of the deliverance of the church and the ruin of its enemies, in due time, but carefully avoiding all personal animosities, and not mixing the leaven of malice with our sacrifices."

Give your resentments to God. Trust Him to work things out properly, in His own time.

Lord, please take my resentments and replace them with Your love.

CREATURE VERSUS CREATOR

Then the Lord answered Job out of the whirlwind, saying, Gird up your loins now like a man; I will demand of you, and you answer Me.

JOB 40:6–7 AMPC

God Himself illustrated the absurdity of created beings questioning their Creator's ways. "Shall what is formed say to the one who formed it, 'You did not make me'?" He asked. "Can the pot say to the potter, 'You know nothing'?" (Isaiah 29:16 NIV). That's an error we've probably all committed at some time. Even as great a man as Job.

He certainly faced extreme trials. And he refused to renounce God, as his wife once suggested (Job 2:9). But in his frustration and pain, Job did say some careless things, like "I cry to You, [Lord,] and You do not answer me; I stand up, but You [only] gaze [indifferently] at me. You have become harsh and cruel to me; with the might of Your hand You [keep me alive only to] persecute me" (Job 30:20–21 AMPC).

God will defend His own honor, and with Job He basically said, "Man up! If you think you're so smart, now answer *My* questions."

God is a patient, loving Father who puts up with a lot from His kids. Let's be sure we never push Him to the point that He has to say, "Okay, buddy, now gird up your loins."

Lord God, I want to respect You even when I don't understand Your ways. Please help me.

Ecclesiastes 1:1–3:15 / 1 Corinthians 12:1–26 / Psalm 139:1–6

CONTENTMENT ISSUES

No matter how much we see, we are never satisfied.
No matter how much we hear, we are not content.

ECCLESIASTES 1:8 NLT

Ecclesiastes is a strange book, apparently written by a strange king. What else can you say about Solomon, blessed by God with wisdom beyond any other person (1 Kings 3:12), who ended up marrying seven hundred women (1 Kings 11:3)?

Sounds like Solomon had contentment issues.

Ecclesiastes takes a dark view of life, describing it as "completely meaningless" (1:2 NLT). The ongoing (and unsatisfying) pursuit of money and pleasure struck the author as a heavy burden. The constant desire for more is "like chasing the wind" (4:4 NLT).

Jesus addressed this issue of discontent, teaching, "Beware! Guard against every kind of greed. Life is not measured by how much you own" (Luke 12:15 NLT). Thankfully, the apostle Paul indicated that contentment can be gained: "I have learned how to be content with whatever I have. I know how to live on almost nothing or with everything. I have learned the secret of living in every situation, whether it is with a full stomach or empty, with plenty or little. For I can do everything through Christ, who gives me strength" (Philippians 4:11–13 NLT).

Just remember this: You can only be content with what you *have*. If you think you'll be content with what you *want*, you'll never be.

Heavenly Father, You give me everything I need.
Help me to learn contentment like Paul did.

Ecclesiastes 3:16–6:12 / 1 Corinthians 12:27–13:13 / Psalm 139:7–18

DON'T SAY IT. . .

Do not be quick with your mouth. . .
many words mark the speech of a fool.
Ecclesiastes 5:2–3 niv

The story is told of a famed British actor at a fancy party. Guests are mingling on the main level when two women, one older and one younger, appear on the second floor. As they descend the grand staircase, the actor nudges a man beside him and whispers, "That's the ugliest woman I've ever seen." Taken aback, the man replies, "That's my wife." The actor quickly shifts gears: "No, no, I mean the other one." To this, the man says, "That's my daughter!" With no graceful escape, the actor simply declares, "I didn't say it," and walks away.

True or not, the story undoubtedly resonates with many guys. . . those of us who wish we could *truly* claim, "I didn't say it."

Scripture indicates that Christian men should be "quick to listen, slow to speak" (James 1:19 niv). We have to allow God to change our hearts, where evils like slander arise (Matthew 15:19). The deeper we go with God, the more control we'll have over our tongues, which figuratively hold the power of life and death (Proverbs 18:21).

Today's scripture specifically addresses vows made to God. But the principle, which appears throughout the Bible, is broad: if there's any doubt at all, just don't say it.

Lord God, please purify my heart so that whatever
crosses my lips is true and good.

Ecclesiastes 7:1–9:12 / 1 Corinthians 14:1–22 / Psalm 139:19–24

RESPECTING GOD'S NAME

They speak of you with evil intent; your adversaries misuse your name.
PSALM 139:20 NIV

Sadly, the use of God's name as a curse word is nothing new. Neither is its careless use as an interjection in everyday speech. But that virus does seem to be spreading.

And the misuse of God's name goes beyond simply speaking it casually or in anger. Today, how many professing Christians use His name as a cover for behaviors that contradict His Word? How many claim God's name when they won't pursue His ways?

The problem goes back at least to the time of King David. Psalm 139, famous for its description of God's intimate knowledge of our lives, also contains a few sentences expressing David's anger with evil people. He lamented their misuse of the Lord's name, as today's scripture indicates. Then David wrote, "Do I not hate those who hate you, LORD, and abhor those who are in rebellion against you? I have nothing but hatred for them; I count them my enemies" (verses 21–22 NIV).

David lived in a different time, when God instructed His people to literally battle the wicked. Our battles are spiritual, and though we're expected to love our enemies (Matthew 5:43–48), we still hate the disrespect they show to our Lord. Whatever anyone else may do, let's commit ourselves to the most profound esteem of His name.

*Your name, Lord God, excels all. May I reverence
Your name, today and every day.*

Ecclesiastes 9:13–12:14 / 1 Corinthians 14:23–15:11 / Psalm 140:1–8

EFFECTS OF GRACE

*I am the least of the apostles and do not even deserve to be called an
apostle, because I persecuted the church of God. But by the grace of
God I am what I am, and his grace to me was not without effect.*

1 Corinthians 15:9–10 niv

What Christian man hasn't struggled with sin or regretted a choice
he's made?

These are big issues—but God's grace is bigger. Don't derail your
faith by focusing on your weakness rather than God's strength.

Consider David, the man after God's own heart (1 Samuel 13:14),
chosen to lead God's people. David achieved marvelous things in
God's strength. . .then committed adultery with a neighbor and had
her husband killed (2 Samuel 11). But David repented (Psalm 51),
and God still used him. His story and psalms are still part of our faith
three thousand years later.

For a New Testament example, there's John Mark. He deserted
Paul's first missionary journey (Acts 15:38), and though his cousin
Barnabas wanted to try again on the next trip, the apostle opposed
the idea—so strongly that he and Barnabas split up (Acts 15:39–40).
In the long run, though, Paul recognized Mark's helpfulness to his
ministry (2 Timothy 4:11). . .and like Paul, Mark contributed to the
Bible we read today.

We'll all fail at times, but that's what God's grace is for.

*Lord, I thank You for grace. Keep me close
and use me in spite of my weakness.*

Song of Solomon 1–4 / 1 Corinthians 15:12–34 / Psalm 140:9–13

GOD WILL REPAY

Those who are fencing me in raise their heads; may the mischief of their own lips and the very things they desire for me come upon them.

PSALM 140:9 AMPC

This psalm may refer to King Saul's persecution of David, the anointed but not yet crowned ruler of Israel. Though the young man was honored to be leader of God's chosen people, David would travel a long, difficult road to the throne.

Initially, Saul appreciated David. The former shepherd boy had felled the Philistine giant Goliath, who terrified Saul's seasoned warriors. But when Israel's women celebrated the victory by singing, "Saul has slain his thousands, and David his ten thousands" (1 Samuel 18:7 AMPC), the king lost his mind. Saul himself tried to murder David with a spear and often sent men in pursuit of him.

That's why David prayed, "Deliver me, O Lord, from evil men; preserve me from violent men" (Psalm 140:1 AMPC). And in verse 9, David asked God to turn his enemies' evil intentions back on their own heads.

In a sense, that's simply an acknowledgment of the biblical principal of sowing and reaping (Galatians 6:7). Unless Saul and his henchmen stopped their hateful, hurtful pursuit of David, they would inevitably reap trouble themselves. And they did.

So will Jesus' enemies today, unless they change their ways. We should pray for their salvation. But we can be sure that if they resist, God will repay.

Lord, I pray for Your ultimate, perfect justice.

Song of Solomon 5–8 / 1 Corinthians 15:35–58 / Psalm 141

BETTER THINGS AHEAD

So it is with the resurrection of the dead: Sown in corruption, raised in incorruption; sown in dishonor, raised in glory; sown in weakness, raised in power; sown a natural body, raised a spiritual body.

1 CORINTHIANS 15:42–44 HCSB

Spiritual growth generates an increasing unease—even hatred—of our natural selves. As we come closer to Jesus, we see more clearly our own sinfulness and need of God's grace.

We all have a long list of sins, past and present. Often, as we gain ground in one area, we lose in another. More and more, we recognize the pride and self-sufficiency in our hearts. The Christian life is a never-ending battle against our old nature.

But that shouldn't surprise us. Jesus said that following Him requires the denial of ourselves (Matthew 16:24). Peter taught, "As obedient children, do not be conformed to the desires of your former ignorance" (1 Peter 1:14 HCSB). The apostle Paul, in today's scripture, indicated we're all on a journey, from lesser to greater—from nothing to everything.

If you sometimes feel corrupt, dishonorable, weak, or all too human, know that something better—perfection—lies ahead. When you commit to Jesus, He commits to you, promising incorruption, glory, and power in a new body that will never fail in any way.

Don't let the daily struggle get you down. We Christians have better things ahead.

Thank You, Lord, for this growing process.
I trust You to see me through to heaven.

Isaiah 1–2 / 1 Corinthians 16 / Psalm 142

YOUR MISSION: SERVE

I was glad when Stephanas, Fortunatus and Achaicus arrived,
because they have supplied what was lacking from you. For they
refreshed my spirit and yours also. Such men deserve recognition.

1 CORINTHIANS 16:17–18 NIV

Many men crave recognition. One guy buys a hot car to turn other people's heads. Another guy makes a ton of money, then donates toward a building that will carry his name.

But even the guys who don't pursue flashy, public notoriety would like to be recognized in some way. The apostle Paul, in today's scripture, describes a beautiful method for being remembered, one with lasting value: service.

Stephanas and his family were the first Christian believers in Achaia, the region surrounding the city of Corinth (1 Corinthians 16:15). He was one of just a handful of people baptized by Paul, who saw his mission primarily as preaching (1:14–17). Along with Fortunatus and Achaicus, men named only in today's scripture, Stephanas served—and Paul said that was deserving of recognition.

You don't have to be rich, famous, or good-looking to serve—nor should those qualities stand in the way of service. You might have business, athletic, musical, or medical skills—or you may not. You can serve either way. Any committed Christian man, following God's leading, can refresh another believer's spirit. When you do, you're guaranteed notice and appreciation—by the other person and God. And that's plenty.

I'd like You to recognize me, Lord. . .please empower me to serve.

Isaiah 3–5 / 2 Corinthians 1:1–11 / Psalm 143:1–6

NOT JUSTICE, GRACE

Don't put your servant on trial, for no one is innocent before you.
PSALM 143:2 NLT

Kids love to complain, "It's not fair!" Adults often make statements like, "I want justice!"

Recommendation: Don't say such things to God.

Every one of us is a rebel against our Creator. We were sinful from conception (Psalm 51:5), and throughout our lives we've taken many opportunities to do our own thing. God, whose word is law, has patiently borne our disrespect and disobedience, giving us countless opportunities to return to His good graces.

Do that humbly, and all is well. Try to argue that you've been handled unfairly or can make some special claim on justice? No. If God has eyebrows, you can be sure they'll be raised.

The psalmist David begged God's protection from and vindication against his many enemies. But within his prayer, David spoke the words of today's scripture. He knew he was entirely dependent on God's mercy and grace. David recognized, as did the apostle Paul a thousand years later, that "nothing good lives in me, that is, in my sinful nature" (Romans 7:18 NLT).

This is true of us as well. So let's take our frustrations to God carefully. Yes, He loves us and wants to hear our prayers. But beware of demanding "fairness" and "justice" from Him. What we all need is *grace*.

Lord, I thank You for dealing with me better than my sins deserve. Please keep me humble and show me grace.

Isaiah 6–8 / 2 Corinthians 1:12–2:4 / Psalm 143:7–12

IT BEARS REPEATING. . .

In the year that King Uzziah died, I saw the Lord, high and exalted, seated on a throne; and the train of his robe filled the temple. Above him were seraphim, each with six wings: With two wings they covered their faces, with two they covered their feet, and with two they were flying. And they were calling to one another: "Holy, holy, holy is the LORD Almighty."

ISAIAH 6:1–3 NIV

Other people have made this observation, but it bears repeating: in heaven, angels worship God by declaring—three times—His holiness.

God is merciful (Deuteronomy 4:31), but we have no record of angels crying, "Merciful, merciful, merciful!" God is love (1 John 4:8), but scripture carries no threefold celebration of that attribute, either. Nor do we see triple repetitions of characteristics like His power, grace, wisdom, or even goodness. All of these qualities comprise our awesome God, but His holiness is the one trait that's shouted three times.

That holiness defies a full explanation. Because He is God—the one eternal, all-powerful, all-knowing, all-everything being—He is infinitely beyond our human experience. Yet He tells us, "Be holy, because I am holy" (1 Peter 1:16 NIV, quoting Leviticus 11:44–45).

People are "holy" when they're set apart by and for God. Then we can aspire to greater God-likeness by the choices we make. Today, let's choose to be holy.

It bears repeating, Lord—You are holy. Empower me to be holy like You.

Isaiah 9–10 / 2 Corinthians 2:5–17 / Psalm 144

CAPTIVE TO WHOM?

Thank God! He has made us his captives and continues to lead us along in Christ's triumphal procession. Now he uses us to spread the knowledge of Christ everywhere, like a sweet perfume.
2 CORINTHIANS 2:14 NLT

Like it or not, you are not your own man. No matter how smart and successful you are, no matter how hard you've worked to distinguish yourself from the pack, you're actually a slave. It's either to Satan and sin or to God for good.

> *Don't you realize that you become the slave of whatever you choose to obey? You can be a slave to sin, which leads to death, or you can choose to obey God, which leads to righteous living. Thank God! Once you were slaves of sin, but now you wholeheartedly obey this teaching we have given you. Now you are free from your slavery to sin, and you have become slaves to righteous living.*
> ROMANS 6:16–18 NLT

In the words of today's scripture, we are "his (God's) captives," being led in a victorious procession through a conquered land. But this is no humiliating ritual for us—it's a high honor that God is using to draw others to Himself. As Christians, we are a sweet perfume "to those who are being saved" (2 Corinthians 2:16 NLT).

It's okay—fantastic, actually—to be God's captive. Accept your role happily. The alternative is terrible.

Thank You, God, for taking me captive. There's no better way to be.

Isaiah 11–13 / 2 Corinthians 3 / Psalm 145

REALIZE THAT GOD IS FAR BEYOND

Great is the LORD and most worthy of praise;
his greatness no one can fathom.

PSALM 145:3 NIV

We can be saved with relatively little knowledge of God. Just accepting certain facts—that He *is*, that we don't live up to His standards, and that He sent Jesus to die on the cross for our sins—is enough to get us into God's family. But then we have the opportunity and responsibility to grow in the understanding of "our Father in heaven" (Matthew 6:9 NIV).

The Bible tells us everything God saw fit to disclose about Himself. It's more than enough to occupy our finite human minds through decades of careful study—but still only a tiny fraction of who God actually is.

As we grow spiritually, we recognize more and more that God is far beyond His creation…that He is far beyond *us*. While holding tightly to the plainly revealed truths of scripture, we stop trying to squeeze God into any kind of box. Many of our cultural, denominational, and personal expectations must fall away as we allow God to be God— which He will be, no matter what we might think of Him. But by acknowledging His immense greatness, which "no one can fathom," we lessen the stress of this broken world—and prepare ourselves for the time when we'll be in His perfect presence.

You are great, Lord, and most worthy of praise.
No one can fathom Your greatness!

Isaiah 14–16 / 2 Corinthians 4 / Psalm 146

HARD TIMES

For our light affliction, which is but for a moment, is working
for us a far more surpassing and eternal weight of glory,
while we look, not at the things that are seen, but at the
things that are not seen. For the things that are seen are
temporal, but the things that are not seen are eternal.

2 CORINTHIANS 4:17–18 SKJV

Christian guys of advancing age probably remember when the world seemed calmer, more logical, less crazed than today. Many long for "simpler times" that younger Christians have never experienced. Whatever our age, we all feel the stress of this broken world.

The apostle Paul could relate. He lived in difficult times, when the government, religious leaders, everyday people—even nature—opposed him: "Five times I received from the Jews forty lashes less one. Three times I was beaten with rods. Once I was stoned. Three times I endured shipwreck. A night and a day I have been in the deep. I have been on journeys often, in peril from waters, in peril from robbers, in peril by my own countrymen, in peril by the Gentiles, in peril in the city, in peril in the wilderness, in peril in the sea, in peril among false brothers" (2 Corinthians 11:24–26 SKJV).

But reread 2 Corinthians 4:17–18 and really contemplate Paul's reaction. Think you could take that perspective today?

Forgive me, Lord, when I complain. Remind me
that You use hard times to make me better.

Isaiah 17–19 / 2 Corinthians 5 / Psalm 147:1–11

MORE TO THE STORY. . .

In that day there will be a highway from Egypt to Assyria.
The Assyrians will go to Egypt and the Egyptians to Assyria.
ISAIAH 19:23 NIV

If you're familiar with Old Testament history, today's scripture may have a frightful ring. From far back in Israel's history—dating to Moses' time—Egypt was often a powerful enemy of God's people. Assyria came on the scene much later, as the world power that wiped out the northern Jewish tribes in 722 BC. If those countries are communicating and mobilizing, things must be very bad for God's chosen nation.

Well, actually, there's more to the story.

The end of Isaiah 19:23 reads, "The Egyptians and Assyrians will worship together." And the passage continues by saying, "In that day Israel will be the third, along with Egypt and Assyria, a blessing on the earth. The LORD Almighty will bless them, saying, 'Blessed be Egypt my people, Assyria my handiwork, and Israel my inheritance'" (verses 24–25 NIV).

The people and situations that so trouble us today can be completely turned around in God's good time. The circumstances that frighten and oppress us will have a totally different appearance on the other side of Jesus' return.

Whatever is bothering you today, know this: it's absolutely within God's knowledge and power. There is always more to the story than you see right now.

I'm grateful, Lord, for Your sovereign control over
all things. Please give me peace and hope.

Isaiah 20–23 / 2 Corinthians 6 / Psalm 147:12–20

THE FORECAST

He sends the snow like white wool; he scatters frost upon
the ground like ashes. He hurls the hail like stones. Who
can stand against his freezing cold? Then, at his command,
it all melts. He sends his winds, and the ice thaws.

PSALM 147:16–18 NLT

If you're reading this devotional in a northern climate, today's scripture is a reminder: in weeks to come, it's going to get cold. Maybe you enjoy wintertime. The psalm writer didn't seem to—"who can stand against [God's] freezing cold?" he asked.

But after God sends cold, frost, and snow, He provides warm breezes that melt the winter's ice. It's all part of an orderly weather cycle that's endured since Noah stepped off the ark—and will continue till the end of time (see Genesis 8:22).

Certainly, there are the occasional extremities—tornadoes, hurricanes, blizzards, floods, and droughts—but these too have occurred for millennia and are under God's control.

Finite human beings will never fully understand why God allows destructive weather that kills and maims and leaves people homeless. Nor can we understand why He gives us so many pleasant days, weeks, years, and decades.

As Christians, we simply trust that God has reasons for everything He does. . .whether He sends stormy or pleasant days. A time is coming when every traumatic event—in either our physical or emotional environments—is part of the forgotten past.

Thank You for the forecast of good things
ahead. Come quickly, Lord Jesus!

Isaiah 24:1–26:19 / 2 Corinthians 7 / Psalm 148

TREACHERY!

The treacherous act treacherously; the treacherous deal very treacherously.
ISAIAH 24:16 HCSB

Treachery encompasses betrayal, disloyalty, and faithlessness. In marriages and corporate boardrooms, in churches and Christian organizations and all the way up to the highest levels of government, treachery seems to be the spirit of the age. Faithful people look like a dwindling minority anymore.

Well, that's depressing.

But it's also a realistic, biblical perspective on life. We don't do ourselves any favors by complaining about things or trying to convince ourselves that "people are basically good."

Today's verse comes from a chapter describing God's coming judgment. Because of all their treachery—their disloyalty to the God who made and keeps them—sinful people are heading for disaster. But for those who wait on Him, God "will wipe away the tears from every face and remove His people's disgrace" (Isaiah 25:8 HCSB).

Don't let the evil of this world surprise you. Pray that it doesn't bring you down. Treacherous people will act treacherously, but your job is to stay faithful—to God, to your family commitments, to what is moral and legal and good.

It won't be easy, but it's definitely worth it. You'll bless your own family, friends, neighbors, and coworkers, and honor the God who deserves complete loyalty. And then you can look forward to His ultimate reward.

Please help me to stay faithful, Lord. You deserve it, and this world needs my example.

Isaiah 26:20–28:29 / 2 Corinthians 8 / Psalm 149–150

LET'S GET THIS STRAIGHT

"I will make. . .righteousness the plumb line."
Isaiah 28:17 niv

An elderly farmer enjoyed rejecting a nearby businessman's ongoing interest in the old man's land. Apparently, the neighbor's bank balance exceeded his integrity. "He's so crooked," the farmer exclaimed, "that when he dies they won't bury him. They'll have to screw him into the ground!"

Sometimes, a person's crookedness is obvious. Other times—perhaps deep within ourselves—it's more subtle. Human beings, even those of us who follow Jesus and have His Holy Spirit in our lives, are often tempted to cut ethical corners and then justify ourselves. That's why God gave us a clear standard: His Word. It describes and prescribes our Lord's righteousness, the plumb line by which we measure our own "straightness."

To be clear, we don't obey biblical rules to earn salvation—that's purely the gift of God, received by faith in Christ. But once we're saved, once we've been adopted into God's family, we have a responsibility to become more and more like Jesus. We are to "work out [our] salvation with fear and trembling" (Philippians 2:12 niv). That's not a terror of God, who accepts us "in the Beloved" (Ephesians 1:6 skjv) and welcomes us to His "throne of grace" (Hebrews 4:16 niv). It's a fear of the sin we're still capable of committing.

Let's get this straight: God's standard is the only one that matters.

Lord, please help me to know Your Word and then live it out.

Isaiah 29–30 / 2 Corinthians 9 / Proverbs 1:1–9

BIG BLESSING

God is able to bless you abundantly, so that in all things at all times,
having all that you need, you will abound in every good work.
2 CORINTHIANS 9:8 NIV

Look at the superlatives in today's scripture: God is able to bless you *abundantly*, so that in *all* things at *all* times, having *all* that you need, you will *abound* in *every* good work.

Our God is very rich (He owns the whole universe, you know) and also very generous. According to the apostle Paul, the Lord is eager to lavish blessing on His people. The catch? He blesses those who bless others by their giving.

Paul encouraged the Christians of Corinth to give toward the needs of poor believers in and around Jerusalem. The example had already been set by the churches of Macedonia. "In the midst of a very severe trial," Paul wrote, "their overflowing joy and their extreme poverty welled up in rich generosity" (2 Corinthians 8:2 NIV). This unselfish sowing would lead to a large harvest of blessing (9:6). But don't think it's all about money. Paul wrote that God would "enlarge the harvest of your *righteousness*" (2 Corinthians 9:10 NIV, emphasis added).

God can (and possibly will) return the money you give, with interest. But He really wants to meet your physical, emotional, and spiritual needs so that "you will abound in every good work."

Lord, You gave me all I have. Now help me to
share generously with those in need.

Isaiah 31–33 / 2 Corinthians 10 / Proverbs 1:10–22

FORGET EGYPT. . .

*Woe to those who go down to Egypt for help, who rely on
horses and trust in chariots because they are many and in
horsemen because they are very strong, but they look not to
the Holy One of Israel, nor seek and consult the Lord!*

ISAIAH 31:1 AMPC

Historically, Isaiah 31 is a warning to God's people in Judah. Assyria
was threatening Jerusalem, and Isaiah demanded his countrymen not
look to Egypt for help.

For years, God had warned His people—both in Judah and
the northern kingdom of Israel—against their idolatry, greed, and
oppression. His patience ran out with Israel around 722 BC, when
He allowed Assyrian soldiers to overrun the nation and scatter its
people. Now, about twenty years later, with Assyria threatening Judah,
God's people chose not to "seek and consult the Lord." They wanted
an alliance with Pharaoh.

Through Isaiah, God declared that "the Egyptians are men and
not God, and their horses are flesh and not spirit; and when the
Lord stretches out His hand, both [Egypt] who helps will stumble,
and [Judah] who is helped will fall, and they will all perish and be
consumed together" (Isaiah 31:3 AMPC).

What does this mean for us? Well, ask yourself: *What is my "Egypt,"
that escape route I turn to before I seek God?* Whatever it is, it won't save
you. Look only to the Holy One of Israel.

Help me, Lord, to bring You my problems immediately, every time.

Isaiah 34–36 / 2 Corinthians 11 / Proverbs 1:23–26

LISTEN UP

*Turn at my rebuke. Behold, I will pour out my spirit
to you; I will make my words known to you.*

PROVERBS 1:23 SKJV

Though the words above sound like God's, they are actually attributed to "Wisdom" (Proverbs 1:20). Personified as a woman, "she cries in the chief place of gathering, in the openings of the gates; she utters her words in the city, saying, 'How long, you simple ones, will you love simplicity, and the scorners delight in their scorning, and fools hate knowledge?'" (verses 21–22 SKJV).

Of course, Wisdom originates with God, so whatever "she" tells us will be what He would say. And in today's scripture, Wisdom implores, "Turn at my rebuke."

A rebuke is an expression of strong disapproval. Haven't we all heard that at some time, from a friend, pastor, wife—or within our own spirit? Not every negative voice should be heeded, but God will often send Wisdom to turn us from some foolish path. If the voice you're hearing confirms what you know God's Word says, listen up.

When we stop to consider Wisdom's call, she then pours out her spirit and makes her words known. All of this is true of Wisdom's source too.

When you hear Wisdom's rebuke, stop. Change direction. There's a reward for listening but trouble for plowing ahead (see the nine verses following today's scripture).

*I don't want to be a fool, Lord. Tune my ear to
Wisdom's call and strengthen me to obey.*

Isaiah 37–38 / 2 Corinthians 12:1–10 / Proverbs 1:27–33

GROW UP TO BE. . .WEAK?

So for the sake of Christ, I am well pleased and take pleasure
in infirmities, insults, hardships, persecutions, perplexities
and distresses; for when I am weak [in human strength],
then am I [truly] strong (able, powerful in divine strength).
2 CORINTHIANS 12:10 AMPC

The Christian life should be an ongoing process of growth. But that growth may not take the form we first assume it will.

Yes, we should engage in "spiritual training" (1 Timothy 4:8 AMPC) in order to "resist the devil" (James 4:7 AMPC). The strength we develop, however, doesn't grow out of ourselves—it is entirely God's power, working through us.

We probably think of the apostle Paul as a paragon of strength. He suffered incredible hardships to boldly preach the gospel to people who hated and often attacked him. But here's how he described other people's impressions of himself: "his personality and bodily presence are weak, and his speech and delivery are utterly contemptible" (2 Corinthians 10:10 AMPC). Later in that same letter to the Corinthian Christians, as you see in today's opening scripture, Paul admitted to being infirm, perplexed, and weak. That's okay—and not only okay, but truly a good thing, because his human weakness made way for *God's* strength.

If you feel like you're not strong enough to succeed in the Christian life, congratulations! You're right where God wants you. . .where *He* can provide the strength you need.

Please be my strength, Lord. I need You.

Isaiah 39–40 / 2 Corinthians 12:11–13:14 / Proverbs 2:1–15

NO ONE

*Who else has held the oceans in his hand? Who has measured off
the heavens with his fingers? Who else knows the weight of the
earth or has weighed the mountains and hills on a scale?*

ISAIAH 40:12 NLT

Most Christians have heard—if they haven't memorized—Isaiah
40:31 (NLT): "Those who trust in the LORD will find new strength.
They will soar high on wings like eagles. They will run and not grow
weary. They will walk and not faint." Isaiah 40:12, quoted above, is the
opening verse of the passage that culminates in this incredible promise.

God's promises are backed by His own power and goodness. Only
God can do what He does, so the answer to the questions above is
"no one." Who could possibly teach God or give Him advice (verses
13–14)? Again, no one. He knows everything—in fact, He defines
reality.

Compared to God, "All the nations of the world are but a drop
in the bucket" (Isaiah 40:15 NLT). He sits high above the earth,
observing all of us like so many grasshoppers (verse 22). "To whom
will you compare me?" God asks. "Who is my equal?" (verse 25 NLT).

No one. Our God is absolutely unique, supreme above all other
things—because all other things came from Him. When He promises
strength to those who trust in Him, believe it. No one else could
make such a promise.

I trust You, Lord. No one else can renew my strength!

Isaiah 41–42 / Galatians 1 / Proverbs 2:16–22

CHANGE IS POSSIBLE

*"The man who formerly persecuted us is now
preaching the faith he once tried to destroy."*
GALATIANS 1:23 NIV

In the years following Jesus' crucifixion and resurrection, nobody
would have bet on Saul of Tarsus becoming a Christian. In his own
words, "You have heard of my previous way of life in Judaism, how
intensely I persecuted the church of God and tried to destroy it. I
was advancing in Judaism beyond many of my own age among my
people and was extremely zealous for the traditions of my fathers"
(Galatians 1:13–14 NIV). Yet that "Hebrew of Hebrews" (Philippians
3:5 NIV) did become a follower of Jesus. . .and, known as Paul, went
on to change the world for Christ.

It took a miracle to convert Saul the persecutor into Paul the
apostle. But God specializes in miracles. While Saul's Damascus road
experience (Acts 9) is extreme, it's still just an example of the change
God works in every person who believes. Whether it's a five-year-old
"asking Jesus into his heart" before bedtime or a belligerent, drunken
fifty-something finally humbling himself before the Lord, salvation
is always a miracle that takes a person "out of darkness into [God's]
wonderful light" (1 Peter 2:9 NIV).

If someone you care about—even yourself—doesn't seem capable
of positive change, remind yourself of the former persecutor "now
preaching the faith he once tried to destroy."

Only You, Lord, make change possible. Help me live up to my new life.

Isaiah 43:1–44:20 / Galatians 2 / Proverbs 3:1–12

WHEN YOU'RE DISCIPLINED

My child, don't reject the LORD's discipline, and don't be upset
when he corrects you. For the LORD corrects those he loves,
just as a father corrects a child in whom he delights.

PROVERBS 3:11–12 NLT

Perhaps your parents put a younger version of you in time-out. Maybe they grounded you or took away privileges. Maybe they even spanked you at times.

If you experienced any of those forms of discipline, did you enjoy them? Probably not. Looking back now, do you appreciate what your parents were trying to accomplish, however imperfectly? Probably so.

Meting out discipline is one of a parent's most important duties. Accepting and learning from that discipline is one of the child's. When both parties take their duties seriously, everyone benefits—the kid grows into a responsible adult, mom and dad enjoy the positive result of their labors.

This is as true in the spiritual realm as it is in the physical. God, as the perfectly wise, all-knowing Father, disciplines His kids for their eternal benefit. It is sensible—even for grown men—to accept and learn from this discipline.

When things aren't going your way, ask yourself, *Could this be God's discipline? If so, what is He trying to teach me? What should I be doing differently?* Whatever you do, don't whine and complain and try to run away. God is training up a son in whom He delights.

Father God, help me to accept Your wise discipline with appreciation.

Isaiah 44:21–46:13 / Galatians 3:1–18 / Proverbs 3:13–26

ALL BY FAITH

*Just as Abraham believed God, and it was credited
to him for righteousness, then understand that
those who have faith are Abraham's sons.*

GALATIANS 3:6–7 HCSB

Paul wrote to the churches of Galatia to counteract a brewing heresy—that anyone who wanted to follow Jesus needed to obey the requirements of Jewish law.

"I am amazed that you are so quickly turning away from Him who called you by the grace of Christ and are turning to a different gospel," Paul wrote (Galatians 1:6 HCSB). Of course, it wasn't a *gospel* (meaning "good news") at all. By adding works to the simplicity of faith in Jesus, these Galatians risked missing salvation entirely. Paul noted that Abraham's belief in God "was credited to him for righteousness." *Then* he was then free to do the good works that proved his faith was real.

The same is true for us. Church attendance is an excellent thing—but it is not what saves us. Service to our fellow man is wonderful—but does not cancel out our sins. Giving money to missions and social needs is great—but no amount of money could ever purchase God's pardon. He offers salvation freely, and we can only accept it by faith.

Nobody is saved by good works. But once we are saved, good works should follow. Let's be sure to keep everything in its proper order.

*Lord, I believe—thank You for saving me.
Now help me do good works out of gratitude.*

Isaiah 47:1–49:13 / Galatians 3:19–29 / Proverbs 3:27–35

GOD'S CREATION

*Yes, My hand has laid the foundation of the earth, and My
right hand has spread out the heavens; when I call to them,
they stand forth together [to execute My decrees].*

ISAIAH 48:13 AMPC

Drive through the Corn Belt in summertime, and you'll understand
the nickname. Every year, this swath of the American Midwest from
the Dakotas to Ohio produces billions of corn plants, perfectly spaced
from each other and from row to row. Nobody would ever think those
ranks and files of corn happened by accident.

But many tell themselves that corn plants—as well as trees and
people and things in the sky—developed by chance, without input
from any divine being. In today's scripture, *the* divine being corrects
that foolishness.

In His wisdom and power, God created all things for His
purpose and glory. Many unbelievers resist that truth, hoping to
absolve themselves of responsibility to God. But even Christians
can become distracted, failing to give the Lord His due respect.

Today, as you step outside, consciously consider creation—not for
nature's sake, but as a reminder of the powerful God who made all
things. Whether your view is farm country, an ocean, the mountains,
open plains, or the concrete jungle of a city, God's design can be seen
if you'll look. Recognize it and give Him all the credit.

*You are amazing, God—I can see that in the beauty, variety,
and order of Your world. Help me never to forget Your greatness.*

Isaiah 49:14–51:23 / Galatians 4:1–11 / Proverbs 4:1–19

RAGS TO RICHES

Because you are his sons, God sent the Spirit of his Son into our hearts, the Spirit who calls out, "Abba, Father." So you are no longer a slave, but God's child; and since you are his child, God has made you also an heir.

GALATIANS 4:6–7 NIV

As we grow in our Christian lives, many things change. We learn more about God's Word and want to spend greater time in it. We recognize how deeply sinful we are and increasingly appreciate Jesus' work on the cross. And we develop a growing awe of the transformation God brings to our lives, swapping the rags of our broken, rebellious humanness for the infinite riches of His heavenly family.

The apostle Paul scolded the Galatians for foolishly overlooking this grace of God. They were listening to false teachers who told them salvation required the observance of old Jewish rules. But salvation is purely by faith in Jesus Christ, who came "to redeem those under the law" (Galatians 4:5 NIV). Jesus bought us from the slave market of sin not to become our new owner but to be our *brother*. And as Jesus' heavenly Father becomes our Father too, we can cry out to Him in the familiar, loving term that Jesus Himself uses: *Abba*.

The study of this incredible rags-to-riches story will take us through all eternity. But you know what? Eternity starts today.

I am grateful to be Your son, Father.
Thank You, Jesus, for redeeming me!

Isaiah 52–54 / Galatians 4:12–31 / Proverbs 4:20–27

THE GUARDED HEART

Guard your heart above all else, for it determines the course of your life.
PROVERBS 4:23 NLT

The Bible mentions "the heart"—meaning the inner part of each man where his thoughts, emotions, and desires dwell—almost 1,000 times. Though we may not understand even our own hearts, God does, and He knows that our hearts are "deceitful above all things and beyond cure" (Jeremiah 17:9 NIV).

The good news, though, is that God, through Jesus Christ and the indwelling Holy Spirit, has not just healed but renewed the hearts of men whose faith is in Jesus. But we still are prone to sin and to wandering from Him. That is why it is so important that we commit ourselves to zealously guarding our hearts against any thoughts, emotions, or speech that could lead us to sin and bad decisions.

Worldly thinking today tells us that we find true happiness by following our hearts. But today's scripture verse warns that we must guard our hearts above everything else, for the heart "determines the course of your life."

So make sure that you diligently guard yourself from images, words, and other outside influences that can pollute your heart and stunt your growth as a man of faith and negatively alter the course of your life.

Father, thank You for teaching me the importance of guarding my heart. Please give me an awareness of things in this life that could compromise my purity of heart.

WAITING EAGERLY

But we who live by the Spirit eagerly wait to receive by faith the righteousness God has promised to us.

GALATIANS 5:5 NLT

In the Bible, the word *wait* can mean different things. For example, the people of Israel were commanded to wait in place until the Lord gave them the visual go-ahead to get up and move out (Exodus 13). And throughout the psalms, we read of the writers' pledges to wait on God to act on their behalf.

In Galatians 5:5, "wait" suggests something different. This verse tells us that we Christians are to *eagerly* wait to fully receive something God has already given those whose faith is in Jesus Christ. This is an *active* waiting, for it includes a decision to live by the leading of the Holy Spirit.

We believers will one day get to live in a perfect relationship with God, who will fulfill His promise to make everything about us right and perfect. In the meantime, we get to live in a type of expectation that can profoundly affect our lives—at home, at work, everywhere—in amazing, world-changing ways.

Are you waiting eagerly for God to make His promises your reality? How does that kind of waiting affect your daily life?

Heavenly Father, thank You for saving me and setting me on the path to Your kingdom in heaven. As I eagerly wait to receive my eternal inheritance, may I live and grow every day in faith and in righteousness.

Isaiah 58–59 / Galatians 6 / Proverbs 5:15–23

WHY WE DO GOOD

*Let us not become weary in doing good, for at the proper
time we will reap a harvest if we do not give up. Therefore,
as we have opportunity, let us do good to all people, especially
to those who belong to the family of believers.*

GALATIANS 6:9–10 NIV

When you came to faith in Jesus Christ, God gave you His Holy Spirit and guaranteed you a place in His eternal kingdom. But He didn't take you home right away. Instead, He gave you a wonderful assignment: to do good for others here on earth.

The Bible is crystal clear: good works here don't earn you an eternal home with God in heaven (Ephesians 2:8–9). But as a man who has been saved through faith in Jesus, you have the privilege of blessing others through your words and actions in the here and now.

You aren't saved *by* good works—you are saved *for* good works!

Doing good for others does wonders for your heart and mind. Not only that, it thwarts the devil's evil plans, shows others a real picture of Jesus' work in you, and glorifies your Father in heaven.

*Lord God, I want to be a source of good in this fallen world.
Please provide for me opportunities to do good for hurting people
who need to see You in what I do for them. I also ask that You
use the good I do to open doors for me to share the gospel.*

Isaiah 60–62 / Ephesians 1 / Proverbs 6:1–5

SEALED WITH THE HOLY SPIRIT

*And you also were included in Christ when you heard the message
of truth, the gospel of your salvation. When you believed, you
were marked in him with a seal, the promised Holy Spirit, who
is a deposit guaranteeing our inheritance until the redemption
of those who are God's possession—to the praise of his glory.*

EPHESIANS 1:13–14 NIV

Some incredible things happened when you came to saving faith in
Jesus Christ. Today's scripture verses tell us that at the very moment
you first believed, God marked you with His own "seal"—the promised
Holy Spirit.

This "seal" is a sort of down payment on what God has already
given you as one who has been saved by grace through faith and who is
therefore guaranteed the inheritance Jesus both promised and secured
through His willing sacrifice on a Roman cross. The Holy Spirit is
God's claim on us as His very own.

What an amazing fulfillment of an eternity-altering promise!

Jesus promised His followers abundant life (John 10:10) in the
Spirit, a life of power, joy, and assurance of a home in heaven with Him.

All that because we've believed and received!

*Father God, thank You for sending Your Son to earth to live a
perfect life and then die on the cross so that all my sins could
be forgiven. And thank You for putting the Holy Spirit inside
me as a pledge of my eternal inheritance in heaven.*

Isaiah 63:1–65:16 / Ephesians 2 / Proverbs 6:6–19

ALL GOD'S DOING

*God saved you by his grace when you believed. And you can't take
credit for this; it is a gift from God. Salvation is not a reward for
the good things we have done, so none of us can boast about it.*

Ephesians 2:8–9 nlt

Many men have a difficult time believing that they can receive something
for nothing. In their minds, they have to contribute *something* when
someone gives them a gift of great value. But the Bible teaches that we
can do *nothing*—can contribute *nothing*—to our salvation, that Jesus
did everything to pay for our salvation when He died on the cross and
was raised from the dead three days later.

But we can take this truth a step further by recognizing that we
bring God *less than nothing* when we come to Him. When we first
came to Jesus, we bring nothing of value—only our lives of sin and
lostness. In exchange for our mess, God showers us with His grace
and gives us forgiveness of sin and eternal life.

Once we are saved, God begins working in us, enabling us to
do good works for Him. But those works don't save us; rather, they
are expressions of gratitude for doing for us what we could never
do for ourselves.

*Lord Jesus, when I first came to You in faith, I had
nothing to offer but my life of sin and two empty hands
extended to receive from You. Thank You!*

WHAT GOD LOOKS FOR

"For My hand has made all those things, and all those things have been," says the LORD. "But I will look to this man, even to him who is poor and of a contrite spirit and who trembles at My word."

ISAIAH 66:2 SKJV

It's amazing to think that the same God who created all things actually looks for certain qualities in each man, isn't it? Isaiah 66:2 offers a promise and a challenge to a man who desires a stronger faith and a deeper walk with God. It tells us that the Lord looks to the man who is humble, who confesses his sins regularly, and who carefully listens to what God says to him.

God is faithful to His promises and to His people because faithfulness is part of who He is. We men, on the other hand, aren't naturally inclined toward faithfulness to the Lord. That's why we must decide *daily* to seek humility, to confess our sins to God, and to seek out what God says to us in His Word.

Those are the actions of the man God looks to and seeks to bless!

Dear Lord, I want my life of faith to be marked by humility and contrition and a high regard for Your Word. I know that You look with favor on a man who knows he needs Your favor and who knows what it takes to receive it. I choose today to believe Your promise to look to me.

Jeremiah 1–2 / Ephesians 4:17–32 / Proverbs 6:27–35

FALLING IN LOVE AGAIN

The word of the Lord came to me: "Go and proclaim in the hearing of Jerusalem: This is what the Lord says: 'I remember the devotion of your youth, how as a bride you loved me and followed me through the wilderness, through a land not sown.'"

Jeremiah 2:1–2 NIV

Remember the last time you attended a wedding? As the bride and groom stand before their friends and family to recite their vows, it's almost as if they forget that anyone is in the room with them as they fix their gaze on one another. They are *that* much in love with one another.

Sadly, many married couples don't maintain that level of love and devotion. In time, they fall out of love and the relationship becomes joyless and sterile.

That's also what happened to the people of Jerusalem.

In today's scripture verses, the Lord remembered how His people had loved Him and how they were so willing to follow Him anywhere. But now, the people's passion for their God was no more. Now, they weren't willing to follow Him with their whole hearts.

Take a good look at your relationship with the Lord as it is today. Do you love Him the way you did when you began your life of faith? Or has the fire begun to wane? If it's the latter, it may be time to renew Your commitment to Him today.

Lord God, help me renew my passionate love for You today.

Jeremiah 3:1–4:22 / Ephesians 5 / Proverbs 7:1–5

PREPARING THE GROUND

This is what the Lord says to the people of Judah and to Jerusalem:
"Break up your unplowed ground and do not sow among thorns."

Jeremiah 4:3 niv

If you've ever successfully grown a backyard vegetable garden, you probably understand the importance of preparing the soil before you plant the seeds. You need to break up the hardened soil, discard some rocks, and pull weeds. If you don't do those things, the seeds may sprout but will quickly die because the young plants can't take root.

The Bible likens the human heart to soil (see Jesus' Parable of the Sower in Luke 8:1–15). In today's scripture verse, God calls His people to "Break up your unplowed ground," meaning that the people needed to soften their hearts toward the Lord and His Word.

What was true in Jeremiah's day is true now: God wants His people to make sure that the soil of their hearts is ready to receive what He has for them. He wants them to search themselves and then confess and repent of their sins. And He wants them to recommit themselves to a living, growing relationship with Him.

Commit yourself today to doing those things, and God will soften your heart and bring you closer to Himself.

> *Lord God, please give me a soft heart so that You can*
> *mold me and make me the man You want me to be.*
> *Help me to break up the unplowed ground of my heart.*

Jeremiah 4:23–5:31 / Ephesians 6 / Proverbs 7:6–27

READY FOR WAR

For we are not fighting against flesh-and-blood enemies, but against evil rulers and authorities of the unseen world, against mighty powers in this dark world, and against evil spirits in the heavenly places.

EPHESIANS 6:12 NLT

Any warrior knows that he and his comrades in arms can succeed in war only when they do two things: know their enemy *and* arm themselves for battle.

This is true in the physical realm and even more so in the spiritual.

Paul knew that the Ephesian Christians were in a war, and not one against mere men. This was a spiritual battle with the devil and his forces, which is why he encouraged his friends in Ephesus to arm themselves.

In Ephesians 6:13–17 (NLT), the apostle encouraged the Ephesians to "put on every piece of God's armor so you will be able to resist the enemy in the time of evil." That full armor included:

- the belt of truth (verse 14)
- the body armor of God's righteousness (verse 14)
- for shoes, the peace that comes from the good news of Christ (verse 15)
- the shield of faith (verse 16)
- the helmet of salvation (verse 16)
- the sword of the Spirit, which is the word of God (verse 16)

We're in a constant state of life-and-death spiritual battle here on earth. But it's a battle God has prepared us to win.

Father in heaven, I understand that I'm in a spiritual battle here on earth. Help me to always be prepared for the enemy's attacks.

A NO-LOSE ARRANGEMENT

For to me, living means living for Christ, and dying is even better.
But if I live, I can do more fruitful work for Christ. So I really
don't know which is better. I'm torn between two desires: I long
to go and be with Christ, which would be far better for me.
PHILIPPIANS 1:21–23 NLT

Paul wrote his letter to the church at Philippi while sitting in a prison cell in Rome. He was in great discomfort, and he knew his life could end soon. Yet Paul still expressed his passionate love for Jesus and his assurance that whether he lived or died, God would be glorified. If Paul lived, he would have more time to tell people about Jesus. But if his physical life was taken, he would be in the very presence of his precious Savior.

Paul understood the frailty of our physical lives. He knew that God alone determined his days here on earth. That's why he was committed to living every day as though it was the last he'd have to preach the message of salvation through Jesus.

God has predetermined the number of days we get to live on this earth. Let's determine in our hearts to proclaim His truth each and every day.

Jesus, whether I live another forty years or whether I die
tomorrow, I want to use each day to glorify You and tell
people about You and what You've done for me.

Jeremiah 7:26–9:16 / Philippians 1:27–2:18 / Proverbs 8:12–21

THE EXAMPLE JESUS SET

*Who, being in very nature God, did not consider equality
with God something to be used to his own advantage;
rather, he made himself nothing by taking the very nature
of a servant, being made in human likeness.*

PHILIPPIANS 2:6–7 NIV

Take a few minutes today and think about the love that motivated Jesus, who had lived for all eternity past with His Father in heaven as the second person of the Trinity, to come to earth and live a simple, humble life here on earth.

Jesus could have come to earth and forcibly set everything right just by willing it to be so. But instead, He came in love and humility, becoming a man and serving others with His every word and action. In doing that, He set the perfect example for every Christian man to observe and follow.

Jesus was God in the flesh. He never ceased to be God, but He chose to give up some of the privileges of deity. Not only that, He died a grisly, horrifically painful death on a wooden cross—a death reserved for the worst malefactors of the time—so that humans could be forgiven and eternally saved.

What an example Jesus set for us all!

*Lord Jesus, thank You for leaving Your Father's side in heaven
and coming to earth to live a humble, obedient life as a man and
for giving Your life so that I could live with You for all eternity.*

Jeremiah 9:17–11:17 / Philippians 2:19–30 / Proverbs 8:22–36

LISTEN!

"Blessed are those who listen to me, watching daily at my doors, waiting at my doorway. For those who find me find life and receive favor from the LORD. But those who fail to find me harm themselves; all who hate me love death."

PROVERBS 8:34–36 NIV

Many of us men aren't as highly skilled at listening as we should be. Sure, we may *hear* what our wives, our children, or our friends say to us, but when it comes to understanding what's behind the words, we often fall short.

The art of listening is vital to building and maintaining a quality relationship with anyone. That includes our relationship with the Lord. The Bible repeatedly promises that God hears us when we come to Him in prayer. But that listening must be a two-way street, and that's why today's scripture verses promise blessings—another way of saying "happiness"—for those who listen to what God has to say.

God wants a growing, vibrant relationship with His people. That means we must learn to listen to Him. It also means not just hearing Him but also understanding and acting on what He says (James 1:22–25).

Learn to listen to what God says in His Word, and then act on it. This will both build you up in your faith and lead to His blessings.

Lord, help me to learn to listen to You more and more closely each day. I never want to miss out on Your blessings.

Jeremiah 11:18–13:27 / Philippians 3 / Proverbs 9:1–6

THE MOST IMPORTANT THING

*I consider everything a loss because of the surpassing worth of
knowing Christ Jesus my Lord, for whose sake I have lost all
things. I consider them garbage, that I may gain Christ and be
found in him, not having a righteousness of my own that comes
from the law, but that which is through faith in Christ—the
righteousness that comes from God on the basis of faith.*

PHILIPPIANS 3:8–9 NIV

What sorts of things do you consider important and valuable in this
life? Your family? Your career? Your home? Your bank accounts? You
can rightly consider all those things blessings from the Lord. But they
should all take a distant backseat in your life when compared with
the privilege of knowing the Lord Jesus Christ.

That is how the apostle Paul approached his life's accomplishments
and blessings. Before Paul met Jesus, he was an accomplished,
respected Jewish religious leader who believed he was doing God's will
(Philippians 3:5–6). His accomplishments meant everything to him. . .
until he met Jesus. After that, he saw his previous life as "garbage"
when compared with the blessings of knowing and serving his Lord.

Nothing this life has to offer can compare to the most important
thing: knowing Jesus and serving Him with everything you have.

*Lord Jesus, knowing You is of greater value than
anything this world could possibly offer. May my
desire to know You continue to grow each day.*

Jeremiah 14–15 / Philippians 4 / Proverbs 9:7–18

DON'T WORRY!

Do not be anxious about anything, but in every situation, by prayer and petition, with thanksgiving, present your requests to God. And the peace of God, which transcends all understanding, will guard your hearts and your minds in Christ Jesus.

PHILIPPIANS 4:6–7 NIV

At some point in the life of every Christian man, something will come up to cause worry, stress, or doubt. If it's not money—or the lack thereof—then it's a health problem...or conflicts in your human relationships...or....

Worry is one of the spiritual weapons the devil likes to use to trip up men of God, but we have a weapon of our own that the enemy just can't overcome: prayer (Ephesians 6:18).

When we fail to pray, our problems tend to magnify themselves to the point where they seem too big and too insurmountable for us to see past them. That's when worry can turn into something we can't overcome on our own.

When we pray about the problems we face, however, we begin to see things through eyes of faith, not through eyes of worry. Suddenly, things come into perspective.

When you're tempted to worry, pray instead.

Father in heaven, I confess that I sometimes give in to the temptation to worry. Please forgive me and help me to leave the things that cause me to worry in Your able hands. May I always dwell on Your goodness and power, not on things I cannot control.

Jeremiah 16–17 / Colossians 1:1–23 / Proverbs 10:1–5

HOPE AND CONFIDENCE

This is what the LORD says: "Cursed are those who put their trust in mere humans, who rely on human strength and turn their hearts away from the LORD. . . . But blessed are those who trust in the LORD and have made the LORD their hope and confidence."

JEREMIAH 17:5, 7 NLT

God's chosen people had steadily fallen into idolatry and had turned from their God and His promises. In today's scripture verses, the prophet Jeremiah chided the people for turning away from their loving God and putting their trust in their own wisdom and strength.

God's message to the people was both dire and simple: *If you want My blessings and not My cursing, come back to Me, trust Me, and make Me your only hope and confidence.*

Sadly, that same message applies to far too many professing Christian men today.

Your talents and abilities are gifts from the Lord, and you should be grateful for them. Same regarding the material blessings. But those things can be gone in an instant and can't be fully trusted. So place your full trust in the Lord and in His unfailing love and promises of provision—not on the things that will surely pass away.

Heavenly Father, thank You that You alone are worthy of my complete, unwavering trust. Search my heart today and let me know if there are areas in my life where I'm prone to relying on my own strength, talents, and abilities instead of You.

Jeremiah 18:1–20:6 / Colossians 1:24–2:15 / Proverbs 10:6–14

DEEPLY ROOTED FAITH

And now, just as you accepted Christ Jesus as your Lord, you must continue to follow him. Let your roots grow down into him, and let your lives be built on him. Then your faith will grow strong in the truth you were taught, and you will overflow with thankfulness.

COLOSSIANS 2:6–7 NLT

In a place called Echo Caves in South Africa is an old wild fig tree whose roots penetrate the earth to a depth of almost 400 feet. This tree may die at some point, but it won't because the wind uprooted it.

As you might expect, trees with deep, strong root systems are trees that survive and thrive under the harshest conditions. Floods, drought, and wind may come, but these deeply rooted trees carry on.

In today's scripture verses, Paul writes that we believers should "let [our] roots grow down into [Christ]" so that we can grow in our faith. When we choose to do that, we'll continue to grow stronger and deeper in our faith no matter what kinds of difficulties we face. Then, instead of complaining and fretting about our circumstances, we'll walk daily with gratitude toward the Lord.

When you come before the Lord in daily prayer, don't forget to ask Him to help you become more and more rooted in Jesus every day.

Jesus, help me to grow in my faith in You. Give me deep, strong faith so that nothing can shake me or move me.

Jeremiah 20:7–22:19 / Colossians 2:16–3:4 / Proverbs 10:15–26

A DIFFICULT CALLING

But the LORD stands beside me like a great warrior. Before him my persecutors will stumble. They cannot defeat me. They will fail and be thoroughly humiliated. Their dishonor will never be forgotten.

JEREMIAH 20:11 NLT

God called the prophet Jeremiah to a very difficult life. He was commissioned to speak a very difficult and unpopular message, and even his family and close friends came against him with threats of violence if he didn't stop preaching God's message (Jeremiah 20:10).

But Jeremiah didn't stop preaching. He *couldn't* stop: "But if I say, 'I will not mention his word or speak anymore in his name,' his word is in my heart like a fire, a fire shut up in my bones. I am weary of holding it in; indeed, I cannot" (Jeremiah 20:9 NIV).

We, like Jeremiah, today are called to speak the Word of God whenever He gives us the opportunity. Real faith gives us that fire to pray for people and to speak to them the truth of the gospel. It may not be easy to do so—in fact, we may face ridicule and scorn when we talk about Jesus. But our faith and our convictions drive us so that we cannot remain quiet.

Heavenly Father, I know that I'm not necessarily called to an easy life. Following You faithfully and speaking Your truth in this fallen, sinful world will bring ridicule, opposition, and maybe even persecution. Strengthen me and embolden me so that I can stand for Your truth.

THE PEACE OF CHRIST

Let the peace of Christ rule in your hearts, since as members
of one body you were called to peace. And be thankful.

COLOSSIANS 3:15 NIV

In Romans 5:1 (NIV), Paul communicates this wonderful promise: "Therefore, since we have been justified through faith, we have peace with God through our Lord Jesus Christ." The phrase *peace with God* gives us the assurance that we are no longer enemies with the Lord, that He has forgiven our sins, and that He has reserved for us an eternal home with Him in heaven.

No *one* or no *thing* can change our status of being at peace with God (Romans 8:31–39). But there is another kind of peace—the "peace of Christ"—that today's scripture verse suggests is a result of an act of the will.

True inner peace is the result of daily abiding in Christ, of trusting God's written Word, of obeying God's commands, of keeping short accounts with Him when it comes to sin, of communicating with Him daily in prayer, and of dying to self and living for Him.

Neglect any of those things, and you will lack inner peace. Do them, and the peace of Christ will rule in your heart—guaranteed!

Lord Jesus, I want Your peace to rule in my heart and mind
at all times. Reveal to me anything that prevents me from
allowing Your peace to guard my heart every day.

Jeremiah 24–25 / Colossians 4:2–18 / Proverbs 11:1–11

DEVOTED TO PRAYER

Devote yourselves to prayer, being watchful and thankful. And
pray for us, too, that God may open a door for our message, so
that we may proclaim the mystery of Christ, for which I am
in chains. Pray that I may proclaim it clearly, as I should.

COLOSSIANS 4:2–4 NIV

God may not have called you to serve on a foreign mission field, and you may not have the means to help out as much as you'd like financially. But you can still offer important support by doing one simple thing: praying daily for those God has sent overseas.

In Colossians 4:2–4, Paul, the greatest missionary of all time, entreats the Christians in Colossae to devote themselves to prayer at all times, but he also asks them to pray that God would open doors for his ministry so that they could preach the message of salvation through Jesus to new people in new places.

First John 5:14 (NIV) promises, "This is the confidence we have in approaching God: that if we ask anything according to his will, he hears us." Prayer is an expression of faith in a God you know wants to do what you request.

So devote yourself to prayer, keeping in mind those whose life work is preaching the good news.

Lord Jesus, I confess that I don't pray for Your workers as
much as I should. May I be devoted to praying about all things,
including the spread of the gospel message throughout the world.

Jeremiah 26–27 / 1 Thessalonians 1:1–2:8 / Proverbs 11:12–21

THE WHOLE TRUTH

This message came to Jeremiah from the LORD early in the reign of Jehoiakim son of Josiah, king of Judah. "This is what the LORD says: Stand in the courtyard in front of the Temple of the LORD, and make an announcement to the people who have come there to worship from all over Judah. Give them my entire message; include every word."

JEREMIAH 26:1–2 NLT

In the first two verses of Jeremiah 26, God commanded the prophet to speak every word of His message to the people of Judah. God had given Jeremiah some harsh words for the people, and it's not hard to imagine him thinking, *The people will probably accept part of the message, but other parts of it might make them angry with me.*

But Jeremiah was committed to speaking all of God's Word. And he obeyed God's command to, "give them my entire message; include every word." And doing so cost him greatly as he was subjected to intense persecution.

How would you respond if God called you to speak hard truth to a brother in Christ who needed a course correction? Would you find yourself watering down the message, or would you boldly speak the whole truth in love?

Lord God, please give me boldness to speak all of Your truth when You give me the opportunity. Strengthen and embolden me to speak difficult truth to my brothers in Christ who need to hear it.

Jeremiah 28–29 / 1 Thessalonians 2:9–3:13 / Proverbs 11:22–26

SEEKING AND FINDING

"If you look for me wholeheartedly, you will find
me. I will be found by you," says the LORD.
JEREMIAH 29:13–14 NLT

In today's scripture verses, God promises His chosen people—the people of Israel—that they would find Him. . .if they sought Him with their whole hearts.

That promise still applies to us today. Jesus put it like this: "Ask and it will be given to you; seek and you will find; knock and the door will be opened to you. For everyone who asks receives; the one who seeks finds; and to the one who knocks, the door will be opened" (Matthew 7:7–8 NIV).

The "finding" God spoke of through Jeremiah and through the words of Jesus doesn't happen when you limit yourself to Sunday church services, weekly Bible studies, or even daily devotionals. It only happens when we lay aside everything else and focus our hearts and minds 100 percent on seeking to know Him on a deeper and deeper level.

God loves you with a deep and everlasting love, and He would never hold out on you as you seek Him with your whole heart. On the contrary, He delights in sharing more of Himself with you as you draw near to Him and seek Him out.

Lord, today I will take time to seek You. I've walked with
You, loved You, and received Your promises, but I still want
more. . .more of You. Only You can satisfy my soul.

Jeremiah 30:1–31:22 / 1 Thessalonians 4:1–5:11 / Proverbs 11:27–31

FOREVER!

For the Lord himself will come down from heaven, with a loud command, with the voice of the archangel and with the trumpet call of God, and the dead in Christ will rise first. After that, we who are still alive and are left will be caught up together with them in the clouds to meet the Lord in the air. And so we will be with the Lord forever.

1 Thessalonians 4:16–17 niv

Most people fear physical death because of its finality *and* because they don't know what—if anything—awaits them on the other side. Though death is the inevitable end for every man, those of us who have been saved by God's grace through faith know that after our bodies cease functioning, our spirits and souls will live on forever in a place called heaven.

Today's scripture verses, however, promise that there is one generation of believers whose bodies will never die, for the Lord Jesus will return to earth to take Christians home to be in the Lord's presence forever. At that moment, God will do away with death, sorrow, and pain (Revelation 21:4), and we will take up eternal residence in a place Jesus, the Creator of all things once called "paradise" (Luke 23:43).

Thank You, Jesus, for the comforting promise of a forever life with You in an eternal kingdom called heaven. I will be in Your very presence after I die—maybe before that if You return while I'm still living on this earth.

Jeremiah 31:23–32:35 / 1 Thessalonians 5:12–28 / Proverbs 12:1–14

THE WORD AT WORK

And may the very God of peace sanctify you wholly.
And I pray that God will preserve your whole spirit and
soul and body as blameless at the coming of our Lord Jesus
Christ. Faithful is He who calls you, who will also do it.

1 THESSALONIANS 5:23–24 SKJV

When you first came to faith in Jesus Christ, God began an amazing work in you, a work in which He transforms you into the image of His Son, the Lord Jesus Christ. This is a post-conversion process the Bible calls "sanctification."

This process involves effort and action on the part of the believing man. It involves an act of the will in submitting to the Holy Spirit and making God's Word a part of our very being. As we do that, we'll see ourselves grow into spiritual men who become "more and more like [Jesus] as we are changed into his glorious image" (2 Corinthians 3:18 NLT).

Before He went to His death on a cross, Jesus prayed for His disciples, "Sanctify them by the truth; your word is truth" (John 17:17 NIV). Later, Paul wrote that God's Word is "useful for teaching, rebuking, correcting and training in righteousness" (2 Timothy 3:16 NIV).

God has called you to grow into a spiritually mature follower of Jesus, and "Faithful is He who calls you, who will also do it."

Heavenly Father, thank You for Your faithfulness and for
Your work within me to bring me to spiritual maturity.

FAITH, LOVE, AND PERSEVERANCE

*We ought always to thank God for you, brothers and
sisters, and rightly so, because your faith is growing
more and more, and the love all of you have for one
another is increasing. Therefore, among God's churches
we boast about your perseverance and faith in all
the persecutions and trials you are enduring.*

2 THESSALONIANS 1:3–4 NIV

The Christians in Thessalonica had been suffering severe persecution
for their faith by Roman oppressors, and to make matters worse, they
feared that they missed out on the Rapture, Jesus' gathering of all
believers in the end times. Paul wrote his second letter to the church
to encourage them, to calm their fears, and to set the record straight
concerning end-time events.

Paul voiced his pride in the Thessalonians' endurance and
increasing faith in the face of intense suffering, telling them that
"among God's churches we boast about your perseverance and faith
in all the persecutions and trials you are enduring."

That's high praise indeed for the Thessalonians!

It has been pointed out that when you squeeze a sponge, what is
inside is sure to come out. When persecution and suffering "squeezed"
the Thessalonians, their faith, their love for one another, and their
perseverance poured forth.

When trials and troubles squeeze you, what do you think will
come out of you? Faith, love, and perseverance. . .or something else?

*Lord, when I must endure trials and tribulations,
help me to stand firm in my faith.*

Jeremiah 34:8–36:10 / 2 Thessalonians 3 / Proverbs 12:21–28

CONFIDENCE IN A FAITHFUL GOD

But the Lord is faithful, and he will strengthen you and protect you from the evil one. We have confidence in the Lord that you are doing and will continue to do the things we command. May the Lord direct your hearts into God's love and Christ's perseverance.

2 THESSALONIANS 3:3–5 NIV

How would you define the word *faithful?* In the context of marriage, that word brings to mind fidelity between a man and his wife. But in a broader sense, faithfulness suggests the quality of being true to one's own promises or vows.

In 2 Thessalonians 3:3–5, Paul wrote with great confidence in the great faithfulness of the Lord when it came to strengthening and protecting His people from attacks from the devil. Because God is faithful, each man who has placed his trust in Jesus can be assured of victory over our spiritual enemies.

The Bible lists many of God's qualities, and one of the most important is His faithfulness. The Lord is 100 percent faithful to His own promises, which means that the Christian man can count on Him, without reservation, to do everything He has said He will do.

In what area of life do you need God to come through for you today?

Heavenly Father, thank You for Your promises and for faithfully keeping every one of them. Thank You for strengthening me when I am weak, protecting me when I feel threatened, and encouraging me when my faith falters.

Jeremiah 36:11–38:13 / 1 Timothy 1:1–17 / Proverbs 13:1–4

FIT FOR GOD'S SERVICE

He considered me trustworthy and appointed me to serve him,
even though I used to blaspheme the name of Christ. In my insolence,
I persecuted his people. But God had mercy on me because I did it in
ignorance and unbelief. Oh, how generous and gracious our Lord was!
He filled me with the faith and love that come from Christ Jesus.

1 TIMOTHY 1:12–14 NLT

The apostle Paul—the greatest Christian missionary of all time and the writer of much of the New Testament—had a complicated past. He was a blasphemer, and a persecutor of that first generation of Christians.

Humanly speaking, it's hard to believe that God would use a guy like Paul in such a mighty way. But He did. He took a man who was once Jesus' sworn enemy and made him His most trusted and dedicated servant.

Paul still stands as an example of how a man's credentials and past sins aren't what's important to God. Rather, it's what God can do in the life of a man He's chosen for a specific purpose.

Maybe you have a messy, complicated past. But that doesn't matter to God—not any longer. When you came to Him through faith in Jesus, He made you a new creation (2 Corinthians 5:17) and made you fit to serve Him (Ephesians 2:10).

Just like the apostle Paul!

Thank You, Jesus, for making a sinner like me a new
creation and for making me fit to serve You.

Jeremiah 38:14–40:6 / 1 Timothy 1:18–3:13 / Proverbs 13:5–13

PRAYING FOR AUTHORITIES

I urge, then, first of all, that petitions, prayers,
intercession and thanksgiving be made for all people—
for kings and all those in authority, that we may live
peaceful and quiet lives in all godliness and holiness.

1 TIMOTHY 2:1–2 NIV

We in America live under a two-party political system, which naturally leads to some division, often along party lines. But many observers hold that over the past decade or so, Americans have become more divided than ever, even to the point where those on opposite sides of the political aisle barely talk to one another—and when they do talk, the communication is filled with hostility and recriminations.

As Christians, how should we respond to such division among our leaders? Today's scripture verses give us a simple yet powerful answer: pray for them!

God has called us Christian men to pray for those in positions of authority: our political leaders, our bosses, our law enforcement, and others.

It may be difficult for you to thank God for and pray for leaders with whom you disagree—especially if their positions are opposed to the Word of God. But remember that it is ultimately God who places people in positions of authority (Romans 13:1). Therefore, your duty as a man of faith is to pray for them, to ask God to bless them and direct them.

Which leader can you pray for today?

Sovereign Lord, remind me daily to pray for those
in positions of leadership and authority.

Jeremiah 40:7–42:22 / 1 Timothy 3:14–4:10 / Proverbs 13:14–21

TRAINING IN GODLINESS

"Physical training is good, but training for godliness is much better,
promising benefits in this life and in the life to come." This is a
trustworthy saying, and everyone should accept it. This is why we
work hard and continue to struggle, for our hope is in the living God,
who is the Savior of all people and particularly of all believers.
1 TIMOTHY 4:8–10 NLT

Track and field enthusiasts look with great admiration at distance runners, athletes who push their bodies to limits the average man can't begin to comprehend—each day and every day in preparation for the actual race. Without that grueling training, runners can't compete on race day.

In today's scripture verses, Paul contrasts physical training with "training for godliness"—meaning taking part in spiritual disciplines such as prayer and Bible reading. But there is a comparison to be made, as self-discipline and commitment go a long way in keeping the man on track and growing in his faith.

If you want to increase your faith and deepen your love for God, there can be no substitute for making a commitment to God's Word—which contains everything you need to live a godly life—and to spending time with your heavenly Father in prayer.

Father in heaven, thank You for giving me everything I need for
training in godliness through Your written Word. Help me to properly
discipline myself and apply biblical truth to my life of faith every day.

Jeremiah 43–44 / 1 Timothy 4:11–5:16 / Proverbs 13:22–25

DOCTRINE MATTERS

*Be diligent in these matters; give yourself wholly to them,
so that everyone may see your progress. Watch your life
and doctrine closely. Persevere in them, because if you
do, you will save both yourself and your hearers.*
1 TIMOTHY 4:15–16 NIV

Many Christian men today find themselves tuning out quickly when they hear the word *doctrine*. But when you consider that "doctrine" simply means a set of beliefs—specifically beliefs drawn from scripture—then you'll get a strong idea of how important sound doctrine really is.

In today's scripture verses, Paul encourages his young protégé Timothy to guard both the way he lived and his doctrine—in other words, what he believed. He expected young Timothy to pay close attention to what the Holy Spirit had inspired Paul to write and teach and then to put those writings and teachings into action. That way, others would hear and believe what the young pastor had to say.

There's no way around it: what we believe will have a profound effect on how we think, how we live, and what we say. That's why it's so important that we seek out sound doctrine and avoid all unbiblical teaching.

*Dear Jesus, may I never stop learning from You, advancing
in my faith, or growing in my love for You and the truths
You've revealed in Your written Word. Please guard
my heart and mind against unsound doctrine.*

Jeremiah 45–47 / 1 Timothy 5:17–6:21 / Proverbs 14:1–6

THE FOLLY OF GREED

*Those who want to get rich fall into temptation and a trap
and into many foolish and harmful desires that plunge people
into ruin and destruction. For the love of money is a root of all
kinds of evil. Some people, eager for money, have wandered
from the faith and pierced themselves with many griefs.*

1 Timothy 6:9–10 niv

Ask most men what the Bible says is the root of all sorts of evil, and they'll likely say, "That's easy! It's money!" But that's not what the Bible says. Not at all!

First Timothy 6:10 (niv, italics added) states that "the *love of money* is a root of all kinds of evil," further warning that some greedy believers had fallen away from the faith.

Greed kills!

Money, in and of itself, is neither good nor evil. It all depends on how it's used and the importance men place on having lots of it.

In this same passage, Paul offered the antidote for greed when he wrote, "Godliness with contentment is great gain" (verse 6 niv). As God's people, we can defeat greed by clinging to His promises to meet all our needs (Philippians 4:19).

God is your Master, not money. Depend fully on Him for all things, and you'll defeat greed.

Heavenly Father, help me to see my money and material possessions the way You want me to—as servants and not my master. Cleanse my heart of even the smallest hint of greed.

BE LIKE PAUL

*So do not be ashamed of the testimony about our Lord or of me his
prisoner. Rather, join with me in suffering for the gospel, by the power
of God. He has saved us and called us to a holy life—not because of
anything we have done but because of his own purpose and grace.*

2 TIMOTHY 1:8–9 NIV

Paul wrote to Timothy, his "son in faith," to encourage and challenge
him never to be ashamed of the gospel of Christ but instead to be bold
and fearless in his testimony about Jesus. Going a big step further,
Paul challenged Timothy not to be ashamed of Paul's imprisonment,
as Paul considered himself a prisoner for the sake of Jesus Christ.

Paul could write such things because he was firmly convinced that
God had saved both himself and Timothy "not because of anything
we have done but because of his own purpose and grace."

Paul was not even the slightest bit ashamed or fearful, for he knew
that the gospel of Christ "is the power of God that brings salvation to
everyone who believes: first to the Jew, then to the Gentile" (Romans
1:16 NIV).

Paul was an incredible example for Timothy, and for us today, of
the kind of faith that puts the gospel message above even his own life.

*Lord Jesus, may I never be ashamed of the testimony of Your gospel,
and may I always be ready and willing to suffer for Your name's sake.*

Jeremiah 49:7–50:16 / 2 Timothy 2 / Proverbs 14:23–27

CIVILIAN AFFAIRS

No one serving as a soldier gets entangled in civilian affairs,
but rather tries to please his commanding officer.

2 TIMOTHY 2:4 NIV

Politicians. Pop singers. Famous actors. What do these professions have in common? All can be used to influence the world for good. . . but usually serve as mere traps for the wealthy.

A dash of fame can season a person's life with greed and self-importance, leading to unrestrained hubris and an increasing lack of accountability. Even worse, the masses who follow these people often bicker and fight amongst themselves about which famous individual is the smartest or most good-looking or most skilled or. . .you get the idea.

In short, it's easy for people who care about fame and fortune to become "entangled in civilian affairs," forgetting the very reason for their existence here on earth. God placed each of us in this life to be a soldier for Him, but just as a soldier forgets his duty the moment he involves himself in the petty disputes of those he's supposed to protect, so Christians often forget their ultimate purpose in favor of pointless arguments and futile obsessions.

So today, don't place your hope in pop stars or politicians. Seek God's will instead—He's got a reward that's far better than any earthly fame.

Lord, help me plant my roots in Your deep purpose—
not in some shallow vision of popularity. I want to
rise, not through the ranks but up toward You.

Jeremiah 50:17–51:14 / 2 Timothy 3 / Proverbs 14:28–35

CHANGING THE PAST

*You, however, know all about my teaching, my way
of life, my purpose, faith, patience, love, endurance,
persecutions, sufferings—what kinds of things happened
to me in Antioch, Iconium and Lystra, the persecutions I
endured. Yet the Lord rescued me from all of them.*

2 TIMOTHY 3:10–11 NIV

As the clock springs back one hour, do you find yourself wishing that the minute hand would keep going in reverse? Maybe you feel trapped, as if each choice you made in the past has led you to this moment of pain. What you wouldn't give for a second chance!

Perhaps this desperate, impossible longing crossed Paul's mind a time or two, especially when he was being stoned to death or beaten or shipwrecked. But then, the moment he started feeling regret in the face of pain, he would remember one truth that kept him going: God was the one who'd led him here, and God would be the one to lead him through. His current predicament was no accident—it was divinely appointed.

No matter what you're going through today, know that God can use your broken pieces to build a masterpiece. Shift your focus away from the unchangeable past and toward the promises that lie in the future. As time marches on, join it, locking step with God toward your ultimate goal.

God, help me move on from the past, appreciate the present, and anticipate the future. I know You're working to make it all worthwhile.

Jeremiah 51:15–64 / 2 Timothy 4 / Proverbs 15:1–9

SOLACE IN WEAKNESS

God alone is powerful enough to create the earth.
He alone is wise enough to put the world together.
He alone understands enough to stretch out the heavens.

JEREMIAH 51:15 VOICE

Strangely enough, it's sometimes comforting to dwell on all the things we *can't* do.

When you look out at the vast cosmos each night and try to imagine the unfathomable distances between each star, ask yourself, *Could I have done any of this?* The answer is clear: of course not! Not even the most powerful person in history could create a star. . .let alone a universe that's filled with them. When compared to God, we're little more than ants, crawling blindly on a small hill of dirt in the middle of an island in the middle of the Pacific Ocean.

And that's okay.

Why? Because imagine the pressure we'd experience if we could change any of this—if we were responsible for keeping the gears of the universe running. The fact that God alone can do this should fill us with overwhelming relief. Our goal shouldn't be to change the unchangeable. . .but rather to better trust in God's ability to do all that and more.

We can't give life to a dying star. . .but we *can* kindle the fires of faith in our souls.

Thank You, God, for handling life's biggest mysteries so that I don't have to. I trust Your decisions on everything, even in things I can't see.

Jeremiah 52–Lamentations 1 / Titus 1:1–9 / Proverbs 15:10–17

WISDOM OF THE ELDERS

*He must have a strong belief in the trustworthy message he was
taught; then he will be able to encourage others with wholesome
teaching and show those who oppose it where they are wrong.*

TITUS 1:9 NLT

Today's verse is describing an appointed elder of the church. It gives
guidelines on who to look for when choosing someone to help lead
God's people.

But these qualifications aren't just limited to elders; they're
applicable to any Christian man who desires a closer walk with God.
So when you read today's verse, ask yourself, *Do I have these qualities?
Is my faith strong enough to weather the doubts that the world throws
my way? Do I encourage others or disappoint them? Am I able to discern
between truth and error?*

Nobody wakes up one morning with all these qualities at once.
It takes a lifetime of honing your spiritual skills, digging deeply into
God's Word and regularly seeking His will, to reach this place. That's
why the leaders in question are known as "elders"—they've lived their
lives seeking godliness and slowly acquiring wisdom.

So, in your quest to become like them, don't be afraid to learn from
them. Find Christians who embody these traits, ask them questions,
and remember their example each time you face hard decisions yourself.

*Lord, thank You for providing not only Your Word
but solid examples of people who put Your Word into
action. Help me learn from their wisdom.*

Lamentations 2:1–3:38 / Titus 1:10–2:15 / Proverbs 15:18–26

LONG-TERM CONSEQUENCES

So it is good to wait quietly for salvation from the LORD. And it is good for people to submit at an early age to the yoke of his discipline.

LAMENTATIONS 3:26–27 NLT

It's no secret that rebellion is more rampant today than ever. When you were a teen, you might've even been unruly yourself, flaunting the wishes of your superiors in hopes of gaining recognition.

But as you grew older, you probably saw through the adrenaline rush that these short, thrilling adventures provided. You started seeing the real long-term consequences of disobedience. Skipping classes leads to bad grades. . .which leads to decreased opportunities for higher education. Drug use leads to addiction, which leads to shattered lives and homelessness. Dangerous activities lead to sickness, injury, or even death.

In short, disobedience is often self-sabotage.

God's laws are no different—except for the fact that His rules are *always* perfect. Disobeying God might give you some worldly recognition or more immediate results. . .but it won't take long before the final consequences start rearing their ugly heads. Temporary happiness changes to long-term guilt and pain, and soon enough, you start deeply regretting the day you decided to step out of line.

So today, practice patience and don't discount obedience. Shape your future by letting God shape you.

God, fill me with a desire to obey, not to rebel. Mold me into the man You want to be, not the man I once foolishly dreamed of becoming.

WORD GUSHERS

The heart of the righteous weighs its answers,
but the mouth of the wicked gushes evil.
PROVERBS 15:28 NIV

Reading today's verse, you can probably name at least five people who fall in the second category, and probably a few who fall in the first. Those who *don't* weigh their answers—the "word gushers"—are usually heard a mile away, and your muscles tense at the thought of putting up with them again. You know every time one of these people walks into the room, the next ten minutes will be a painful exercise in balancing the conversation on a knife's edge of civility—somewhere between lashing back in rage and darting out the door.

But for those who are considerate and thoughtful, it's a joy to see their faces. You know that this conversation will be pleasant and insightful, no matter how many twists and turns it takes. Individuals like this make life easier, and they make us better people for just speaking with them.

So. . .which one are you? Do you regularly practice holding your tongue and responding with kindness, or are you unafraid to speak your mind, no matter how ugly the thoughts within it get?

Never forget that you, as a child of God, are also His ambassador—His representative to this world. What image do you want to convey?

Lord, grow my self-control so that I can speak life instead of poison—
comfort and wisdom instead of cynicism and hasty words.

Ezekiel 1:1–3:21 / Philemon 1 / Proverbs 16:1–9

DANGEROUS FANTASIES

"I am sending you to the Israelites, to the rebellious pagans who have rebelled against Me. . . . The children are obstinate and hardhearted."

EZEKIEL 2:3–4 HCSB

Have you ever heard of the Jovian-Plutonian effect? If not, don't worry: it doesn't actually exist. This pseudoscientific idea began as an April Fool's prank when the astronomer Patrick Moore announced over the radio in 1976 that Jupiter and Pluto would be aligning, creating a period of weakened gravity.

Apparently, the fact that it was a hoax didn't stop people from experiencing it. One woman even called in and claimed she and a group of friends "wafted" up from their chairs and "orbited gently around the room." Hundreds of similar calls came pouring in that day.

This is a more innocent example of the kind of delusion the Israelites were under. They'd tricked themselves into believing a lie for so long that they fought against anyone who disagreed. These "obstinate" people didn't want to hear the truth. . .and they wouldn't believe it if they did.

Such delusion is easy to fall into—most of us would rather float in our sinful ignorance than be brought back to earth by the truth. But God's truth, in the long run, is far better than any wild fantasy we could ever dream up.

> *God, help me accept Your teaching, even if it goes against my own notions. I want to grow in Your reality, not get lost in my own deception.*

Ezekiel 3:22–5:17 / Hebrews 1:1–2:4 / Proverbs 16:10–21

CHANGELESS

"In the beginning, Lord, you laid the foundations of the earth,
and the heavens are the work of your hands. They will perish,
but you remain; they will all wear out like a garment. . . .
But you remain the same, and your years will never end."

HEBREWS 1:10–12 NIV

How would it feel to know that everything you hold dear will last forever? The sting of death and decay, gone. The dread of the end, never to be felt again.

That's the kind of life God calls us to live in Him. Here on earth, everything we see is temporary. Even the largest stone or the most impressive skyscraper will crumble under the massive weight of time. But God's love? It's existed for all of eternity—it's just as strong today as it was at the dawn of time. In a life full of passing pleasures and crushing finality, it's great to have a hope that will never slip away or get snuffed out by the hand of death.

Today, try putting a little less emphasis on the fading shadows of this life and focus more on the eternal light that awaits you just around the corner. What's seen is temporary, but what's unseen is forever (2 Corinthians 4:18). So keep looking!

Father, it's so hard to focus on Your eternal truth when these
fleeting shadows seem so convincing. Give me eyes that can
pierce the veil that separates this life from my life to come.

Ezekiel 6–7 / Hebrews 2:5–18 / Proverbs 16:22–33

RIGHT'S STILL RIGHT

"I will leave a remnant when you are scattered among the nations."
EZEKIEL 6:8 HCSB

A strange experiment was once performed in Arizona's Petrified Forest National Park.

To prevent theft, signs had been posted that read: "Your heritage is being vandalized every day by theft losses of petrified wood of 14 tons a year, mostly a small piece at a time." But the experiment began when a researcher removed the signs from certain paths. Shockingly, the theft rate went *down* on the paths without the signs!

Why? Because the signs gave the impression that stealing was a common action, so visitors were naturally more inclined to do it themselves.

In a world full of peer pressure and socially constructed morality, it can be hard to see the point in following God's laws—nobody else is, so why bother? But as today's verse says, God will always preserve a remnant of the faithful, and it's up to us to decide whether we want to be a part of it.

By burying ourselves in God's Word rather than in the world's boiling confusion, we can strengthen our resolve to do His will, even if we're the only believers in sight. As St. Augustine said, "Right is right even if no one is doing it; wrong is wrong even if everyone is doing it."

What have you chosen to do?

Father, help me see morality through Your eyes,
not through the eyes of a lost and confused world.

Ezekiel 8–10 / Hebrews 3:1–4:3 / Proverbs 17:1–5

HARD CHOICES

*We have come to share in Christ, if indeed we hold
our original conviction firmly to the very end.*

HEBREWS 3:14 NIV

Some Christians might read this verse and, with a gulp, think, *That's
a pretty big if!* After all, we know just how long and confusing life can
be. Who's to say that you, no matter how devout you may be today,
won't turn your back on God twenty years down the line?

While it's certainly true that people do turn back from God,
keep in mind that He won't let you go without a fight. As Paul said
in 2 Timothy 1:12 (NLT), "I know the one in whom I trust, and I am
sure that he is able to guard what I have entrusted to him until the
day of his return." Even if our own hearts turn against us, as human
hearts tend to do, "we know that God is greater than our hearts"
(1 John 3:20 NIV).

Matters of salvation—both leaving and staying—involve
intentional decisions, the results of a mind that's firmly made up. As
long as you have the desire to fight for what's right, God won't let
you fall. You still have to choose each day. . .but God will always be
by your side, encouraging you to choose Him.

*Father, help me grow in You so that the temptation to fall becomes less
each day. Thank You for gripping me—may I never resist Your pull.*

Ezekiel 11–12 / Hebrews 4:4–5:10 / Proverbs 17:6–12

RELATABLE SAVIOR

[Jesus] has been tested in every way as we are, yet without sin.
HEBREWS 4:15 HCSB

In a 1930 movie titled *All Quiet on the Western Front* (an adaptation of a semi-autobiographical book of the same name) young Paul Bäumer joins the German army after being inspired by his professor's grandiose description of the battlefield. Needless to say, the realities of war soon shatter those idealistic notions, and he later returns home with scars too deep to fathom.

Deciding to visit the classroom where he was recruited, Bäumer is shocked to see the professor still misleading his class, filling their heads with naive optimism. But when Bäumer tells them what war is really like, they and the professor ridicule him, calling him a coward.

Why couldn't they empathize with him? Because they'd never experienced what he'd experienced. In his inward suffering, Bäumer was all alone.

That feeling is what today's verse can remedy. Jesus has experienced the worst this world has to offer. He knows this life isn't pretty. He knows how blisters form and fingernails break, how resolve wears thin. He knows. . .because He's *been there*.

Today, don't hesitate to tell Jesus about your weariness. He'll never shame you for your honesty; rather, He's always willing to offer the comfort of companionship, joining you as you travel the darkest paths.

Lord Jesus, thank You for being relatable. May I always turn to You for strength whenever I feel nobody knows or cares.

Ezekiel 13–14 / Hebrews 5:11–6:20 / Proverbs 17:13–22

CHEERFUL HEARTS

A cheerful heart is good medicine, but a crushed spirit dries up the bones.
PROVERBS 17:22 NIV

In this world of cynicism and hopelessness, a truly cheerful heart seems about as easy to find as a five-leaf clover. Despair and weariness are the default emotions, fed by a constant influx of bad news concerning everything from the state of the nation to the state of one's bank account. In short, while there are good things in this life, you can't count on them to outweigh the bad. . .unless you're a Christian.

A relationship with God is the key ingredient that makes a cheerful heart possible. Without it, any hint of cheerfulness is either fake or manufactured. What hope is there for someone who believes this world is all there is? For that person, life is just a gallery of tiny tragedies and triumphs, lumped together in no particular order and then snuffed out by the weight of inevitable oblivion.

But, thankfully, God offers a better way. By reflecting on His promises and strengthening your relationship with Him, you can grow closer to the root of all purpose—the one who created your life and gave it the meaning we all so desperately crave.

You don't have to live with a crushed spirit any longer—your Father holds the cure.

> *Lord, may I remember hope when things seem*
> *hopeless—joy when happiness seems to leave.*
> *Teach me to look to You for the meaning of life.*

Ezekiel 15:1–16:43 / Hebrews 7:1–28 / Proverbs 17:23–28

"COOL SPIRIT"

He who has knowledge spares his words,
and a man of understanding has a cool spirit.
PROVERBS 17:27 AMPC

Think back on your high school days for a minute and try remembering a day when your class had to give an oral presentation. As students stood up one by one, you could usually tell which ones had prepared and which ones were winging it. How? By noticing which ones talked the most. . .without really saying anything.

There's nothing wrong with being passionate about a topic and wanting to share it with others, of course. But whenever we find ourselves doing *all* the talking, it's usually a sign that we're insecure about our knowledge and want to cover up the gaps with more words.

But there's an even bigger downside to having a "big mouth"—the more we talk, the more we tend to like hearing ourselves talk. . .making it easier to tune out anyone else's voice or opinion. So whenever God speaks to our souls, telling us the right path to take, we're too busy maintaining an inner (or outer) monologue to pay attention.

Sometimes, when presented with a problem you can't solve, it's okay to sit back, stay silent, and wait on God to show you the answer. Silence is a sign of a cool spirit.

Lord, give me the patience and humility to keep quiet when
You have something to say. May I listen more than I speak.

Ezekiel 16:44–17:24 / Hebrews 8:1–9:10 / Proverbs 18:1–7

JUST A SHADOW

*If [Jesus] were on earth, he would not be a priest, for there are
already priests who offer the gifts prescribed by the law. They serve
at a sanctuary that is a copy and shadow of what is in heaven.*

HEBREWS 8:4–5 NIV

Human nature can be tricky sometimes. We're hardwired to stick with
what we know, even when new and potentially better solutions present
themselves. Sure, this has the biological benefit of keeping us safe
in our routines, but it can also lead to self-destructive stubbornness.

Take the first-century Jews, for example. They'd spent thousands
of years serving God in the temple, but when God literally came down
and told them, face-to-face, about His new and better way, they were
so committed to their old way of life that they chose to cling to a
mere shadow of His ultimate plan.

Today, the Church is full of traditions and "habits"—some good,
others not so much. But no matter how valuable your upbringing or
your church's rich history may be, you should never let it overshadow
God's plan for you today.

Be attentive to God's voice. Study His Word deeply and regularly.
Dwell on the purpose He's given you. And then. . .go out and live the
real thing, not just a shadow of it.

*Father, Your plans reach so much higher beyond my
comfort zone. May I always be willing to leave familiarity
behind in pursuit of a richer relationship with You.*

Ezekiel 18–19 / Hebrews 9:11–28 / Proverbs 18:8–17

PROJECTING

Yet the people of Israel continue to complain, "The Lord's way is not fair at all!" You think My way is unfair, people of Israel? Don't you think you are the ones with perverted ways?

EZEKIEL 18:29 VOICE

In psychology, there's a concept known as "projecting." This happens when people with deeply engrained negative attitudes "project" their feelings onto others in order to subconsciously shift the blame. A manipulative man, for instance, might believe everyone else is manipulating him.

Well, judging by today's verse, the Israelites were doing a lot of projecting. Even worse, the target of their foolish accusations was none other than God Himself.

Whenever life goes wrong, it's tempting for many Christians to use God (or their feeble understanding of God, at least) as a punching bag—a scapegoat upon whom they can pin all the wickedness that actually lies within their own hearts. But all this does is create a world in which nobody owns up to their own mistakes.

In order to grow in our faith in God, we've got to first have a right understanding of who He is. So whenever we feel as if God's laws are unfair or too stifling, it's probably time to look inward, searching for the place where we've gone wrong. If someone is at fault, rest assured: it's *never* God.

Lord, forgive me for the times I've held wrong opinions about You. Teach me to own up to my own failures instead of shifting the blame.

Ezekiel 20 / Hebrews 10:1–25 / Proverbs 18:18–24

TURN AROUND WHEN POSSIBLE

*"I am the LORD your God; follow my decrees
and be careful to keep my laws."*

Ezekiel 20:19 niv

God's commands aren't suggestions. After two thousand years, you'd think Christians would've figured that out by now, but it seems many stray further from God's will each day, chasing their own visions instead of the Lord's perfect revelation. No wonder this world is collapsing!

For an illustration, imagine for a moment if you treated your GPS like some people treat the Bible. "Take the third right" becomes "Go straight if you feel like it." Pretty soon, the computerized voice is repeating things like "Turn around when possible," but you just shut it off, annoyed by its constant bickering. And when you find yourself thirty miles out in the land of nowhere, you blame the GPS for not being clear enough.

If that sounds ridiculous, that's because it is. . .yet for many Christians, it's their way of life. Wanting to have God by their side but not wanting Him to tell them what to do, they miss the point entirely, derailing their own lives and then blaming the one who tried to help.

Today, don't ignore the Spirit's gentle plea whenever you need to course correct. Follow God's decrees, and you'll never be lost again.

*Lord, You are the only one who can hold my life together.
Teach me to follow Your rules, even when I don't see
the point. I know You're leading me home.*

Ezekiel 21–22 / Hebrews 10:26–39 / Proverbs 19:1–8

ABUSING GRACE

Just think how much worse the punishment will
be for those who have. . .insulted and disdained
the Holy Spirit who brings God's mercy to us.
HEBREWS 10:29 NLT

Right now, think of the most amazing technology that currently exists—the internet, fast transportation, etc. Next, think of all the ways these things are *supposed* to be used. . .compared with all the ways people have *abused* them.

An avenue for long-distance relationships becomes a highway for cyberbullying. A convenient subway system becomes a target for terrorists. A search engine designed to expand people's knowledge becomes an outlet for the darkest desires of the wicked.

It's one thing to do wrong—it's another thing to do so by intentionally hijacking something that was intended for good.

It's no different when it comes to God's grace. Some people, always looking to exploit the system, try using this wonderful gift as an excuse to sin even more, living a reprehensible lifestyle under the guise of "magnifying God's forgiveness." Such perversion will never result in spiritual growth—in fact, it's a surefire way to kill your walk with God altogether.

So today, don't abuse God's gift of salvation. Strive for holiness at all times, seek forgiveness when you fail, and grow closer to the one who saved you.

Thank You, Jesus, for saving my soul. May I always appreciate
this salvation as something to be cherished, not exploited.
May I never intentionally grieve the Spirit who lives within me.

Ezekiel 23 / Hebrews 11:1–31 / Proverbs 19:9–14

NATURAL FAITH

*Now faith is confidence in what we hope for and
assurance about what we do not see.*

HEBREWS 11:1 NIV

Many people mistakenly believe that faith is something unrelated to the rest of our lives—an outlier in the human range of emotions and opinions. But if you think about it, faith shows up everywhere we look. When we sit in a restaurant to eat dinner, for example, we have faith that our chair won't collapse, that the food won't be poisoned, that the waiter won't spill the soda on us. . .and so on.

Why do we have faith in these things? Because of our experience. We've been to countless restaurants throughout our lives, so we know exactly what to expect.

Similarly, faith in God can only grow through experience. When you first come to Him, He gives you just the faith you need to believe the gospel. . .and then He works alongside you as you discover more about His character. Each trial, painful as it may be at the time, adds another reinforcement to your faith as you watch God bring you through. Each hour spent in Bible study and prayer adds to your understanding of God's faithfulness, thereby growing your confidence in Him.

Strong faith isn't reached overnight—it's a journey that will only end when faith becomes sight.

*God, make me confident in the things I can't see by helping
me recognize Your patterns in the things I can.*

Ezekiel 24–26 / Hebrews 11:32–40 / Proverbs 19:15–21

FAMOUS LAST WORDS

The one who keeps commands preserves himself;
one who disregards his ways will die.

PROVERBS 19:16 HCSB

It was The Battle of Spotsylvania Court House, May 9, 1864. Major General John Sedgwick was leading the Sixth Corps near Brock Road, where a group of enemy sharpshooters were stationed. Various soldiers had warned Sedgwick not to go onto the road…but he didn't listen. As bullets whizzed by, his men warned him frantically to take cover, to which Sedgwick quipped, "They couldn't hit an elephant at that distance."

Those were his last words.

Out of all the vices that can befall a Christian man, there's a reason pride always takes the first spot. Arrogance has a way of clouding one's judgment, discounting the wisdom of those who know best in favor of a misplaced sense of self-confidence. That's why spending time with God is so important—it creates a better understanding of the depths of God's wisdom…and the reality of your limitations.

Growing in your faith often means tearing down the faith you had in yourself. In order for God's rules to take precedence in your life, you first have to dispose of the "nothing can hurt me" mentality. If you don't, the next defiant action might just be your last.

When You speak, Father, help me pay attention.
Your rules are more than just background noise—they're the
only chance I have to survive this sin-stricken world.

Ezekiel 27–28 / Hebrews 12:1–13 / Proverbs 19:22–29

ALL EYES ON YOU

"I will be proved holy through them in the sight of the nations."
EZEKIEL 28:25 NIV

The theater of Epidaurus is one of the few structures of ancient Greece that is preserved almost in its entirety. It's well known for quite a few things—it's size, its capacity (up to 14,000 people), and its breathtaking aesthetic. But perhaps the most amazing feature of this theater lies not in sight but in sound.

The acoustics of Epidaurus are said to have been so good that even people in the back row could hear a coin drop on stage. The theater had been so crafted that anyone who stood onstage became the center of focus for 14,000 pairs of eyes and ears. If you happened to forget your lines, *everyone* would know.

Similarly, God has entrusted us with an astounding position of influence—a sobering responsibility to draw all eyes to Him. He's set us on the stage, like a "city on a hilltop" (Matthew 5:14 NLT), and it's our choice whether we want to recite the lines God has given us or improvise our way through, making fools out of ourselves as we go.

Today, don't hide your faith or stifle it through disobedience—shout it out for the people in the back.

Father, make me aware of my position of influence,
and help me use this opportunity for Your glory.
This is all Your stage—give me the words to say.

Ezekiel 29–30 / Hebrews 12:14–29 / Proverbs 20:1–18

BAD PLANS

Finalize plans with counsel, and wage war with sound guidance.
PROVERBS 20:18 HCSB

In 53 BC, Marcus Licinius Crassus led his Roman legion into a crushing defeat. Marching his men out into the desert, Crassus soon realized his mistake as the dry heat weakened his troops, making his army vulnerable to attack by the fierce Parthians. In the end, he lost roughly half of his 40,000 troops. . .as well as his own life.

The two biggest reasons for his failure were these: lack of knowledge about the terrain and lack of knowledge about the enemy's skills. If he'd only spent more time studying either of these factors, the battle would've probably played out much differently.

As soldiers for Christ, it's imperative that we spend time vigorously studying our battle plan for this war against the enemy. By seeking wisdom in the Bible, asking God for guidance, and looking for ways to apply these lessons into our own lives, we'll have all we need to face new battles each day.

Armed with the sword of the Spirit and carrying the life-giving water of God's peace, we'll never have to worry about being ambushed in the desert. We can take the fight all the way to the devil's home turf. . .and win.

*Father, may I take advantage of the battle plans You've
given me. Strengthen my shield of faith in the face of doubt,
and give me the stamina to endure the heat of temptation.*

Ezekiel 31–32 / Hebrews 13 / Proverbs 20:19–24

BITTER REVENGE

Do not say, "I will get even for this evil."
Wait for the Eternal; He will defend you.
PROVERBS 20:22 VOICE

In one of the greatest ironies of this life, hardly anything causes a spirit to become more imbalanced than the desire to get even.

Think of a time when someone said something hurtful or cheated you out of something you believed was yours. Now, think of a time when you chose to react to one of these situations with revenge in your heart instead of forgiveness. Chances are, the emotional turmoil you felt during and after this moment of "payback" was greater than the hurt caused by the original action itself. Why? Because instead of pulling out this splinter in your mind, you chose to drive it deeper with every angry thought. Soon, the only torment left was of your own making.

God knows how the human mind works. He created humanity with the instinct to love and forgive…but our fallen nature now draws us into hatred and long-held grudges. That's why having His Spirit in our lives—communing with Him daily and learning to listen to His voice—is so important: it strengthens that part of us that God always intended to prevail.

You are made in the image of Love Himself—what room is there for revenge?

God, without Your mercy, I'd have no hope. Help me
extend this mercy to others, whose crimes against
me are far smaller than mine against You.

Ezekiel 33:1–34:10 / James 1 / Proverbs 20:25–30

TESTED FAITH

For you know that when your faith is tested, your endurance has a chance to grow. So let it grow, for when your endurance is fully developed, you will be perfect and complete, needing nothing.

JAMES 1:3–4 NLT

Christianity was built on the foundation of suffering. Jesus, our Savior, was killed for His teaching, and His death and subsequent resurrection are the reason the Church exists today.

So why do Christians today act like Christianity is all about doing what makes us happy? Why do some preach a gospel of "health and wealth"? Sure, in a perfect world, having everything we want would bring us closer to God. . .but that perfect world is called heaven, and we're not there yet. In this life, suffering is often the only thing that can propel us fallen humans into a closer relationship with God. As C. S. Lewis said, pain is "[God's] megaphone to rouse a deaf world."

So today, don't let pain destroy your walk with God. Instead, start viewing each trial that comes along—each financial uncertainty, each sickness, each strained relationship—not as an obstacle but as a path that leads you closer to God.

Walking this path may be hard and filled with thorns and pitfalls, but the moment you break through the thicket and step into the light, the view of God's joy will make it all worthwhile.

> *Lord Jesus, You endured unimaginable pain for me—*
> *help me endure this small discomfort for You.*

Ezekiel 34:11–36:15 / James 2 / Proverbs 21:1–8

FIRST THING'S FIRST

As the body without the spirit is dead, so faith without deeds is dead.
JAMES 2:26 NIV

The great Reformer Martin Luther had a problem with the book of James. He referred to it as the "epistle of straw," fit for being removed from the Bible altogether. Why? Because of the emphasis James put on works.

But let's take a closer look. James isn't saying that a person can win God's favor through good deeds—if he were, then Luther might've had a point. No, James is saying that true faith will always create a change in a person's life.

For example, think of a healthy tree with hundreds of apples. Does the abundance of apples make the tree healthy. . .or do the apples grow *because* the tree is healthy? Clearly, it's the latter. Similarly, salvation isn't caused by good works any more than the health of a tree is caused by the fruit it bears. It's precisely the other way around.

So what about you? Is your life thriving and filled with the fruits of the Spirit, or is it withered and dry, a shadow of what it once was? If so, don't spend your life trying to make your exterior look better than your interior—ask God to work on your heart first, and the rest will follow.

Lord, may I draw nutrients from Your teachings, growing my faith and, as a result, producing fruit that will point others to You.

Ezekiel 36:16–37:28 / James 3 / Proverbs 21:9–18

REMADE

*And they shall say, This land that was desolate has become
like the garden of Eden, and the waste and desolate
and ruined cities are fortified and inhabited.*

Ezekiel 36:35 AMPC

In his brilliant book *Mere Christianity*, C. S. Lewis explains the profound effect that God's salvation has on a believer. "Our Lord is like the dentists," he says. "If you give Him an inch, He will take an ell. Dozens of people go to him to be cured of some one particular sin. . . . Well, He will cure it all right: but He will not stop there. . . . He will give you the full treatment."

Of course, the "full treatment" is often the last thing on our minds whenever we ask God for help! We may come to Him seeking a solution to a particular issue or the strength to overcome a temptation. . .but the moment He starts correcting other aspects of our lives, how often do we resist and say, "Whoa, God, that's enough!"?

God isn't interested in fixing your gutters—He's interested in tearing down your old life and building a new one from scratch. If you've accepted Jesus, then this process has already begun—and it will only be finished when you wake up on the shores of glory.

Are you willing to be remade?

*Lord God, remake me each day with Your Spirit. Tear down my
sinful inclinations and replace them with Your power and holiness.*

Ezekiel 38–39 / James 4:1–5:6 / Proverbs 21:19–24

TRUE NORTH

So humble yourselves before God. Resist the devil, and he will flee from you. Come close to God, and God will come close to you. Wash your hands, you sinners; purify your hearts, for your loyalty is divided between God and the world.

JAMES 4:7–8 NLT

As mere humans, one of the greatest lies we often tell ourselves is that we have full control over spiritual matters—that we can turn sin and righteousness on and off like a faucet whenever we please.

But in reality, each human is like a magnet. To the south of this magnet lies the army of evil. . .and to the north lies God's glorious kingdom. The individual's responsibility—his sole power in this life— is to choose which direction he wants to face. Will he turn toward his Creator, thus attracting the righteousness and blessings that only God can provide, or will he repel God. . .and thereby draw in all the forces of darkness? There's no middle option. Neither side of the spiritual battle will remain in place—one will always move in relationship to each man, either toward or away.

As you read this, you are making a choice to invite either God or Satan into your life. Who will it be?

Lord, direct my heart toward You whenever I feel myself gradually rotating toward the enemy. You're my true north— my only hope for gaining the grace I don't deserve.

Ezekiel 40 / James 5:7–20 / Proverbs 21:25–31

THANKSGIVING

Is anyone among you suffering? He should pray.
Is anyone cheerful? He should sing praises.

JAMES 5:13 HCSB

Most Christians have no problem practicing the first part of today's verse. When disaster strikes and grief grips the heart, prayer is often just as natural as breathing. Even hardened atheists, when presented with a problem too big for them to handle, might subconsciously mumble a prayer to the God they've spent their lives denying.

But what about thanksgiving? Sure, there's an entire holiday devoted to it, but how many of us practice it on the other 364 days of the year? When God works powerfully in our lives, how eager are we to jump at the chance to praise Him for His intervention? Sadly, it seems the answer is usually "not eager enough." Living in a first-world culture has taught us to expect comfort and complain when it's taken away. It's dulled our senses to the spiritual reality all around us, making us care more about preserving the status quo than strengthening our souls.

Sometimes growing your faith means enduring a trial that's been thrust upon you. Other times, it means actively calling to mind the God that has given you so much beyond what some people could even imagine. Both routes are necessary for a Christian man to become the person God meant him to be.

How are you showing thanksgiving to God?

Father, may my life be a continual song of
thanksgiving for Your grace and blessings.

Ezekiel 41:1–43:12 / 1 Peter 1:1–12 / Proverbs 22:1–9

SHADOWS IN A CAVE

"Son of man, describe the temple to the people of Israel, that they may be ashamed of their sins. Let them consider its perfection."

EZEKIEL 43:10 NIV

The famous philosopher Plato once gave an allegory about a group of people who had been chained up in a dark cavern all their lives. Their only light source was a small fire behind them, which projected their shadows on the wall in front. All they knew were these shadows. . . until someone from outside the cave came in, broke their chains, and led them into the sunlight. This new and sudden revelation caused them to retreat back into the cave, seeking the familiarity of shadows over the truth of the light. The sun was just too bright.

To those who've spent their entire life in sin, God's perfection often seems like the sunlight—wonderful but too bright to handle. It puts to shame their former life, leaving them with a choice: learn to adjust to God's light or settle for the shadows.

This choice is a continual one—it only finds its fulfillment once we've reached the Sun Himself. But the further we travel toward Him, the more our eyes will adapt, and the more clearly we'll see our past life for the shameful shadow it was.

Are you moving into the light?

God, adjust my eyes to Your holiness, helping me to see how much better Your truth is compared to the lies I once believed.

Ezekiel 43:13–44:31 / 1 Peter 1:13–2:3 / Proverbs 22:10–23

NO SEPARATION

*Do not exploit the poor because they are poor
and do not crush the needy in court.*

PROVERBS 22:22 NIV

Having the right relationship with God isn't just the first and most important commandment—it's the one that dictates whether you follow all the others with the right mindset.

Take stealing, for example—the topic of today's verse. If you truly love God and are seeking a closer relationship with Him, how could you possibly treat His image-bearers with disdain? Every time you look at another human being, you see a reflection of God Himself, so if your relationship with God is truly where it needs to be, you'll want to treat others the way God has treated you—with mercy, love, and generosity.

C. S. Lewis once said, "If you are right with [God] you will inevitably be right with all your fellow-creatures, just as if all the spokes of a wheel are fitted rightly into the hub and the rim they are bound to be in the right positions to one another."

God doesn't want us to separate our faith in Him from our interactions with others. These two worlds are inextricably linked, and it's up to us to choose which direction we want to take them.

*Lord, fill me with a desire to know You more and more
each day. I know that the closer I draw to You, the closer
I will draw to those whom You want me to love.*

Ezekiel 45–46 / 1 Peter 2:4–17 / Proverbs 22:24–29

SILENCING THE CRITICS

*For so is the will of God, that with doing good you
may put to silence the ignorance of foolish men.*

1 PETER 2:15 SKJV

Let's be honest, guys—honor is a tricky subject when it comes to living like Jesus. Sure, we may give lip service to humility and "turning the other cheek," but the moment someone attacks our character, we often turn into a bunch of Spartans, hurling verbal weaponry in a last-ditch effort to defend our wounded pride.

But usually, all we succeed in doing is making fools out of ourselves. Why? Because we fail to remember the classic but time-honored adage: actions speak louder than words.

If someone insults you by calling you a liar, the best way you can prove him wrong is by telling the truth. If a coworker falsely accuses you of laziness, don't fulfill his prophecy by spending all your time bickering with him. Simply work, trusting that God and your actions will stand up for you in the court of others' opinions. Once you focus on allowing God to change you into the man He wants you to be, the wrong opinions of others won't matter as much.

Don't focus on getting the last word; focus on living in the Word Himself.

*Father, help me silence my critics by first silencing the reactionary
part in me. I don't want to waste time proving these naysayers
right—teach me to let my actions speak for themselves.*

Ezekiel 47–48 / 1 Peter 2:18–3:7 / Proverbs 23:1–9

SHARE IN SUFFERING, SHARE IN GLORY

*When you do what is good and suffer, if you endure it, this brings favor
with God. For you were called to this, because Christ also suffered for
you, leaving you an example, so that you should follow in His steps.*

1 PETER 2:20–21 HCSB

Peter's first letter is about hope. Christians were being persecuted,
even killed, for their faith, and he wanted them to understand that
God was using their suffering in ways they could barely imagine—to
make them more like Jesus.

Peter knew firsthand what that looked like. He believed that
after Jesus built a base through His healing, teaching, and preaching,
He would overthrow Rome and establish His kingdom. He never
imagined that Jesus would let Himself be unjustly arrested, tortured,
and executed—or that He would rise again. The best possible scenario
for all mankind came through what looked like the worst.

That's the model for Christian suffering. That's why Peter later
added, "Don't be surprised at the fiery trials you are going through
. . .for these trials make you partners with Christ in his suffering, so
that you will have the wonderful joy of seeing his glory when it is
revealed to all the world" (1 Peter 4:12–13 NLT).

As you partner with Jesus in the hard times, remember: His
suffering ended. Yours will too.

*Jesus, I can't wait for You to return and make everything right.
Until then, help me to suffer with Your glory in mind.*

Daniel 1:1–2:23 / 1 Peter 3:8–4:19 / Proverbs 23:10–16

ALL IN ALL

*"Praise be to the name of God for ever and ever; wisdom
and power are his. He changes times and seasons; he deposes
kings and raises up others. He gives wisdom to the wise and
knowledge to the discerning. He reveals deep and hidden things;
he knows what lies in darkness, and light dwells with him."*

DANIEL 2:20–22 NIV

The world feels increasingly divided, violent, and beyond human
control. Politics are as contentious as they've been in generations,
culture is bent on calling good evil and evil good, and natural disasters
grab headlines weekly. But God is still in control.

God gave Daniel understanding that no one else had because
Daniel trusted Him. Nothing is a mystery to God. No catastrophe
confuses Him, no disaster discourages Him, and no fatigue fouls
His mind.

In a place and culture where God was foreign and unknown,
Daniel held on to his faith. More than merely surviving or going with
the flow, he chose to honor God. That required wisdom, strength, and
peace higher and greater than anything he had on his own—and God
never let him down.

God was his only chance to survive the upriver swim, but Daniel
didn't waste energy worrying. He channeled his fears into faith,
knowing God is greater than anything this world could do to him.

*God, You are faithful to the faithful. By Your strength and
wisdom, I will do what is right, not what is easy.*

Daniel 2:24–3:30 / 1 Peter 5 / Proverbs 23:17–25

GOOD FEAR

Don't envy sinners, but always continue to fear the LORD.
You will be rewarded for this; your hope will not be disappointed.

PROVERBS 23:17–18 NLT

The world wears us down. The way running water eats away solid ground, the world, the flesh, and the devil collaborate to create moments of doubt. We see it repeatedly in the psalms and here in Proverbs, this fear that those who follow God are having a much harder time in life than those who don't.

But scripture also regularly gives God's promises of a reward for our perseverance. In the daily struggle to provide for ourselves and our families, to deal with a steady stream of troubles, to try and make something better of the world through our work and ministry, we can lose sight of the big picture. At times, it would be easier not to worry about what God thinks or has said—but that way always ends in disaster.

There is no greater tragedy than a lost soul staying lost—someone choosing the world over God, expedience over righteousness, ambition over service. The Bible promises the ultimate loss for those who never choose the narrow way: the loss of true self—everything God wants them to be. When we're tempted to take the wide path, respect for God and fear of letting Him down will steady us.

Lord, You are my reward. To see You face-to-face will be
worth everything this broken world throws at me.

Daniel 4 / 2 Peter 1 / Proverbs 23:26–35

ESCAPING THE WORLD

He has given us very great and precious promises, so that
through them you may share in the divine nature, escaping
the corruption that is in the world because of evil desires.

2 PETER 1:4 HCSB

God's promises to His children are like His grace—no strings attached.
If you embrace His Son, everything Jesus inherits—glory, power,
peace—is yours too. Your calling in this life is liberation from the
world system—the anti-God philosophy of self-sufficiency and self-
worship. You are to walk in and by the Spirit, not the world, and to
help others do the same.

That's an uphill climb, but one that takes you closer with each
faithful step toward heaven—and one that God empowers you to do.
That's Peter's point: you have tools for the job. It takes time to learn
what they are and how to use them. You'll stumble along the way, but
God will never let you fail in any final sense.

"The more you grow like this, the more productive and useful
you will be in your knowledge of our Lord Jesus Christ" (verse 8
NLT). Bible study won't save you, but it will help you grow in grace
and protect you from the lure of the world and the flesh.

God, Your grace astounds me. Thank You for preserving me against
the world and the privilege of being one with You through Jesus.
Help me stay connected to You, my only source of true life.

Daniel 5 / 2 Peter 2 / Proverbs 24:1–18

WHEN YOUR FOES FALL

*Don't rejoice when your enemies fall; don't be happy
when they stumble. For the LORD will be displeased with
you and will turn his anger away from them.*
PROVERBS 24:17–18 NLT

One of the toughest tests of Christian character is to love our enemies. These include God's enemies in the broad sense of all those who haven't received Christ's gift of salvation (a position we once held), and personal enemies, those who are against us for whatever reason but especially if we have been obedient to God and are hated because of it.

Proverbs 24:18 makes it clear: rejoicing when an enemy falls displeases God. It reveals un-Christlike character, forgetting that Christ has overcome our default setting—revenge. He wants no one to waste their lives without Him and then suffer the ultimate destruction.

Even harder is that it may invite God's mercy on that person, if only to show you that you have fallen to their level. An enemy rejoices when you stumble, but God only sees someone who is suffering the consequences of mistakes as one who may be drawn to Him through these errors. Crowing over an enemy's fall only says you don't appreciate what God rescued you from—your own sin. As His adopted son, seek to bless where others curse.

*Lord, revenge is Yours, and so is perfect justice.
Help me to forgive, to pray that my enemies would
come to know Your powerful, cleansing love.*

Daniel 6:1–7:14 / 2 Peter 3 / Proverbs 24:19–27

JUSTICE IS COMING

*The Lord does not delay His promise, as some
understand delay, but is patient with you, not wanting
any to perish but all to come to repentance.*

2 PETER 3:9 HCSB

We love a story when the bad guy gets what's coming to him, that sense of justice being served. God loves justice too, but He is incredibly patient when it comes to meting it out. We all have moments when we ask, "How long, Lord?" We long for Jesus' return because He will bring justice.

If you stand before God in Christ's righteousness, that judgment holds no fear for you. Since only Jesus can judge fairly, you'll rejoice when He makes things right. That deep sense you've carried for so long of all that's wrong and unjust will be satisfied.

One day, all believers will celebrate the final fall of our true enemies—Satan and his world system. Until then, anyone can be redeemed, even the most unlikely of us. That's God's plan, to save anyone who will be.

Judgment Day is coming. That knowledge should keep you from becoming cynical and help you stand for justice where you can. When the time is right, God will make everything right. Carry that peace with you as you face the world's wrongs.

*God, one day You will make everything right. Until then,
help me to rest, knowing that Your judgment is coming,
and to stand, knowing that justice matters to You.*

Daniel 7:15–8:27 / 1 John 1:1–2:17 / Proverbs 24:28–34

TO KNOW HIM IS TO LOVE LIKE HIM

*Those who obey God's word truly show how completely they
love him. That is how we know we are living in him.*

1 JOHN 2:5 NLT

The clearest sign of someone living a Christian life is that they live
like Jesus did. That boils down to simple obedience to what Jesus
called the two greatest commandments: love God with all you are,
and love others as yourself.

Neither is easy. You can only love well with God's help—His
Spirit inside you, drawing you back to Him when you want to go
your way instead. And you can only be aware of such love because
God loved you first. But because He did, you are now called to love
like He does—sacrificially, with your motivation being the good of
others, even over your own.

That's the light that Jesus brought into the world—the torch
that He passed to us as His church, His people, His priesthood. To
live in His light is to love like He did, finding that rhythm of grace
and truth. We don't back down from the truth of our desperate need,
nor do we back off the good news that God's grace covers all our sin.
Anyone living like that can truly lay claim to loving God.

*Jesus, thank You for loving me first. Help me to love
God and others like You do, whatever the cost.*

Daniel 9–10 / 1 John 2:18–29 / Proverbs 25:1–12

THE WARFARE IS REAL

"From the moment you decided to humble yourself to receive
understanding, your prayer was heard, and I set out to come to
you. But I was waylaid by the angel-prince of the kingdom of
Persia and was delayed for a good three weeks. But then Michael,
one of the chief angel-princes, intervened to help me."

DANIEL 10:12–13 MSG

Recognizing the reality of spiritual warfare resembles acknowledging
fear: we don't feel afraid the way we did as kids, but the things that
worry us are almost always rooted in fear. Fear recognizes threats.
Once we see it for what it is, we can replace fear with faith, trusting
God with those troubles.

Similarly, spiritual warfare recognizes the reality of a world we
can't see. Not only are angels and demons real, they fight over us. Your
unanswered prayer literally might be held up by an angel battling a
demon to come to your aid.

But don't be afraid: angels outnumber demons two to one, and
any hold evil has in the world will be broken—either by constant and
fervent prayer or when Jesus returns. Till then, hold on to the angel's
words to Daniel in verse 11 (HCSB): "You are a man treasured by God."
Keep praying with the expectation that God sees you and He is moving.

Lord, I will rest knowing I matter to You. I will pray in faith that Your
power is unsurpassed and Your will is going to be accomplished.

Daniel 11–12 / 1 John 3:1–12 / Proverbs 25:13–17

MY DAD'S STRONGER THAN YOUR DAD

*When people do what is right, it shows that they are
righteous, even as Christ is righteous. But when people
keep on sinning, it shows that they belong to the devil,
who has been sinning since the beginning. But the Son
of God came to destroy the works of the devil.*

1 JOHN 3:7–8 NLT

How did Jesus destroy the works of the devil? At the cross. His defeat of death, sin, and hell means His people operate from a position of triumph. How does He destroy the devil's attempts to keep us from living in that victory? Through our obedience to His commands.

The power that resurrected Jesus is alive in everyone who puts their faith in Him. His authority enables us to live righteously, to stand for truth and love others well. Every time we obey Jesus and do the right thing, we defeat something Satan intended for evil.

To do that, though, we must surrender control of every part of our lives to God's scrutiny and authority. Make no excuses for sin. In a sin-broken world, it's an uphill battle, but it's one that Jesus has already overcome. We aren't fighting for victory but from it. Honor God's superiority by giving Jesus control in every part of your life.

*Jesus, Your victory over evil fuels me every day,
giving me what I need to represent You well. I will stand
by and on Your truth today and every day to come.*

Hosea 1–3 / 1 John 3:13–4:16 / Proverbs 25:18–28

BURNING COALS

If you see your enemy hungry, go buy him lunch; if he's thirsty, bring him a drink. Your generosity will surprise him with goodness, and GOD will look after you.

PROVERBS 25:21–22 MSG

Jesus' command to love our enemies often feels unreasonable—because it's not the world's way. Yet that's exactly what He did, healing them, speaking the truth to them, even praying for their forgiveness from the cross. Jesus always took the long view, always had the mission in mind—filling the kingdom of God with as many as will receive Him.

That's the mission He gave us too, and He furnishes the strength and the heart to seek good for those who have wronged us, annoyed us, betrayed us, wounded us. He paid to redeem us from sin's grip but also from all those hurts. Could there be a more Christlike action than to go against every bone in your body and be kind to the difficult guy next door?

Many translations of Proverbs 25:22 call this putting "burning coals" on an enemy's head. Strange phrase but totally scriptural: don't repay evil for evil but pay back evil with good. Your decency might shame them, but that shame might bring them to Christ. It's the essence of what Jesus did: His kindness leads us to repentance (Romans 2:4).

Jesus, let my undeserved kindness to others—
like Yours to me—play a part in Your work to
convict them and bring them to repentance.

Hosea 4–6 / 1 John 4:17–5:21 / Proverbs 26:1–16

WORLD-BEATER

Whatever has been born of God conquers the world. This is the victory that has conquered the world: our faith. And who is the one who conquers the world but the one who believes that Jesus is the Son of God?

1 JOHN 5:4–5 HCSB

John defined the spirt of antichrist as "everyone who refuses to confess faith in Jesus" (1 John 4:3 MSG). The idea of antichrist isn't so much about opposites, because that implies Jesus Christ has an equal opponent, which He doesn't. Rather, it's the spirit of *instead of*, rejecting Him and putting anything else in His rightful place as the center of it all (Colossians 1:16–17).

So, when John says that Christians—those who have "been born of God"—are conquerors, he means that our faith in Jesus helps us to overcome our default setting, which is to put anything but God first in our lives. *Anything* but God is an idol—even otherwise good things like marriage, parenting, or ministry. Put them first and they become bad things, simply because they were never meant to fully satisfy us. Only God can.

The only way to overcome the pull of such things is to trust in Jesus as God's Son more than anything or anyone else. Jesus is the world-beater and in Him the world holds no power over us.

Jesus, You overcame the world so that I can too. Be my center, my strength, and my ultimate goal and reward.

Hosea 7–10 / 2 John / Proverbs 26:17–21

LOVE PRESERVES YOUR REWARD

Look to yourselves. . .that you may not lose. . .all that we and you have labored for, but that you may. . .receive back a perfect reward [in full].

2 JOHN 1:8 AMPC

John warns us to adhere to Jesus' commandment to "walk in love" (2 John 1:6 AMPC). We can only recognize and overcome false teachings when we "walk in accordance with and guided by His commandments" (verse 6 AMPC)—that is, when we unselfishly seek what's best for each other.

Christ telling us to love one another isn't optional. It's a command. It's also doctrine—teaching that keeps us aligned with God's will. To understand that love, we must adhere to biblical teaching about Jesus—that He is the second person of the godhead, come in flesh to offer Himself for our sin, risen again and ascended to the Father's right hand, and returning one day to rule with a rod of iron.

Many people calling themselves Christians move away from these truths. John gives them a name: antichrists (verse 7). They put their own understanding, experiences, and opinions ahead of biblical truth, but they will be exposed because they will fail to love like Jesus loves.

Loving well requires God's help, and staying faithful to His command brings His reward.

God, give me discernment and knowledge to recognize false teachers, but most of all, let me love others the way You do, so I can show I am Yours.

WALKING WISELY

*Who is wise? Let them realize these things. Who is discerning?
Let them understand. The ways of the LORD are right; the
righteous walk in them, but the rebellious stumble in them.*

HOSEA 14:9 NIV

Hosea's ministry focused on God's faithfulness to Israel despite its ongoing infidelity. Verse 9 is the book's final verse, and it asks if we get the point: wisdom obeys God. God gives us grace when we stray off His path, but He expects us to honor His grace by getting back on track when we see our error.

The Bible is clear that the only way to stay true to God is to keep obeying His Word. Only He Himself is enough to keep us faithful, but to know Him we must constantly refamiliarize ourselves with who He is and what matters to Him. Right now, you're doing just that: seeking God so you can make sure your words and actions line up with what's in your heart.

In Hosea's day, godly wisdom was based on the law and the prophets. Christians, though, are to go beyond that: Jesus' teachings aren't just wisdom, they are "full of the Spirit and life" (John 6:63 NIV). We are to take in Jesus' words like they are food and drink—they go deep inside us, become part of us, guide and redirect us, and sustain us.

*Lord, nourish me with Your words so I can live for
You. Help me to walk wisely in Your ways.*

Joel 1:1–2:17 / Jude / Proverbs 27:10–17

STAY TOGETHER, STAY ON TARGET

*Carefully build yourselves up in this most holy faith by praying
in the Holy Spirit, staying right at the center of God's love,
keeping your arms open and outstretched, ready for the mercy of
our Master, Jesus Christ. This is the unending life, the real life!*

JUDE 1:20–21 MSG

Jude encourages us to be intentional about our faith. If the Christians
of the early church were infiltrated by those who pretended to follow
Jesus but instead served themselves, how much more is that true today?

Recent years have seen many successful pastors and ministries
exposed for exactly the kinds of behavior Jude warns against: those
"grabbing for the biggest piece of the pie, talking big, saying anything
they think will get them ahead" (verse 16 MSG). It's a sobering reminder
of how easy it is to cover natural human ambition and desire with a
veneer of Christianity.

Jude's remedy is to "build yourselves up in this most holy faith."
Build implies deliberate, ongoing action—praying, letting the Holy
Spirit guide and direct, honoring God as the highest priority, and
seeking His best for others. It's also directed to us corporately: we
build our faith by living life with each other. There should be no
place like the church for finding wisdom, encouragement, comfort,
and accountability.

*God, I want to keep growing in my faith, and to help the people around
me grow in theirs. Guide us all by Your Spirit into Your truth and life.*

Joel 2:18–3:21 / Revelation 1:1–2:11 / Proverbs 27:18–27

EYES ON THE PRIZE

*"Don't be afraid of what you are about to suffer. The devil will
throw some of you into prison to test you. . . . But if you remain
faithful even when facing death, I will give you the crown of life."*

REVELATION 2:10 NLT

If someone told you, "You're about to suffer," you'd probably consider
staying in bed. But Jesus said just that to the church in Smyrna. The
devil was gunning for them, and their lives, already characterized by
poverty, were about to get worse. However, He also promised a reward
for staying faithful: the crown of life.

Crown refers to a winner's prize in an athletic event—in those
days, usually a laurel wreath. But even today's diamond rings and gold
medals pale next to the eternal prize God has for us (1 Corinthians
9:25).

God doesn't promise to protect us from persecution, but He does
promise to accompany us while we go through it. The worst people
can do is pretty bad, but it's nothing compared to the best Jesus has
for us when we stay true to Him.

Jesus praised the church at Smyrna for staying faithful under
duress. By the world's standards, they were poor and downtrodden.
But by God's, they were rich! Jesus said their suffering would have a
limit, but victorious life with Him does not.

*Jesus, as the world's hatred for You grows, let me stay
faithful to You. Help me run my race for Your glory.*

Amos 1:1–4:5 / Revelation 2:12–29 / Proverbs 28:1–8

STICK TO THE PLAN

The Sovereign LORD never does anything until he
reveals his plans to his servants the prophets.

AMOS 3:7 NLT

Amos prophesied judgment against both Israel and its enemies for their sins. But God's judgment is always intended to bring repentance and restoration. That's the theme of Scripture: God's faithful rescue mission, and God used prophets to get the word out.

Both Old and New Testaments center on one person and two events: Jesus Christ and His first and second comings. Every prophecy reveals that purpose, one way or another, and through His prophets in the Bible, God has told us everything we need to know.

Hebrews 1:1–2 (NIV) says, "In the past God spoke to our ancestors through the prophets at many times and in various ways, but in these last days he has spoken to us by his Son." Our work nowadays is to share Christ's good news, which includes sticking to what He has already said through His prophets in the Bible.

There is no other plan for humanity's salvation, no matter what some who claim to be prophets have said. All who trust in Jesus hold to and speak what He has already said—no adding, subtracting, or revising to fit the current culture. Jesus is the center of Scripture, history, and creation itself, and God's words show Him to us.

Lord, thank You for revealing Your good plans in the Bible.
Fill me with Your Spirit to be Your messenger today.

Amos 4:6–6:14 / Revelation 3 / Proverbs 28:9–16

NO MORE HIDING

*People who conceal their sins will not prosper, but if they
confess and turn from them, they will receive mercy.*

PROVERBS 28:13 NLT

Hide and-seek was a fun game to play with friends, but it's a dangerous, destructive game to play with God. Sin separates us from God. Although He is saddened by our sin, He is not surprised by it, and has even provided a process to deal with it. According to Proverbs 28, the process is twofold: confess and turn.

Biblical confession involves God and His people. First John 1:9 tells us to confess our sin to God for forgiveness, and James 5:16 instructs us to confess sin to one another for healing. Forgiveness and healing are only possible through honest confession to God and to godly people.

Although confession is the first step, it's not the end. Proverbs 28 reminds us that the final step is to turn from sin. You will not be sinless, but by God's grace, you will sin less and less as you pursue God more and more.

Stop playing games with God. It's time to come out of hiding so you can live seeking the Lord!

*God, please forgive me for selfishly following my own desires
and help me to live for You. Although sin is inevitable on this side
of eternity, I want to be quick to confess and turn from it.*

Amos 7–9 / Revelation 4:1–5:5 / Proverbs 28:17–24

THE FOCAL POINT

I saw a throne in heaven and someone sitting on it.
REVELATION 4:2 NLT

Even a cursory read of Revelation 4 reveals a clear focal point. In the opening verses, we see five mentions of a throne, demonstrating that all the action of heaven centers around the one seated on it. In heaven, God is constantly glorified, honored, and praised—in other words, given with joy what is rightfully His.

In Matthew 6:10, Jesus instructed the disciples to pray "on earth, as it is in heaven." Unfortunately, our default mode is "on earth, as I want it," which directly contradicts the focus and arrangement of heaven.

Instead of instinctively turning inward, we must aim at focusing outward and upward, like heaven. After all, since all of heaven is focused on the one seated on the throne, it only seems right that our lives on earth should be lived similarly. We can't realize a fully Jesus-centric life until heaven, but we can get a taste of it as we focus every area of our lives on Him: relationships, finances, dreams, and decisions. A life lived for Jesus is how we bring a little taste of heaven to earth.

Jesus, help my life on earth to mirror the throne room of heaven: centered on You. Forgive me for the times I have selfishly turned inward, and help me to keep my life focused on You.

Obadiah–Jonah / Revelation 5:6–14 / Proverbs 28:25–28

LET'S TRY THAT AGAIN

Then the word of the LORD came to Jonah a second time.
JONAH 3:1 HCSB

Jonah 1:2 and Jonah 3:2 are almost exactly the same: God tells Jonah to go to Nineveh and speak against it. In between these verses are two chapters of hypocrisy, disobedience, and outright rebellion—all from a man who claimed to "worship GOD, the God of heaven who made sea and land" (Jonah 1:9 MSG)!

Although God could have justifiably allowed Jonah to drown, He graciously saved him and let him try "a second time," just as He has for each of us. God wants holiness and obedience from us, but He also factors in our humanity and disobedience. God will get His work done whether we're on board or not. It's just better to obey the first time, even when we don't understand what He's doing, and trust what He will do.

Aim to live a life where God does not have to repeat Himself. Rest in His grace, trusting that He will replay the instructions when needed, patiently allowing you to attempt it yet again. The best part is that when you step out in obedience, you can trust Him with the details and the outcome.

> *God, thank You for giving me more chances. I confess that I have failed You, and at times, even lived hypocritically and rebelliously. However, today I choose to do what You have told me to do, trusting You every step of the way.*

Micah 1:1–4:5 / Revelation 6:1–7:8 / Proverbs 29:1–8

NO ONE WILL MAKE THEM AFRAID

*Nation will not take up sword against nation, nor will
they train for war anymore. Everyone will sit under their
own vine and under their own fig tree, and no one will
make them afraid, for the LORD Almighty has spoken.*

MICAH 4:3–4 NIV

Micah 4 provides a preview of coming attractions—a picture of life
on the renewed earth when Jesus returns and reigns. During His
thousand-year rule, Jesus will establish Jerusalem as the world's capital,
and people will freely come and go, seeking His wisdom and justice.

No one will be able to doubt that Jesus is God. Revelation 2:27
(AMPC) tells us He will rule with "a sceptre of iron"—absolute authority
and power—and the results will include the end of warfare and the
first true era of peace the world has ever known. Everything that
humans have broken and corrupted will be redeemed, and God's
people "will walk in the name of the LORD our God forever and ever"
(Micah 4:5 NIV).

These promises give us hope in the dark times we're living in.
God doesn't waste any of our suffering. Every ounce of pain, hardship,
and injustice will be turned into peace, prosperity, and joy—all these
good things will be even better because we know the suffering that
God created them from.

*Almighty God, I can't wait for Your return when You replace all my
fears and pain with Your glory and goodness. Come soon, Lord Jesus!*

Micah 4:6–7:20 / Revelation 7:9–8:13 / Proverbs 29:9–14

WHAT GOD IS LOOKING FOR

He's already made it plain how to live, what to do, what GOD
is looking for in men and women. It's quite simple: Do what is
fair and just to your neighbor, be compassionate and loyal in your
love, and don't take yourself too seriously—take God seriously.

MICAH 6:8 MSG

Should Christians get involved with a society that makes less and less room for God? Micah 6:8 indicates that it's a question of justice. The broad idea of justice is giving people what they deserve, but once the evildoers have been dealt with, what about those they've oppressed or hurt?

We're all made in God's image, made to know and reflect Him. Sin impacts us all—it's the reason the world is unfair and unjust. Jesus came to meet God's requirements for sin's just punishment but also His desire to save those He loves. Justice requires both truth and love: punishing wrongdoers *and* caring for those who've been hurt by the wrongdoing. Those wrongs are both specific and broad, but to care like God does is to be concerned with justice and mercy.

Only God's grace makes us just. We evangelize to get people to believe in Christ as Lord and Savior, and then, because of what God has done for us, we seek to help others.

Lord, You met my need and Your perfect, holy standard
in Jesus' sacrifice. Help me to find that rhythm today,
representing Your truth and demonstrating Your love.

Nahum 1–3 / Revelation 9–10 / Proverbs 29:15–23

YOUR STRONGHOLD

*The Lord is good, a Strength and Stronghold in the day
of trouble; He knows (recognizes, has knowledge of, and
understands) those who take refuge and trust in Him.*

NAHUM 1:7 AMPC

It's easy to say the Lord is good when things are going well. But when they're not, will you still say God is good? If you will, God will be your strength and fortress. God knows when you're trusting in Him—and when you're not. He knows when you're trusting yourself and your ways instead, and sometimes, He lets you get to the end of your rope so you'll turn back to Him.

Nahum brought God's hammer down on infidelity and injustice, but he also proclaimed the shelter of God's mercy—His desire to be reconciled with any who turn to Him and commit to His ways. The devil doesn't want you to access God's goodness, faithfulness, and wisdom, so he tries to make God seem distant or uninvolved. These tests can backfire against him, though, when you choose to recall who God is and how much He cares about and for you.

God knows everything you're worried about, all the things that cost you sleep, but He has promised never to leave or forsake you. Let Him be your shelter today against whatever you're facing. He won't let you down.

*God, I need You today. Be my refuge. I put my trust
in You, knowing You will always be with me.*

Habakkuk 1–3 / Revelation 11 / Proverbs 29:24–27

REJOICING IN THE HARD TIMES

*Though the fig tree does not bud and there are no grapes on the
vines, though the olive crop fails and the fields produce no food,
though there are no sheep in the pen and no cattle in the stalls,
yet I will rejoice in the LORD, I will be joyful in God my Savior.*

HABAKKUK 3:17–18 NIV

Sometimes God feels distant, especially in the holiday season when the
wonder and promise of Christ's birth feels smothered by the onslaught
of busyness, commercialism, and family get-togethers.

Other trials may compound the isolation. Illness, accidents,
and joblessness don't care about peace and goodwill toward men.
Habakkuk described such a season—fruitless, no return for hard
labor, no promise of renewed life. Maybe it's your marriage or the
choices your kids are making that are making you feel dried up
and abandoned. Maybe everyone around you seems to be doing
great—especially the people who have no time for God—and it's
all wearing you thin.

Whatever you're going through, God is there with you. He knows
and He cares. He will make things right one day in His perfect timing.
Advent is a season of waiting for His salvation and redemption. Don't
give up hoping in Him. You are not alone or forgotten.

*Jesus, You are with me, no matter how I feel or what I'm
going through. Your love and faithfulness never change,
and You are making all things new, even now.*

Zephaniah 1–3 / Revelation 12 / Proverbs 30:1–6

HE CAME TO SHIELD US

*Every word of God proves true. He is a shield
to all who come to him for protection.*
PROVERBS 30:5 NLT

Agur, the author of Proverbs 30, contrasts the understanding of man—"I lack common sense" (verse 2 NLT)—with godly wisdom—"He is a shield to all who come to him." Just as God blew Job away with a whirlwind of rhetorical questions (Job 38–40), Agur's words carry an edge that reveals truth.

Agur's insights includes a startling question about God: "What is His name, and what is His Son's name?" (verse 4 AMPC). In a proverb written a thousand years before Christ was born, Agur understood that God has a Son and the Son has a name.

Jesus humbled Himself to come and show us what God is all about. Do we have the humility to trust that God's revelation tells us all we need to know to live for Him?

Perhaps Jesus had Proverbs 30:4 in mind when he said in John 3:13 (HCSB), "No one has ascended into heaven except the One who descended from heaven—the Son of Man." How much Agur understood about the Messiah is unclear, but he anticipated that almighty God was humble enough to descend from heaven and ascend again to shield us from just judgment.

*Father, I praise You for sending Your Son to be my shield
against sin and death, my protection and my righteousness.
This was always Your plan, and it is good.*

Haggai 1–2 / Revelation 13:1–14:13 / Proverbs 30:7–16

HE CAME TO STEADY US

Here [comes in a call for] the steadfastness of the saints
[the patience, the endurance of the people of God], those who
[habitually] keep God's commandments and [their] faith in Jesus.

REVELATION 14:12 AMPC

As dark as these times are—as divisive and uncertain—they are nothing compared to history's penultimate stage, the tribulation. But if God will strengthen His children to face unprecedented persecution at that time—the daily threat of poverty, imprisonment, and execution—won't He help us to face those and any other challenges we're facing today?

It may be hard to imagine a time when you're asked to choose between meeting your basic human needs and keeping your faith. But that's why Revelation 14:12 (NIV) encourages us to "keep [God's] commandments and remain faithful to Jesus": if we persevere in our hard times, we are promised in verse 13 (NIV) that even if we die, we will "rest from [our] labor, for [our] deeds will follow [us]."

Just as Jesus came to die and return to glory, we will share in His glory when we die to ourselves to follow Him into whatever He allows. This is both the dark nearer edge of Christmas and the glory of its ultimate gift: total life with God forever.

Jesus, You steadied Yourself to face the world You made,
knowing that our rejection of You would make it possible for
any of us to be adopted and embraced by God. I celebrate
Your birth, Your death, and Your glory. Thank You.

HE CAME TO EMPOWER US

"Not by might nor by power, but by my Spirit," says the LORD *Almighty.*
ZECHARIAH 4:6 NIV

Zechariah spoke these stunning words to Zerubbabel, who was rebuilding God's temple upon the people's return from exile in Babylon. The symbols in Zechariah's prophecy point to God's Spirit accomplishing God's purposes: the lampstand with seven lamps (the menorah) was used in the tabernacle and Solomon's temple, a symbol of God's light—His truth, presence, and wisdom—coming to mankind. The two olive trees feeding the lampstand are His anointing, poured out constantly.

Like so many aspects of the temple, the lampstand points to God's ultimate work in Jesus Christ. The temple was where God chose to meet His people then. Now, as part of His Church, you are God's temple, the work of His hands and representative of His light. Just as Zerubbabel's temple wouldn't have been completed without God's help, you need God's Spirit guiding and fueling your faith.

God's greatest works are always done so that only He can receive credit and glory for and from them. You are His workmanship, a testimony to His greatness. He will finish what He has started in you. You're connected like Zechariah's vision of olive trees to God's ongoing, everlasting anointing, empowered to show His grace and works to the world.

Lord God, by Your Spirit in me, let me shine Your light to a hurting world. Deepen my connection to You so my faith continues to grow.

EYES PEELED

*See, I am coming like a thief! Blessed is the person who
watches and waits, dressed and ready to go, so as not
to wander about naked, exposed to disgrace.*

REVELATION 16:15 VOICE

Paul and Peter both said the day of the Lord would come like a thief
in the night—suddenly and without warning. Jesus affirmed this in
Revelation 16, that the tribulation will end similarly, interrupting
Satan's last stand as he gathers the nations of the world to attack
Jerusalem in a futile attempt to thwart God's judgment. The context
matters: Jesus' return will surprise and dismay *unbelievers*, but He
expects His church to heed the signs of the times and always be
ready for His return.

That's the purpose of Jesus' warning to stay clothed. We don't
want to get caught with our spiritual pants down, more focused on
our immediate needs than on God's provision, more concerned about
paying the bills than building His kingdom. First John 2:28 (NIV) says,
"Continue in him, so that when he appears we may be confident and
unashamed before him at his coming."

It feels odd to consider the end of the world in the Christmas
season, but Advent not only celebrates Jesus being born to save us,
it anticipates His return to rule over the earth, to undo all the pain
of this world.

*Lord Jesus, You came and You are coming again.
I'll stand by Your strength till You return. Come soon!*

Zechariah 9–11 / Revelation 17:1–18:8 / Proverbs 30:29–33

PROPHECY'S TWIN PEAKS

Rejoice, O people of Zion! Shout in triumph, O people of Jerusalem!
Look, your king is coming to you. He is righteous and victorious,
yet he is humble, riding on a donkey— riding on a donkey's colt.

ZECHARIAH 9:9 NLT

Zechariah 9:9 prophesied Jesus' first coming, riding into Jerusalem as the humble King astride the back of a peaceful donkey, welcomed by the crowds—yet on His way to buy that peace at the cross. However, verse 10 (NLT) immediately depicts what Jesus will do at His second coming: "I will destroy all the weapons used in battle, and your king will bring peace to the nations."

Old Testament prophecy often pairs an imminent fulfillment and a long-term one. The prophets saw two mountain peaks of prediction, side by side as if on a postcard, but nowadays we have a glimpse of God's bigger view: those peaks are separated by a chasm of time.

Revelation 19:11 says Jesus will return on a white horse as the conquering King, judging justly and waging war. But after He defeats His enemies and begins His unchallenged reign, He will bring about the kingdom Zechariah foresaw—one of peace and harmony, gentleness and humility. We need Him to be both righteous Savior and holy judge, to win our hearts before He conquers the world.

God, You alone see history's beginning, middle,
and end. Thank You for sending Jesus to save us the
first time and again to make everything right.

Zechariah 12–14 / Revelation 18:9–24 / Proverbs 31:1–9

SPEAK UP

Speak out on behalf of those who have no voice, and defend all those who have been passed over. Open your mouth, judge fairly, and stand up for the rights of the afflicted and the poor.

PROVERBS 31:8–9 VOICE

Because justice matters to God, it should matter to us. Justice is about restoring basic human dignity, building relationships based on every person's worth to God. Because we are united with Christ, the King of kings, we should seek a king's role: to defend the helpless and speak for the voiceless.

Start by listening. Only when we know someone's story can we speak with wisdom about it. Prayer is also vital, both to help us examine our own hearts and to seek God's will. His Word doesn't excuse us from action. He may tell us to be still, but there will come a time when He calls us to speak up. We must be prepared to hear and obey.

Jesus will restore everything to His original intentions in Eden—a world of justice, righteousness, and harmonious community. Until then, our mandate as His people is to seek those things the best we can. We won't ever get perfect results or seek with perfect hearts, but with the Holy Spirit inside us, we are not powerless to act.

Father, I need Your wisdom to listen well and speak up when You call me to. Help me represent Your desire for justice with love and truth.

Malachi 1–2 / Revelation 19–20 / Proverbs 31:10–17

THE GLORIOUS RETURN

I saw heaven opened, and there was a white horse. Its rider is called
Faithful and True, and He judges and makes war in righteousness.

REVELATION 19:11 HCSB

There is no more awe-inspiring image in Scripture than the return of Jesus Christ. Along with His first coming, it's what the whole Bible centers on. No donkey this time, riding to give Himself for our peace—here, it's a war charger fit for the King of kings and Lord of lords. It's our time too, as His church, to return with Him and join His reign on earth.

The prophecies about Jesus' second coming outnumber those of His first by a ratio of eight to one. More than 1,800 verses refer to His return, including seventeen Old Testament books and seven of every ten chapters in the New. Finally, at history's worst point, this is it! "Every eye will see Him, including those who pierced Him" (Revelation 1:7 HCSB).

The image of Faithful and True riding a white horse to conquer His foes should give you both goosebumps and a strong urge to cheer. After all, your team has won the ultimate victory at the cross, and this is the winner's ceremony, the coronation of the one who gave His life for you so you could bet your life on Him.

King Jesus, I honor and celebrate Your victory over death
and sin, and Your coming victory lap upon Your return.
All glory and power are Yours, now and forever.

Malachi 3–4 / Revelation 21–22 / Proverbs 31:18–31

HAPPY ENDINGS

*Look! God has moved into the neighborhood, making his home
with men and women! They're his people, he's their God. He'll
wipe every tear from their eyes. Death is gone for good.*

REVELATION 21:3–4 MSG

"I am the LORD, and I do not change."

MALACHI 3:6 NLT

Near the end of each testament, we see the promise of God's ultimate
plan—a new heaven and earth where peace and joy reign—and the
guarantee of His character: He does not change. God is always Himself,
always faithful to keep His promises, to complete what He began, to
do what is good, just, and right.

Malachi presents God's patience with His people despite their
faithlessness: "What's the use of serving God? What have we gained
by obeying his commands?" (Malachi 3:14 NLT). But to those who
listened to God's words and repented, He promises, "On the day when
I act in judgment, they will be my own special treasure" (verse 17 NLT).

God acted on that promise by sending His Son to save all who
would listen, trust, and obey Him by faith. So, when we come to
the end of the story, we grasp how amazing His promise is, that He
should make His home with His people, and we will know justice,
peace, and joy.

*Almighty God, Your plans for redeeming all Your creation are good
from beginning to end. I look back over the past year and ahead
to the coming one and proclaim Your unending faithfulness.*

CONTRIBUTORS

Elijah Adkins is a freelance writer and editor who lives in Ohio. He enjoys reading, hiking, bicycling, and attending church. Elijah's devotions appear in March, July, and November.

Quentin Guy writes from the high desert of New Mexico to encourage and equip people to know and serve God. He currently works in publishing for Calvary Church and has cowritten such books as *Weird and Gross Bible Stuff* and *The 2:52 Boys Bible*, both of which are stuck in future classic status. A former middle school teacher, he serves with his wife as marriage prep mentors and trusts God that his children will survive their teenage years. Quentin's devotions appear in April, August, and December.

Paul Muckley is a long-time editor who, under the pseudonym Paul Kent, has also written several books, including *Know Your Bible, Oswald Chambers: A Life in Pictures,* and *Playing with Purpose: Baseball Devotions.* He and his family live in Ohio's Amish Country. Paul's devotions appear in January, May, and September.

Tracy M. Sumner is a freelance author, writer, and editor in Beaverton, Oregon. An avid outdoorsman, he enjoys fly-fishing on world-class Oregon waters. Tracy's devotions appear in February, June, and October.

READ THROUGH THE BIBLE
IN A YEAR PLAN

1-Jan	Gen. 1-2	Matt. 1	Ps. 1
2-Jan	Gen. 3-4	Matt. 2	Ps. 2
3-Jan	Gen. 5-7	Matt. 3	Ps. 3
4-Jan	Gen. 8-10	Matt. 4	Ps. 4
5-Jan	Gen. 11-13	Matt. 5:1-20	Ps. 5
6-Jan	Gen. 14-16	Matt. 5:21-48	Ps. 6
7-Jan	Gen. 17-18	Matt. 6:1-18	Ps. 7
8-Jan	Gen. 19-20	Matt. 6:19-34	Ps. 8
9-Jan	Gen. 21-23	Matt. 7:1-11	Ps. 9:1-8
10-Jan	Gen. 24	Matt. 7:12-29	Ps. 9:9-20
11-Jan	Gen. 25-26	Matt. 8:1-17	Ps. 10:1-11
12-Jan	Gen. 27:1-28:9	Matt. 8:18-34	Ps. 10:12-18
13-Jan	Gen. 28:10-29:35	Matt. 9	Ps. 11
14-Jan	Gen. 30:1-31:21	Matt. 10:1-15	Ps. 12
15-Jan	Gen. 31:22-32:21	Matt. 10:16-36	Ps. 13
16-Jan	Gen. 32:22-34:31	Matt. 10:37-11:6	Ps. 14
17-Jan	Gen. 35-36	Matt. 11:7-24	Ps. 15
18-Jan	Gen. 37-38	Matt. 11:25-30	Ps. 16
19-Jan	Gen. 39-40	Matt. 12:1-29	Ps. 17
20-Jan	Gen. 41	Matt. 12:30-50	Ps. 18:1-15
21-Jan	Gen. 42-43	Matt. 13:1-9	Ps. 18:16-29
22-Jan	Gen. 44-45	Matt. 13:10-23	Ps. 18:30-50
23-Jan	Gen. 46:1-47:26	Matt. 13:24-43	Ps. 19
24-Jan	Gen. 47:27-49:28	Matt. 13:44-58	Ps. 20
25-Jan	Gen. 49:29-Exod. 1:22	Matt. 14	Ps. 21
26-Jan	Exod. 2-3	Matt. 15:1-28	Ps. 22:1-21
27-Jan	Exod. 4:1-5:21	Matt. 15:29-16:12	Ps. 22:22-31
28-Jan	Exod. 5:22-7:24	Matt. 16:13-28	Ps. 23
29-Jan	Exod. 7:25-9:35	Matt. 17:1-9	Ps. 24
30-Jan	Exod. 10-11	Matt. 17:10-27	Ps. 25
31-Jan	Exod. 12	Matt. 18:1-20	Ps. 26
1-Feb	Exod. 13-14	Matt. 18:21-35	Ps. 27
2-Feb	Exod. 15-16	Matt. 19:1-15	Ps. 28
3-Feb	Exod. 17-19	Matt. 19:16-30	Ps. 29
4-Feb	Exod. 20-21	Matt. 20:1-19	Ps. 30
5-Feb	Exod. 22-23	Matt. 20:20-34	Ps. 31:1-8
6-Feb	Exod. 24-25	Matt. 21:1-27	Ps. 31:9-18
7-Feb	Exod 26-27	Matt. 21:28-46	Ps. 31:19-24
8-Feb	Exod. 28	Matt. 22	Ps. 32
9-Feb	Exod. 29	Matt. 23:1-36	Ps. 33:1-12
10-Feb	Exod. 30-31	Matt. 23:37-24:28	Ps. 33:13-22
11-Feb	Exod. 32-33	Matt. 24:29-51	Ps. 34:1-7
12-Feb	Exod. 34:1-35:29	Matt. 25:1-13	Ps. 34:8-22
13-Feb	Exod. 35:30-37:29	Matt. 25:14-30	Ps. 35:1-8
14-Feb	Exod. 38-39	Matt. 25:31-46	Ps. 35:9-17
15-Feb	Exod. 40	Matt. 26:1-35	Ps. 35:18-28
16-Feb	Lev. 1-3	Matt. 26:36-68	Ps. 36:1-6
17-Feb	Lev. 4:1-5:13	Matt. 26:69-27:26	Ps. 36:7-12
18-Feb	Lev. 5:14 -7:21	Matt. 27:27-50	Ps. 37:1-6
19-Feb	Lev. 7:22-8:36	Matt. 27:51-66	Ps. 37:7-26
20-Feb	Lev. 9-10	Matt. 28	Ps. 37:27-40
21-Feb	Lev. 11-12	Mark 1:1-28	Ps. 38
22-Feb	Lev. 13	Mark 1:29-39	Ps. 39
23-Feb	Lev. 14	Mark 1:40-2:12	Ps. 40:1-8
24-Feb	Lev. 15	Mark 2:13-3:35	Ps. 40:9-17
25-Feb	Lev. 16-17	Mark 4:1-20	Ps. 41:1-4
26-Feb	Lev. 18-19	Mark 4:21-41	Ps. 41:5-13

27-Feb	Lev. 20	Mark 5	Ps. 42-43
28-Feb	Lev. 21-22	Mark 6:1-13	Ps. 44
1-Mar	Lev. 23-24	Mark 6:14-29	Ps. 45:1-5
2-Mar	Lev. 25	Mark 6:30-56	Ps. 45:6-12
3-Mar	Lev. 26	Mark 7	Ps. 45:13-17
4-Mar	Lev. 27	Mark 8	Ps. 46
5-Mar	Num. 1-2	Mark 9:1-13	Ps. 47
6-Mar	Num. 3	Mark 9:14-50	Ps. 48:1-8
7-Mar	Num. 4	Mark 10:1-34	Ps. 48:9-14
8-Mar	Num. 5:1-6:21	Mark 10:35-52	Ps. 49:1-9
9-Mar	Num. 6:22-7:47	Mark 11	Ps. 49:10-20
10-Mar	Num. 7:48-8:4	Mark 12:1-27	Ps. 50:1-15
11-Mar	Num. 8:5-9:23	Mark 12:28-44	Ps. 50:16-23
12-Mar	Num. 10-11	Mark 13:1-8	Ps. 51:1-9
13-Mar	Num. 12-13	Mark 13:9-37	Ps. 51:10-19
14-Mar	Num. 14	Mark 14:1-31	Ps. 52
15-Mar	Num. 15	Mark 14:32-72	Ps. 53
16-Mar	Num. 16	Mark 15:1-32	Ps. 54
17-Mar	Num. 17-18	Mark 15:33-47	Ps. 55
18-Mar	Num. 19-20	Mark 16	Ps. 56:1-7
19-Mar	Num. 21:1-22:20	Luke 1:1-25	Ps. 56:8-13
20-Mar	Num. 22:21-23:30	Luke 1:26-56	Ps. 57
21-Mar	Num. 24-25	Luke 1:57-2:20	Ps. 58
22-Mar	Num. 26:1-27:11	Luke 2:21-38	Ps. 59:1-8
23-Mar	Num. 27:12-29:11	Luke 2:39-52	Ps. 59:9-17
24-Mar	Num. 29:12-30:16	Luke 3	Ps. 60:1-5
25-Mar	Num. 31	Luke 4	Ps. 60:6-12
26-Mar	Num. 32-33	Luke 5:1-16	Ps. 61
27-Mar	Num. 34-36	Luke 5:17-32	Ps. 62:1-6
28-Mar	Deut. 1:1-2:25	Luke 5:33-6:11	Ps. 62:7-12
29-Mar	Deut. 2:26-4:14	Luke 6:12-35	Ps. 63:1-5
30-Mar	Deut. 4:15-5:22	Luke 6:36-49	Ps. 63:6-11
31-Mar	Deut. 5:23-7:26	Luke 7:1-17	Ps. 64:1-5
1-Apr	Deut. 8-9	Luke 7:18-35	Ps. 64:6-10
2-Apr	Deut. 10-11	Luke 7:36-8:3	Ps. 65:1-8
3-Apr	Deut. 12-13	Luke 8:4-21	Ps. 65:9-13
4-Apr	Deut. 14:1-16:8	Luke 8:22-39	Ps. 66:1-7
5-Apr	Deut. 16:9-18:22	Luke 8:40-56	Ps. 66:8-15
6-Apr	Deut. 19:1-21:9	Luke 9:1-22	Ps. 66:16-20
7-Apr	Deut. 21:10-23:8	Luke 9:23-42	Ps. 67
8-Apr	Deut. 23:9-25:19	Luke 9:43-62	Ps. 68:1-6
9-Apr	Deut. 26:1-28:14	Luke 10:1-20	Ps. 68:7-14
10-Apr	Deut. 28:15-68	Luke 10:21-37	Ps. 68:15-19
11-Apr	Deut. 29-30	Luke 10:38-11:23	Ps. 68:20-27
12-Apr	Deut. 31:1-32:22	Luke 11:24-36	Ps. 68:28-35
13-Apr	Deut. 32:23-33:29	Luke 11:37-54	Ps. 69:1-9
14-Apr	Deut. 34-Josh. 2	Luke 12:1-15	Ps. 69:10-17
15-Apr	Josh. 3:1-5:12	Luke 12:16-40	Ps. 69:18-28
16-Apr	Josh. 5:13-7:26	Luke 12:41-48	Ps. 69:29-36
17-Apr	Josh. 8-9	Luke 12:49-59	Ps. 70
18-Apr	Josh. 10:1-11:15	Luke 13:1-21	Ps. 71:1-6
19-Apr	Josh. 11:16-13:33	Luke 13:22-35	Ps. 71:7-16
20-Apr	Josh. 14-16	Luke 14:1-15	Ps. 71:17-21
21-Apr	Josh. 17:1-19:16	Luke 14:16-35	Ps. 71:22-24
22-Apr	Josh. 19:17-21:42	Luke 15:1-10	Ps. 72:1-11
23-Apr	Josh. 21:43-22:34	Luke 15:11-32	Ps. 72:12-20
24-Apr	Josh. 23-24	Luke 16:1-18	Ps. 73:1-9
25-Apr	Judg. 1-2	Luke 16:19-17:10	Ps. 73:10-20
26-Apr	Judg. 3-4	Luke 17:11-37	Ps. 73:21-28
27-Apr	Judg. 5:1-6:24	Luke 18:1-17	Ps. 74:1-3
28-Apr	Judg. 6:25-7:25	Luke 18:18-43	Ps. 74:4-11
29-Apr	Judg. 8:1-9:23	Luke 19:1-28	Ps. 74:12-17

30-Apr	Judg. 9:24-10:18	Luke 19:29-48	Ps. 74:18-23
1-May	Judg. 11:1-12:7	Luke 20:1-26	Ps. 75:1-7
2-May	Judg. 12:8-14:20	Luke 20:27-47	Ps. 75:8-10
3-May	Judg. 15-16	Luke 21:1-19	Ps. 76:1-7
4-May	Judg. 17-18	Luke 21:20-22:6	Ps. 76:8-12
5-May	Judg. 19:1-20:23	Luke 22:7-30	Ps. 77:1-11
6-May	Judg. 20:24-21:25	Luke 22:31-54	Ps. 77:12-20
7-May	Ruth 1-2	Luke 22:55-23:25	Ps. 78:1-4
8-May	Ruth 3-4	Luke 23:26-24:12	Ps. 78:5-8
9-May	1 Sam. 1:1-2:21	Luke 24:13-53	Ps. 78:9-16
10-May	1 Sam. 2:22-4:22	John 1:1-28	Ps. 78:17-24
11-May	1 Sam. 5-7	John 1:29-51	Ps. 78:25-33
12-May	1 Sam. 8:1-9:26	John 2	Ps. 78:34-41
13-May	1 Sam. 9:27-11:15	John 3:1-22	Ps. 78:42-55
14-May	1 Sam. 12-13	John 3:23-4:10	Ps. 78:56-66
15-May	1 Sam. 14	John 4:11-38	Ps. 78:67-72
16-May	1 Sam. 15-16	John 4:39-54	Ps. 79:1-7
17-May	1 Sam. 17	John 5:1-24	Ps. 79:8-13
18-May	1 Sam. 18-19	John 5:25-47	Ps. 80:1-7
19-May	1 Sam. 20-21	John 6:1-21	Ps. 80:8-19
20-May	1 Sam. 22-23	John 6:22-42	Ps. 81:1-10
21-May	1 Sam. 24:1-25:31	John 6:43-71	Ps. 81:11-16
22-May	1 Sam. 25:32-27:12	John 7:1-24	Ps. 82
23-May	1 Sam. 28-29	John 7:25-8:11	Ps. 83
24-May	1 Sam. 30-31	John 8:12-47	Ps. 84:1-4
25-May	2 Sam. 1-2	John 8:48-9:12	Ps. 84:5-12
26-May	2 Sam. 3-4	John 9:13-34	Ps. 85:1-7
27-May	2 Sam. 5:1-7:17	John 9:35-10:10	Ps. 85:8-13
28-May	2 Sam. 7:18-10:19	John 10:11-30	Ps. 86:1-10
29-May	2 Sam. 11:1-12:25	John 10:31-11:16	Ps. 86:11-17
30-May	2 Sam. 12:26-13:39	John 11:17-54	Ps. 87
31-May	2 Sam. 14:1-15:12	John 11:55-12:19	Ps. 88:1-9
1-Jun	2 Sam. 15:13-16:23	John 12:20-43	Ps. 88:10-18
2-Jun	2 Sam. 17:1-18:18	John 12:44-13:20	Ps. 89:1-6
3-Jun	2 Sam. 18:19-19:39	John 13:21-38	Ps. 89:7-13
4-Jun	2 Sam. 19:40-21:22	John 14:1-17	Ps. 89:14-18
5-Jun	2 Sam. 22:1-23:7	John 14:18-15:27	Ps. 89:19-29
6-Jun	2 Sam. 23:8-24:25	John 16:1-22	Ps. 89:30-37
7-Jun	1 Kings 1	John 16:23-17:5	Ps. 89:38-52
8-Jun	1 Kings 2	John 17:6-26	Ps. 90:1-12
9-Jun	1 Kings 3-4	John 18:1-27	Ps. 90:13-17
10-Jun	1 Kings 5-6	John 18:28-19:5	Ps. 91:1-10
11-Jun	1 Kings 7	John 19:6-25a	Ps. 91:11-16
12-Jun	1 Kings 8:1-53	John 19:25b-42	Ps. 92:1-9
13-Jun	1 Kings 8:54-10:13	John 20:1-18	Ps. 92:10-15
14-Jun	1 Kings 10:14-11:43	John 20:19-31	Ps. 93
15-Jun	1 Kings 12:1-13:10	John 21	Ps. 94:1-11
16-Jun	1 Kings 13:11-14:31	Acts 1:1-11	Ps. 94:12-23
17-Jun	1 Kings 15:1-16:20	Acts 1:12-26	Ps. 95
18-Jun	1 Kings 16:21-18:19	Acts 2:1-21	Ps. 96:1-8
19-Jun	1 Kings 18:20-19:21	Acts 2:22-41	Ps. 96:9-13
20-Jun	1 Kings 20	Acts 2:42-3:26	Ps. 97:1-6
21-Jun	1 Kings 21:1-22:28	Acts 4:1-22	Ps. 97:7-12
22-Jun	1 Kings 22:29- 2 Kings 1:18	Acts 4:23-5:11	Ps. 98
23-Jun	2 Kings 2-3	Acts 5:12-28	Ps. 99
24-Jun	2 Kings 4	Acts 5:29-6:15	Ps. 100
25-Jun	2 Kings 5:1-6:23	Acts 7:1-16	Ps. 101
26-Jun	2 Kings 6:24-8:15	Acts 7:17-36	Ps. 102:1-7
27-Jun	2 Kings 8:16-9:37	Acts 7:37-53	Ps. 102:8-17
28-Jun	2 Kings 10-11	Acts 7:54-8:8	Ps. 102:18-28
29-Jun	2 Kings 12-13	Acts 8:9-40	Ps. 103:1-9

30-Jun	2 Kings 14-15	Acts 9:1-16	Ps. 103:10-14
1-Jul	2 Kings 16-17	Acts 9:17-31	Ps. 103:15-22
2-Jul	2 Kings 18:1-19:7	Acts 9:32-10:16	Ps. 104:1-9
3-Jul	2 Kings 19:8-20:21	Acts 10:17-33	Ps. 104:10-23
4-Jul	2 Kings 21:1-22:20	Acts 10:34-11:18	Ps. 104: 24-30
5-Jul	2 Kings 23	Acts 11:19-12:17	Ps. 104:31-35
6-Jul	2 Kings 24-25	Acts 12:18-13:13	Ps. 105:1-7
7-Jul	1 Chron. 1-2	Acts 13:14-43	Ps. 105:8-15
8-Jul	1 Chron. 3:1-5:10	Acts 13:44-14:10	Ps. 105:16-28
9-Jul	1 Chron. 5:11-6:81	Acts 14:11-28	Ps. 105:29-36
10-Jul	1 Chron. 7:1-9:9	Acts 15:1-18	Ps. 105:37-45
11-Jul	1 Chron. 9:10-11:9	Acts 15:19-41	Ps. 106:1-12
12-Jul	1 Chron. 11:10-12:40	Acts 16:1-15	Ps. 106:13-27
13-Jul	1 Chron. 13-15	Acts 16:16-40	Ps. 106:28-33
14-Jul	1 Chron. 16-17	Acts 17:1-14	Ps. 106:34-43
15-Jul	1 Chron. 18-20	Acts 17:15-34	Ps. 106:44-48
16-Jul	1 Chron. 21-22	Acts 18:1-23	Ps. 107:1-9
17-Jul	1 Chron. 23-25	Acts 18:24-19:10	Ps. 107:10-16
18-Jul	1 Chron. 26-27	Acts 19:11-22	Ps. 107:17-32
19-Jul	1 Chron. 28-29	Acts 19:23-41	Ps. 107:33-38
20-Jul	2 Chron. 1-3	Acts 20:1-16	Ps. 107:39-43
21-Jul	2 Chron. 4:1-6:11	Acts 20:17-38	Ps. 108
22-Jul	2 Chron. 6:12-7:10	Acts 21:1-14	Ps. 109:1-20
23-Jul	2 Chron. 7:11-9:28	Acts 21:15-32	Ps. 109:21-31
24-Jul	2 Chron. 9:29-12:16	Acts 21:33-22:16	Ps. 110:1-3
25-Jul	2 Chron. 13-15	Acts 22:17-23:11	Ps. 110:4-7
26-Jul	2 Chron. 16-17	Acts 23:12-24:21	Ps. 111
27-Jul	2 Chron. 18-19	Acts 24:22-25:12	Ps. 112
28-Jul	2 Chron. 20-21	Acts 25:13-27	Ps. 113
29-Jul	2 Chron. 22-23	Acts 26	Ps. 114
30-Jul	2 Chron. 24:1-25:16	Acts 27:1-20	Ps. 115:1-10
31-Jul	2 Chron. 25:17-27:9	Acts 27:21-28:6	Ps. 115:11-18
1-Aug	2 Chron. 28:1-29:19	Acts 28:7-31	Ps. 116:1-5
2-Aug	2 Chron. 29:20-30:27	Rom. 1:1-17	Ps. 116:6-19
3-Aug	2 Chron. 31-32	Rom. 1:18-32	Ps. 117
4-Aug	2 Chron. 33:1-34:7	Rom. 2	Ps. 118:1-18
5-Aug	2 Chron. 34:8-35:19	Rom. 3:1-26	Ps. 118:19-23
6-Aug	2 Chron. 35:20-36:23	Rom. 3:27-4:25	Ps. 118:24-29
7-Aug	Ezra 1-3	Rom. 5	Ps. 119:1-8
8-Aug	Ezra 4-5	Rom. 6:1-7:6	Ps. 119:9-16
9-Aug	Ezra 6:1-7:26	Rom. 7:7-25	Ps. 119:17-32
10-Aug	Ezra 7:27-9:4	Rom. 8:1-27	Ps. 119:33-40
11-Aug	Ezra 9:5-10:44	Rom. 8:28-39	Ps. 119:41-64
12-Aug	Neh. 1:1-3:16	Rom. 9:1-18	Ps. 119:65-72
13-Aug	Neh. 3:17-5:13	Rom. 9:19-33	Ps. 119:73-80
14-Aug	Neh. 5:14-7:73	Rom. 10:1-13	Ps. 119:81-88
15-Aug	Neh. 8:1-9:5	Rom. 10:14-11:24	Ps. 119:89-104
16-Aug	Neh. 9:6-10:27	Rom. 11:25-12:8	Ps. 119:105-120
17-Aug	Neh. 10:28-12:26	Rom. 12:9-13:7	Ps. 119:121-128
18-Aug	Neh. 12:27-13:31	Rom. 13:8-14:12	Ps. 119:129-136
19-Aug	Esther 1:1-2:18	Rom. 14:13-15:13	Ps. 119:137-152
20-Aug	Esther 2:19-5:14	Rom. 15:14-21	Ps. 119:153-168
21-Aug	Esther. 6-8	Rom. 15:22-33	Ps. 119:169-176
22-Aug	Esther 9-10	Rom. 16	Ps. 120-122
23-Aug	Job 1-3	1 Cor. 1:1-25	Ps. 123
24-Aug	Job 4-6	1 Cor. 1:26-2:16	Ps. 124-125
25-Aug	Job 7-9	1 Cor. 3	Ps. 126-127
26-Aug	Job 10-13	1 Cor. 4:1-13	Ps. 128-129
27-Aug	Job 14-16	1 Cor. 4:14-5:13	Ps. 130
28-Aug	Job 17-20	1 Cor. 6	Ps. 131
29-Aug	Job 21-23	1 Cor. 7:1-16	Ps. 132
30-Aug	Job 24-27	1 Cor. 7:17-40	Ps. 133-134

31-Aug	Job 28-30	1 Cor. 8	Ps. 135
1-Sep	Job 31-33	1 Cor. 9:1-18	Ps. 136:1-9
2-Sep	Job 34-36	1 Cor. 9:19-10:13	Ps. 136:10-26
3-Sep	Job 37-39	1 Cor. 10:14-11:1	Ps. 137
4-Sep	Job 40-42	1 Cor. 11:2-34	Ps. 138
5-Sep	Eccles. 1:1-3:15	1 Cor. 12:1-26	Ps. 139:1-6
6-Sep	Eccles. 3:16-6:12	1 Cor. 12:27-13:13	Ps. 139:7-18
7-Sep	Eccles. 7:1-9:12	1 Cor. 14:1-22	Ps. 139:19-24
8-Sep	Eccles. 9:13-12:14	1 Cor. 14:23-15:11	Ps. 140:1-8
9-Sep	SS 1-4	1 Cor. 15:12-34	Ps. 140:9-13
10-Sep	SS 5-8	1 Cor. 15:35-58	Ps. 141
11-Sep	Isa. 1-2	1 Cor. 16	Ps. 142
12-Sep	Isa. 3-5	2 Cor. 1:1-11	Ps. 143:1-6
13-Sep	Isa. 6-8	2 Cor. 1:12-2:4	Ps. 143:7-12
14-Sep	Isa. 9-10	2 Cor. 2:5-17	Ps. 144
15-Sep	Isa. 11-13	2 Cor. 3	Ps. 145
16-Sep	Isa. 14-16	2 Cor. 4	Ps. 146
17-Sep	Isa. 17-19	2 Cor. 5	Ps. 147:1-11
18-Sep	Isa. 20-23	2 Cor. 6	Ps. 147:12-20
19-Sep	Isa. 24:1-26:19	2 Cor. 7	Ps. 148
20-Sep	Isa. 26:20-28:29	2 Cor. 8	Ps. 149-150
21-Sep	Isa. 29-30	2 Cor. 9	Prov. 1:1-9
22-Sep	Isa. 31-33	2 Cor. 10	Prov. 1:10-22
23-Sep	Isa. 34-36	2 Cor. 11	Prov. 1:23-26
24-Sep	Isa. 37-38	2 Cor. 12:1-10	Prov. 1:27-33
25-Sep	Isa. 39-40	2 Cor. 12:11-13:14	Prov. 2:1-15
26-Sep	Isa. 41-42	Gal. 1	Prov. 2:16-22
27-Sep	Isa. 43:1-44:20	Gal. 2	Prov. 3:1-12
28-Sep	Isa. 44:21-46:13	Gal. 3:1-18	Prov. 3:13-26
29-Sep	Isa. 47:1-49:13	Gal 3:19-29	Prov. 3:27-35
30-Sep	Isa. 49:14-51:23	Gal 4:1-11	Prov. 4:1-19
1-Oct	Isa. 52-54	Gal. 4:12-31	Prov. 4:20-27
2-Oct	Isa. 55-57	Gal. 5	Prov. 5:1-14
3-Oct	Isa. 58-59	Gal. 6	Prov. 5:15-23
4-Oct	Isa. 60-62	Eph. 1	Prov. 6:1-5
5-Oct	Isa. 63:1-65:16	Eph. 2	Prov. 6:6-19
6-Oct	Isa. 65:17-66:24	Eph. 3:1-4:16	Prov. 6:20-26
7-Oct	Jer. 1-2	Eph. 4:17-32	Prov. 6:27-35
8-Oct	Jer. 3:1-4:22	Eph. 5	Prov. 7:1-5
9-Oct	Jer. 4:23-5:31	Eph. 6	Prov. 7:6-27
10-Oct	Jer. 6:1-7:26	Phil. 1:1-26	Prov. 8:1-11
11-Oct	Jer. 7:26-9:16	Phil. 1:27-2:18	Prov. 8:12-21
12-Oct	Jer. 9:17-11:17	Phil 2:19-30	Prov. 8:22-36
13-Oct	Jer. 11:18-13:27	Phil. 3	Prov. 9:1-6
14-Oct	Jer. 14-15	Phil. 4	Prov. 9:7-18
15-Oct	Jer. 16-17	Col. 1:1-23	Prov. 10:1-5
16-Oct	Jer. 18:1-20:6	Col. 1:24-2:15	Prov. 10:6-14
17-Oct	Jer. 20:7-22:19	Col. 2:16-3:4	Prov. 10:15-26
18-Oct	Jer. 22:20-23:40	Col. 3:5-4:1	Prov. 10:27-32
19-Oct	Jer. 24-25	Col. 4:2-18	Prov. 11:1-11
20-Oct	Jer. 26-27	1 Thes. 1:1-2:8	Prov. 11:12-21
21-Oct	Jer. 28-29	1 Thes. 2:9-3:13	Prov. 11:22-26
22-Oct	Jer. 30:1-31:22	1 Thes. 4:1-5:11	Prov. 11:27-31
23-Oct	Jer. 31:23-32:35	1 Thes. 5:12-28	Prov. 12:1-14
24-Oct	Jer. 32:36-34:7	2 Thes. 1-2	Prov. 12:15-20
25-Oct	Jer. 34:8-36:10	2 Thes. 3	Prov. 12:21-28
26-Oct	Jer. 36:11-38:13	1 Tim. 1:1-17	Prov. 13:1-4
27-Oct	Jer. 38:14-40:6	1 Tim. 1:18-3:13	Prov. 13:5-13
28-Oct	Jer. 40:7-42:22	1 Tim. 3:14-4:10	Prov. 13:14-21
29-Oct	Jer. 43-44	1 Tim. 4:11-5:16	Prov. 13:22-25
30-Oct	Jer. 45-47	1 Tim. 5:17-6:21	Prov. 14:1-6
31-Oct	Jer. 48:1-49:6	2 Tim. 1	Prov. 14:7-22

1-Nov	Jer. 49:7-50:16	2 Tim. 2	Prov. 14:23-27
2-Nov	Jer. 50:17-51:14	2 Tim. 3	Prov. 14:28-35
3-Nov	Jer. 51:15-64	2 Tim. 4	Prov. 15:1-9
4-Nov	Jer. 52-Lam. 1	Ti. 1:1-9	Prov. 15:10-17
5-Nov	Lam. 2:1-3:38	Ti. 1:10-2:15	Prov. 15:18-26
6-Nov	Lam. 3:39-5:22	Ti. 3	Prov. 15:27-33
7-Nov	Ezek. 1:1-3:21	Philemon 1	Prov. 16:1-9
8-Nov	Ezek. 3:22-5:17	Heb. 1:1-2:4	Prov. 16:10-21
9-Nov	Ezek. 6-7	Heb. 2:5-18	Prov. 16:22-33
10-Nov	Ezek. 8-10	Heb. 3:1-4:3	Prov. 17:1-5
11-Nov	Ezek. 11-12	Heb. 4:4-5:10	Prov. 17:6-12
12-Nov	Ezek. 13-14	Heb. 5:11-6:20	Prov. 17:13-22
13-Nov	Ezek. 15:1-16:43	Heb. 7:1-28	Prov. 17:23-28
14-Nov	Ezek. 16:44-17:24	Heb. 8:1-9:10	Prov. 18:1-7
15-Nov	Ezek. 18-19	Heb. 9:11-28	Prov. 18:8-17
16-Nov	Ezek. 20	Heb. 10:1-25	Prov. 18:18-24
17-Nov	Ezek. 21-22	Heb. 10:26-39	Prov. 19:1-8
18-Nov	Ezek. 23	Heb. 11:1-31	Prov. 19:9-14
19-Nov	Ezek. 24-26	Heb. 11:32-40	Prov. 19:15-21
20-Nov	Ezek. 27-28	Heb. 12:1-13	Prov. 19:22-29
21-Nov	Ezek. 29-30	Heb. 12:14-29	Prov. 20:1-18
22-Nov	Ezek. 31-32	Heb. 13	Prov. 20:19-24
23-Nov	Ezek. 33:1-34:10	Jas. 1	Prov. 20:25-30
24-Nov	Ezek. 34:11-36:15	Jas. 2	Prov. 21:1-8
25-Nov	Ezek. 36:16-37:28	Jas. 3	Prov. 21:9-18
26-Nov	Ezek. 38-39	Jas. 4:1-5:6	Prov. 21:19-24
27-Nov	Ezek. 40	Jas. 5:7-20	Prov. 21:25-31
28-Nov	Ezek. 41:1-43:12	1 Pet. 1:1-12	Prov. 22:1-9
29-Nov	Ezek. 43:13-44:31	1 Pet. 1:13-2:3	Prov. 22:10-23
30-Nov	Ezek. 45-46	1 Pet. 2:4-17	Prov. 22:24-29
1-Dec	Ezek. 47-48	1 Pet. 2:18-3:7	Prov. 23:1-9
2-Dec	Dan. 1:1-2:23	1 Pet. 3:8-4:19	Prov. 23:10-16
3-Dec	Dan. 2:24-3:30	1 Pet. 5	Prov. 23:17-25
4-Dec	Dan. 4	2 Pet. 1	Prov. 23:26-35
5-Dec	Dan. 5	2 Pet. 2	Prov. 24:1-18
6-Dec	Dan. 6:1-7:14	2 Pet. 3	Prov. 24:19-27
7-Dec	Dan. 7:15-8:27	1 John 1:1-2:17	Prov. 24:28-34
8-Dec	Dan. 9-10	1 John 2:18-29	Prov. 25:1-12
9-Dec	Dan. 11-12	1 John 3:1-12	Prov. 25:13-17
10-Dec	Hos. 1-3	1 John 3:13-4:16	Prov. 25:18-28
11-Dec	Hos. 4-6	1 John 4:17-5:21	Prov. 26:1-16
12-Dec	Hos. 7-10	2 John	Prov. 26:17-21
13-Dec	Hos. 11-14	3 John	Prov. 26:22-27:9
14-Dec	Joel 1:1-2:17	Jude	Prov. 27:10-17
15-Dec	Joel 2:18-3:21	Rev. 1:1-2:11	Prov. 27:18-27
16-Dec	Amos 1:1-4:5	Rev. 2:12-29	Prov. 28:1-8
17-Dec	Amos 4:6-6:14	Rev. 3	Prov. 28:9-16
18-Dec	Amos 7-9	Rev. 4:1-5:5	Prov. 28:17-24
19-Dec	Obad-Jonah	Rev. 5:6-14	Prov. 28:25-28
20-Dec	Mic. 1:1-4:5	Rev. 6:1-7:8	Prov. 29:1-8
21-Dec	Mic. 4:6-7:20	Rev. 7:9-8:13	Prov. 29:9-14
22-Dec	Nah. 1-3	Rev. 9-10	Prov. 29:15-23
23-Dec	Hab. 1-3	Rev. 11	Prov. 29:24-27
24-Dec	Zeph. 1-3	Rev. 12	Prov. 30:1-6
25-Dec	Hag. 1-2	Rev. 13:1-14:13	Prov. 30:7-16
26-Dec	Zech. 1-4	Rev. 14:14-16:3	Prov. 30:17-20
27-Dec	Zech. 5-8	Rev. 16:4-21	Prov. 30:21-28
28-Dec	Zech. 9-11	Rev. 17:1-18:8	Prov. 30:29-33
29-Dec	Zech. 12-14	Rev. 18:9-24	Prov. 31:1-9
30-Dec	Mal. 1-2	Rev. 19-20	Prov. 31:10-17
31-Dec	Mal. 3-4	Rev. 21-22	Prov. 31:18-31

SCRIPTURE INDEX
OLD TESTAMENT

NEW TESTAMENT